TOO CLOSE TO CALL

TOO CLOSE TO CALL

Power and Politics –
John Major in No. 10

Sarah Hogg
and
Jonathan Hill

LITTLE, BROWN AND COMPANY

A *Little, Brown* Book

First published in Great Britain in 1995
by Little, Brown and Company

Copyright © 1995 by The Baroness Hogg & Jonathan Hill

The moral right of the authors has been asserted.

A CIP catalogue record for this book
is available from the British Library.

ISBN 0 316 87716 6

Typeset by Palimpsest Book Production Limited,
Polmont, Stirlingshire
Printed and bound in Great Britain by
Clays Ltd, St Ives plc.

Little, Brown and Company (UK)
Brettenham House
Lancaster Place
London WC2E 7EN

For Alex and Douglas

Contents

Preface   ix

Foreword   1
1   PICKING UP THE PIECES   3
2   INSIDE NUMBER 10   16
3   FOREIGN DEVILS AND AMERICAN FRIENDS   37
4   LAUNCHING BIG BERTHA   55
5   EUROPE: HEARTS AND MINDS   71
6   WHERE'S THE BEEF?   83
7   LONG COLD SUMMER   106
8   FALSE ALARM   124
9   AT THE SIGN OF THE GOLDEN TULIP   138
10   'IF THIS IS TUESDAY, IT MUST BE TRANSPORT'   163
11   'THE ECONOMY, STUPID'   183
12   THEY'RE OFF   203
13   BARN OWLS AND BIRTHDAY CAKE   223
14   TOO CLOSE TO CALL   239
15   OPENING THE BLACK BOX   254
Afterword: 'PUT UP OR SHUT UP'   264

Appendix I: The 1992 General Election Result   285
Appendix II: John Major's First Cabinet – and After   287
Picture Credits   293
Index   295

Preface

The idea of this book arose when we left our jobs in Number 10, Jonathan Hill in late 1994, Sarah Hogg in early 1995. There was, we believed, an important story to tell about the way in which John Major – in just under five hundred days – picked up the shattered pieces of his party and, against the odds, put his Government in a position to win another general election.

Our original intention was to end on 10 April 1992. There is another book to be written about John Major's second administration, but that story is not yet completed. However, the events of June 1995 carried such strong echoes of both 1990 and 1992, demonstrating again his remarkable winning streak, that we added a chapter on that part of the John Major story, too.

We did not set out to write a fully rounded history of the Major Government. This is, instead, an impressionistic account of that history in the making, with all the limitations of personal perspective. Rather than producing a book of analysis, what we have tried to do, through the medium of personal experience, is to give the feel of the demanding, relentless, unforgiving but engrossing business of government and politics, and to throw some light on what it was like to work in John Major's Downing Street.

Too many members of the Cabinet, past and present, senior civil servants, party officials and others have helped us write this book to thank individually here. The same applies to all those Ministers, officials, industrialists, think-tankers and others who gave us so much help, advice and support in the Policy Unit and the Political Office.

Many of our closest colleagues in Number 10 do not feature, simply because they fall outside the time-frame of this book, but to all of them we owe thanks: to the secretaries, in particular Gill Keen, Debbie Lewis, Ann Hickinbotham and Debbie de Satgé; to the messengers; to 'Switch', the Number 10 telephone operators; to the drivers and policemen; to officials at every level; to all who work long hours in that strange building, to support the Prime Minister and help those who work for him.

To the Prime Minister our thanks are due above all for the opportunity to work for him. To him and to Norma go our personal thanks for so much kindness, generosity and sheer good fun. Seasoned inside observers of Downing Street have remarked on the lack of in-fighting in Number 10 in his time. That is due to the spirit created in the building by John and Norma Major.

Our special thanks are due to the officials and politicians who were good enough to read all or part of the manuscript in draft; but especially to our two severest critics, who respectively applied an insider's and outsider's eye to the whole text, Nick True and Charles Lysaght. Debbie de Satgé worked miracles on the word processor. Quintin Hogg wrestled with the Colindale newspaper library, the photocopier and his mother's syntax. The House of Lords library and computer room were unfailingly helpful.

But our thanks are due first and last to Alex Hill and Douglas Hogg. During the frenzied weeks in which we completed this book against a tight deadline, Alex became a mother for the third time, Douglas a Cabinet Minister for the first, and neither received from their spouses the support that was due.

This book is dedicated to them both.

TOO CLOSE TO CALL

Foreword

On Monday 13 April 1992, Jonathan Hill went into Sarah Hogg's office at Number 10 waving his copy of the 'float' – the folder of internal papers for the Prime Minister that circulate amongst his officials each day. Jonathan gleefully pointed to the top one. Sarah began reading what seemed to be a tedious litany of coming events in the Prime Minister's diary. Mystified as to why Jonathan wanted her to plough through it, Sarah looked up.

'Go on,' he said.

Finally, she reached the sentence which had caused him so much amusement:

> On this occasion, you will wish to notify your European partners that you intend to sign up to the Social Chapter.

The penny dropped. The 'Prime Minister' for whom the note had been written by one of the Private Secretaries was not John Major, but Neil Kinnock.

During the weeks of a general election campaign, the officials who have been the Prime Minister's life support system simply fade away, to prepare papers for an alternative government. They have to be ready to implement the policies of whichever party wins the election. No difference between the parties was simpler or starker than over the Social Chapter that John Major had fought to keep out of the European Community's Maastricht Treaty. This surviving example of papers prepared for Neil Kinnock, served up by mistake in Monday's batch, was a reminder to both Jonathan and Sarah of what might have been.

And very nearly was.

1

Picking Up the Pieces

It's what I always dreamed of and hoped for.
Margaret Thatcher to Norma Major, on John Major's
election as leader of the Conservative Party,
27 November 1990

It takes three minutes to drive from Buckingham Palace to Downing Street. Sitting with Norma in the back of the official Daimler, John Major pulled from his pocket some cards he had grabbed on his way through the Queen's offices. It was about eleven in the morning on 28 November 1990. He had just kissed hands on his appointment as Prime Minister. When he got back to Number 10 after that short drive, he knew he would have to speak to the press clustered opposite the famous front door.

What would his message be? In 1979, Margaret Thatcher had quoted Saint Francis of Assisi – 'Where there is discord, let us bring harmony . . .' John Major relied on his own words. In his angular, slightly elongated hand, he wrote quickly of his desire to create scope for people to fulfil their potential, and – underlined – 'to build a country that is at ease with itself'. It was this echo of Baldwin that was to stick in people's minds. But his final words were equally typical: brisk, unrhetorical, defiantly flat. He was going to go inside Number 10 and get on with the work in hand, 'starting here and now'.

There was certainly no shortage of work in hand. If Margaret

Thatcher saw him as the man to protect her legacy, in November 1990 the liabilities of this inheritance loomed larger than the assets. There was a war approaching, a big European negotiation ahead, a tax revolt simmering, inflation, a recession – and a general election to fight in eighteen months at most.

In some ways, John Major conformed to the pattern of history. Most Prime Ministers have reached Number 10 via the Treasury or the Foreign Office, and he – unlike Margaret Thatcher – had experience of both. In other ways, he did not fit the pattern. His rise had been unusually rapid. Margaret Thatcher had clearly been thinking more long-term when she told an interviewer that she did not expect to be succeeded by someone from the same generation, but she was proved right. At forty-seven, John Major was the youngest British Prime Minister this century; and had had the shortest parliamentary apprenticeship for the job of any since Pitt and Addington. Margaret Thatcher had been in Parliament twenty years before becoming Prime Minister; John Major had been there only eleven – since 1979 – and had never been in Opposition. In his few months as Foreign Secretary, he had barely had time for one Commonwealth conference; as Chancellor, he had only presented one Budget.

In the dining-room of Tristan Garel-Jones's[1] house in Westminster hangs a group portrait of the 'Blue Chips', a self-selected group of MPs who entered Parliament at the same time as John Major. Amongst these high-flyers of the Tory class of '79, the artist has placed him standing, slightly to the left. The future Prime Minister's hair curls right over his collar, a detail which betrays the fact that it was painted well before he entered Number 10. But Robert Cranborne,[2] who commissioned the painting, knew what he was doing. John Major is one of two figures – the other is

[1]Tristan Garel-Jones was a Foreign Office Minister, former Deputy Chief Whip and unofficial chairman of the Blue Chips.
[2]Robert Cranborne, elected to the Commons in 1979, became Leader of the Lords in 1994, as Lord Cranborne. In June 1995 he headed John Major's campaign for re-election to the leadership of the Tory Party. His sister Rose painted the picture, intended to join the political memorabilia of four centuries accumulated by the house of Cecil at Hatfield.

Chris Patten[3] – on whom the eye naturally lights. John Major was the first Blue Chip, the first of the 1979 intake, to enter the Cabinet.

On the night of the first ballot of the Tory leadership election in 1990, some Blue Chips, and others in the influential middle rank of government, met at that same house in Westminster. They concluded that Margaret Thatcher could not survive. Most of them wanted the Foreign Secretary, Douglas Hurd, to take over from her. Chris Patten and Tristan Garel-Jones went on to run the Foreign Secretary's campaign, in a gentlemanly, leisurely and soon clearly unsuccessful fashion.

Many of the Blue Chips went on to become John Major's closest allies, but they were not, in the leadership election, his power base. He had the support of three much more substantial forces: the Treasury, Margaret Thatcher, and above all, the Tory party's instinct for survival.

A former Chief Secretary to the Treasury as well as Chancellor, John Major had made the Treasury building on the corner of Parliament Square his home base. Treasury Ministers had run his campaign. Treasury officials liked, supported and encouraged him to stand. They relished his success. In Number 10, reduced to the tiny staff Britain provides for its Prime Minister, John Major sometimes clearly missed the Treasury corps. As they spread across Whitehall on promotion to Permanent Secretary, he greeted almost all of them as long-lost friends.

Holding Whitehall's purse-strings gives the Treasury a particular mindset, perhaps characteristic of a group of clever oddballs who are resigned to others' resentment: the Treasury's motto should be *Contra mundum* – Treasury men (almost entirely men) against the world. So they were shocked when Nigel Lawson, John Major's predecessor as Chancellor, came out for Michael Heseltine in the leadership election.

[3]Chris Patten, Environment Secretary at the time, had been Director of the Conservative Research Department from 1974 to 1979, and a junior Minister for many years before Margaret Thatcher finally appointed him to the Cabinet in 1989.

The afternoon of Tuesday 27 November, the day of the final ballot, had been spent by John Major in the Chancellor's magnificent office at the Treasury, doodling Cabinet lists – the politician's favourite parlour game. But by then, he knew he might very soon be doing it for real. This realisation had begun to sink in the previous weekend when Francis Maude, a junior Minister who was amongst the most active of John Major's campaign team, rang him up to give him estimates of support for the candidates. But they didn't add up. It was clear to John Major's sensitive political antennae that Francis was deliberately damping down his expectations. Now, on the day of the ballot, Norman Lamont had just given him the latest lists. John Major called in his Chief Economic Adviser, Sir Terry Burns, and finally risked voicing the thought to an official: 'It looks as if I may win.'

The British system of government, dedicated to the principle that the Queen's business must be carried on, does not stop for a heart-beat. Margaret Thatcher had answered her final Prime Minister's Questions just before 3.30 that afternoon. The last one was, by her count, the 7,500th such question she had answered: a parting shot by Gavin Strang, the member for Edinburgh East, on poverty and unemployment. To the last, however, she gave as good as she got, going down firing on the history of the mid-1980s miners' strike. Then the House went mundanely on with the presentation of a bill to permit the construction of a new bridge over the River Severn. Two days later, John Major would be at the Despatch Box, answering the next set of Prime Minister's Questions.

Less than three hours after Margaret Thatcher's last prime ministerial appearance in the Commons, the result of the leadership ballot was declared. John Major was watching the television, with a crowd of friends, in the big drawing room at Number 11. Shortly after 6.20 p.m., the figures were announced: Major 185, Heseltine 131, Hurd 56.

John Major had hoped for up to seven more votes. With the aid of some very private cross-checking with Douglas Hurd, he had been able to identify some of those MPs who had simply pledged their support to everybody, but he had still under-estimated the number of liars. He was, in fact, two votes short of an overall majority, but a few minutes later, the other two candidates conceded. Shortly after that Cranley Onslow, the Chairman of the 1922 Committee of Tory backbenchers, confirmed there would be no third ballot. John Major had won.

The celebration began in earnest in Number 11. Margaret Thatcher was reported to be 'thrilled', and came through from Number 10 to offer her congratulations. Margaret Thatcher and John Major had had their differences – it was he, after all, who persuaded her to join the European Exchange Rate Mechanism. But she had strongly supported his candidature – so strongly, indeed, that he had been forced to deny on television that he was 'son of Thatcher'. Personally as well as politically, she was closer to John Major than Douglas Hurd – let alone Michael Heseltine. When she had promoted John Major to the Cabinet as Chief Secretary to the Treasury in 1987, the *Daily Telegraph* noted his 'firmly held right of centre views', while the *Sunday Telegraph* called him 'a more moderate version of Norman Tebbit'. However, *The Times* decided that he was 'in the mould of Kenneth Clarke'.

This difficulty in pinning him down was part of John Major's attraction to the parliamentary party, which was desperately in need of unification. By background, he was even less a part of the old Tory hierarchy and squirearchy than the Grantham alderman's daughter, Oxford graduate and businessman's wife whom he succeeded. But he was a Government man, a team player, universally liked. He was the clubbable outsider, the sixteen-year-old school-leaver from Brixton who could more than hold his own among the Blue Chips. His career was Treasury 'dry', Social Security 'wet', a Whip[4], a colleague, a communicator. The Tory parliamentary party understood something real – that John Major was a deeply Conservative man. They also saw that he represented their best hope of electoral salvation.

The party now assembled to celebrate his victory was interrupted

---

[4]The Government's Whips are a team of junior Ministers responsible for securing the successful passage of its legislation, by ensuring that MPs turn up to speak and vote at the right moments (and for the right side). They are the Government's parliamentary intelligence service, and the Whips' office is very much a place for team players. There is a parallel Whips' office on the Opposition side.

by phone calls, most notably from George Bush. The President was calling from aboard his official aircraft, Air Force One, and kept losing contact, while the new Prime Minister was trying to take the call in a noisy kitchen. This scrappy – not to say scatty – conversation was the start of John Major's closest international friendship.

As on election night in 1992, the party on 27 November was composed of the three groups of people who always cluster round the politically victorious. There are the victor's own team, eyes glazed with exhaustion, usually occupying the quietest corners, mobile phones switched off, thankful for an uninterrupted drink. Then there are those whose job it is to serve the ruler of the day, participating with the quiet assurance of those with secure civil service positions. Finally, centre stage, you can always find the courtiers and jackals of public life – by no means all of them politicians – who since time immemorial have deserted the dying monarch just as soon as the succession is beyond doubt. To an old Treasury colleague of John Major like Terry Burns, arriving to offer his congratulations, the presence of this third group was a sharp reminder that the most disturbing guest of all had just entered Number 11: power.

In the political bomb-site left by Margaret Thatcher's defeat, John Major's first task was to form a new Cabinet that would help rebuild the confidence and unity of his party. When he went across to the Commons that night, he had already made it clear that there would be places in his team for the other candidates for the leadership. He was going to have a 'Cabinet of all the talents'. All through the morning and early afternoon of Wednesday 28 November, the leavers, movers and joiners tramped in and out of Number 10. Some decisions took no more than a quick phone call. Douglas Hurd was rather evidently relieved to sail back out of the political firing line into harbour at the Foreign Office. It was much less easy to decide where to anchor that great political privateer, Michael Heseltine. One possible berth was thought to be the Home Office, but 'Hezza' let it be known that his heart's desire was the Board of Trade. He was not, however, to be offered that until after the general election, when Treasury suspicions of his interventionist instincts had waned a little. In the meantime, he could not refuse the Department of the Environment, home of the Community Charge, or poll tax.

It was no easier to decide who to appoint to the two key positions in any government in the run-up to a general election: Chancellor, and Party Chairman. Two big names were in the frame for Chancellor: Kenneth Clarke[5] and Chris Patten. But John Major promoted Norman Lamont to the job, even though he had never headed a government department.

Norman Lamont had been his Chief Secretary, the Chancellor's back-up in Cabinet. He had also run John Major's election campaign, energetically – and successfully. To have appointed anyone else would have seemed like a rebuff to his lieutenant – especially as neither Chris Patten nor Ken Clarke had ever worked in the Treasury. Norman Lamont, an ex-Rothschild's man, had ten years' experience of economic departments behind him, and was, John Major knew, hoping to follow his leader up the Treasury tree.

Unlike the chancellorship, the chairmanship of the Conservative Party is a job that can be everything or nothing. Sometimes – as in the case of John Gummer, Peter Brooke or Sir Norman Fowler – the Chairman is not even in the Cabinet. In the run-up to a general election, however, the Chairman has a crucial job. He had to be a senior figure in John Major's first Cabinet.

Chris Patten had the intellectual strength needed to help the new Prime Minister define his strategy; a vivid turn of phrase; and street-fighting skills sharpened by his time as Environment Secretary, when he had been forced to defend the poll tax. The presence of a strong, thoughtful, articulate Party Chairman in the Cabinet certainly eased the job of running the pre-election Government. But as Chairman, Chris Patten had one great weakness: a marginal seat. At the time of his appointment, however, his electoral

[5]Ken Clarke had been in the Cabinet since 1985, first at Employment, then at Trade and Industry, then as Secretary of State for Health. At the beginning of November 1990, in the reshuffle following Sir Geoffrey Howe's resignation, Margaret Thatcher had moved Ken Clarke to a new battleground, as Secretary of State for Education.

vulnerability did not feature in the Prime Minister's conversation with him.

The Cabinet Secretary, Sir Robin Butler, felt concerned that there were no political wise old heads to help the Prime Minister make out the list. He was echoing the famous Thatcher dictum that 'Every Prime Minister needs a Willie', which has earned Lord Whitelaw a place in every anthology of political anecdote.

Legend has turned Lord Whitelaw into a cross between Merlin and Dr Watson, but contemporary observers give a more modest account of his role in Margaret Thatcher's Government. However, he was there at her elbow, with the Chief Whip Michael Jopling, to help her put together her first Cabinet, and stayed at her side, providing what she called 'ballast', until 1988.

He proved extraordinarily hard to replicate in the 1990s. To begin with, it was intended that his role should be filled by David Waddington, who would leave the Home Office to become Leader of the Lords. The right would be reassured by his 'dry' presence alongside the Prime Minister; and freed from departmental responsibilities, he could also perform the Whitelaw job of arbitrating between colleagues.

In the event, however, this plan faded. John Wakeham, another and more long-lasting of Major's 'Whitelaws', recalls that John Major was much more accessible to his colleagues than his predecessor, so there was less need for another shoulder to cry on. While much liked, Lord Waddington did not tower over his colleagues with Whitelaw authority (or Whitelaw volume).

A first Cabinet says something about a Prime Minister, something about the time, something about the Parliament from which the choice is made. John Major was operating under severe constraints; he made only limited changes. Thirteen Cabinet Ministers stayed in their same jobs, including the three who had been moved only a few weeks before, when Sir Geoffrey Howe had resigned. Only two left the Cabinet, apart from Margaret Thatcher: Lord Belstead and Cecil Parkinson.

But viewed against the backdrop of history, some changes had taken place, even since Margaret Thatcher's first Cabinet in 1979. John Major had more university graduates in his Cabinet than any incoming Prime Minister this century. Oxbridge still predominated, but the balance within it had changed. 1990 was the apotheosis of the Cambridge generation, usurping Oxford's traditional dominance of Conservative Cabinets. The 'Cambridge mafia' – Ken Clarke, John Gummer, Norman Lamont, Michael Howard – were there in force. Douglas Hurd, Peter Lilley, Ian Lang, Tom King and David Mellor were also Cambridge men; so was Richard Ryder, the Chief Whip, who though not formally a member of Cabinet, attended every meeting. Oxford could claim Tony Newton, William Waldegrave, David Waddington, Ken Baker, Michael Heseltine, Chris Patten and Peter Brooke.[6]

For all the Prime Minister's care, that first Cabinet had one glaring presentational flaw. When he had compiled the list, the Prime Minister strolled to Gus O'Donnell's bow-windowed office at the front of Number 10. What did his Press Secretary think? Gus pointed out that 'all the talents' were drawn from one sex, and warned him about the likely reaction. At his very first Prime Minister's Questions on 29 November, the Prime Minister came under fire for appointing the first all-male Cabinet since 1964.

He had not, to be fair, inherited a wide choice of female talent. Since 1964, there had in fact been only one woman in any Tory Cabinet: Margaret Thatcher.[7] There had not been many women on the backbenches: a combination of family unfriendly working hours and unenthusiastic selection committees had limited the inflow of Tory women to the House of Commons. John Major put Virginia Bottomley and Gillian Shephard in key Minister of State jobs, to bring them on for next time. His offer of the deputy chairmanship of the party to Lynda Chalker reached newspaper ears – unfortunately, since she had refused it.

The new Cabinet met for the first time on 29 November – the regular Thursday morning slot. After any reshuffle, let alone a change of leader, the first Cabinet has something of the air of a

[6]By 1995, after John Major's July reshuffle, Oxford was, however, back in the lead, by eleven Cabinet Ministers to seven.
[7]There had been one other woman, for a time, in the Conservative Shadow Cabinet of the late 1970s: Mrs Sally Oppenheim, now Baroness Oppenheim-Barnes.

school prize-giving. The winners stride in from their cars, clutching folders emblazoned with the stamp of their new offices of state – briskly bypassing the cameras, or hanging back to allow a good shot, according to temperament. They gather in the lobby outside the Cabinet Room, chatting self-consciously, pretending to ignore the television crew now allowed to film these preliminaries on special occasions. Officials cluster at the side, watching the show with the tolerant detachment of those whose jobs have not been at risk.

Finally, the new Cabinet is called in to find their places in the new geography of power. The table's curious shape – like a boat with two blunt ends, or an oddly symmetrical coffin – is intended to allow the Prime Minister to see everyone from his central position in front of the fireplace. The old guard sit close to the Prime Minister, the big political beasts opposite him, the new bugs towards the two ends. The Cabinet Secretary sits at his right. On these light-hearted occasions, Robin Butler may allow a schoolmasterly smile to pass over his traditional poker face.

Usually, the Prime Minister is already in the room, seated ready for his Cabinet. On this first occasion, he walked in with them, towards his own new place. He had a good deal to say before normal business began. In traditional style, he began by welcoming the newcomers – David Mellor and Ian Lang. There was also the not-so-newcomer to welcome back: Michael Heseltine. He was, as John Major reminded his colleagues, the sole survivor of both Ted Heath's and Margaret Thatcher's Cabinets. The Prime Minister said he hoped there were no bruises from the leadership contest; they had a lot to do together. There were warm words for the other contender, too, although Douglas Hurd himself was absent at the UN, where the Security Council was agreeing the resolution that would trigger the Gulf War. The Foreign Office had availed itself of the privilege it alone of all departments enjoys: to send a ministerial substitute whenever the Secretary of State is away.

Many have reported John Major's characteristic ice-breaker: 'Well, who'd have thought it?' But an innovation which came later in this Cabinet meeting was more significant. After the traditional tour of the Foreign Office horizon – a serious matter, on the eve of the Gulf War – silence would have been the norm. Margaret

Thatcher did not encourage discussion. But now Michael Heseltine spoke up, with a comment on Jordan, from which he had recently returned.

There was a pause. Ministers eyed each other. There is an old convention that Ministers may report to Cabinet on their overseas trips – a hangover from less travelled days, which can nowadays make for some extraordinarily tedious September Cabinets. Was this convention being revived? Was it Hezza-specific? Or was it a game everyone could play? Then Tom King, as Defence Secretary, came in again. The same happened when Cabinet moved on to Europe, though this time it was not only Michael Heseltine who came in from the sidelines, but also Kenneth Clarke. It was, recorded one of the officials present, like the Prisoners' Chorus from *Fidelio*. One Minister said afterwards, 'Suddenly we were having our first real discussion for years.'

Of course, such discussions were still limited. A group of twenty-plus people, John Major knew quite well, cannot conveniently make complex and detailed decisions. A once-round-the-table of Cabinet on any point can be expected to take up to an hour. Sometimes this is a polite necessity. Sometimes it is necessary for raw political reasons, so that no Minister can afterwards claim not to have been 'signed up' to a decision. But clearly everyone involved – not just the Prime Minister – will try to ensure that the number of issues which require such lumbering treatment, or which will arouse disagreement, are kept to a minimum.

So much of any Cabinet meeting consists of reporting, rather than debating; congratulating, rather than arguing. When Sarah arrived at Number 10, one old hand put it to her this way: 'Ministers,' he said, 'only say two things in Cabinet: "Look, Daddy, no hands," or "Look, Daddy, me too."'

Nevertheless, Ministers did notice a change with the new Prime Minister. 'We got the summing up at the end of Cabinet, rather than the beginning,' is how Chris Patten puts it. John Major's way of doing business, allowing colleagues their say, tempering the blow to those whose arguments did not win the day, kept the Cabinet together. It enabled him to bring Michael Heseltine back into the fold and bury the poll tax with the minimum of disruption. The

Tory party he had to lead was a fragile reconstruction. Yet John Major managed to negotiate a European treaty with full Cabinet backing – and to fight an election at the head of a united team. The process could be time-consuming, leading – as with the slow death of the poll tax – to the charge of 'dithering'. Wary of committing himself too early on any issue, the Prime Minister liked to use Cabinet committee meetings to work his way through the detail first; and this sometimes annoyed his more impatient colleagues. But all acknowledged his skills as a chairman.

These skills carried him through the dark days after Black Wednesday, in the uncongenial basement of the Cabinet Office to which the Cabinet was exiled by repairs to Number 10. They carried him through even more cliff-edge Cabinets in his room at the Commons, when the Government took its life in its hands with the final vote on the Maastricht Bill. They were instinctive. Once Sarah said to him that, even when she knew his game plan, she found it hard during the meeting to spot the moves that would bring results. He looked surprised. 'There wasn't a game plan,' he said.

In Chris Patten's view, the most difficult aspect of John Major's legacy from Margaret Thatcher was her particular style of leadership. The system, he maintains, had got used to being driven at breakneck speed, with no regard for holes in the road, or even corners. When the springs of the jalopy finally broke in the poll tax crater, and her successor began to drive it at a more considerate pace, bits began to fall off. But there were few signs of trouble, in the Cabinet or the party, during those early days. Michael Howard carried the standard for the right to great effect – particularly before Maastricht – because he was always a team player, ready to get involved. Of the other three Ministers who came to be most identified with the Euro-sceptic right, only Peter Lilley was in the Cabinet, at Trade and Industry. John Redwood was one of Peter Lilley's Ministers of State, while Michael Portillo was one of Michael Heseltine's, with hands–on responsibility for the destruction of the poll tax.

At that first Cabinet meeting on 29 November, John Major had, beneath his folder, a list scribbled on one of the scruffy pads provided at each place around the table. On it, he had noted four issues on which he was determined to make an impact: inflation and unemployment (the predictable preoccupations of a former Chancellor); but also, perhaps more revealingly, Northern Ireland and public services. To the Cabinet, however, he pointed up three different and more urgent questions: Europe, the poll tax – and the Gulf. None could wait. Between them, they would absorb most of the energies of John Major's pre-election Government.

2

Inside Number 10

*Never forget, Arthur: the garden belongs to Number Ten and has
nothing to do with Number Eleven.*
Advice given by Lord Rosebery to Arthur Balfour, on his
appointment as Prime Minister; *The Prime Minister* by
George Malcolm Thomson

The three front doors in the plain brick façade of Downing Street
lead into a building like a *Cluedo* board – full of passages, stairs and
doorways that all somehow connect and reconnect with each other.
It was well known to the new Prime Minister – he had worked in
Number 12 as a Whip, and he had been living in Number 11 for
a year as Chancellor – but still, his Press Secretary Gus O'Donnell
recalled later, it felt like alien territory. Margaret Thatcher had lived
there for over eleven years, and it was full of her redecorations, her
choice of pictures, her staff.

The physical oddities of Downing Street reflect its origins. It is
an architectural marriage of Roundhead and Royalist, an allegory
of British constitutional history. George Downing, Cromwell's
chief of intelligence (and one of Harvard's first graduates), was a
successful speculator and political opportunist who, even after the
Restoration, managed to hang on to his claim to the site that bears
his name. To make a suitable residence for Sir Robert Walpole,
the building thrown up on this ground was connected to a much
grander mansion built on land leased by Charles II to the Countess
of Lichfield, his illegitimate daughter by the Duchess of Cleveland.
The black front door (in 1990, before the IRA scored its hit on the

building, still made of wood) so familiar from a thousand evening news programmes, was therefore originally the back entrance: the quick exit through the plebeian, Downing Street end of the building to Parliament. Engraved in brass is the name of the occupant: The First Lord of the Treasury. When George II gave the house to Sir Robert Walpole, it was intended as a personal gift. It was Walpole who wished it to pass to his successors.

The door opens to reveal the central artery of modern British government – the surprisingly long, straight, rather narrow corridor that leads directly to the Cabinet Room. At the Downing Street end, the offices are plain: you are in government rather than in power. Even in the front hall, where world leaders pose with the Prime Minister before the fireplace, you are with Mr Downing, not the Countess. Portraits, a Chippendale hooded chair, a black and white marble floor, the odd pot plant, a glimpse of a Henry Moore down the corridor: all these fight unsuccessfully for command of the atmosphere against the come and go of bureaucratic life. There is none of the imperial grandeur of the Foreign Office, nor even the municipal state of the Treasury.

The unique quality of the entrance to Number 10 is provided by its living history: its kindly, unpretentious, incurably helpful doorkeepers, messengers, police and security staff. They receive scores of petitions and limo-loads of statesmen. Outside the door, living in the intermittent glare of television lights, they line up schoolchildren for photographs, roll red carpets out and back, soften the politician's exit to fame or misfortune, and watch over the Cabinet Office cat. Inside, they dispense coffee, cheerfulness and visitors in a constant stream.

At the far end of the corridor that leads from the front door, you pass from, as it were, the Commons to the Lords, leaving Mr Downing's house and entering the Countess's mansion. The corridor widens into a lobby outside the Cabinet Room. From his portrait over the fireplace, Sir Winston Churchill looks down on the clusters of Ministers who assemble there for meetings;[1] so, from his alcove,

---

[1] This painting was brought to Number 10 by Margaret Thatcher in 1979. It used to hang in her room as Leader of the Opposition in the House of Commons.

does a bust of William Pitt. From a plinth on the other side of the lobby, Benjamin Disraeli keeps an eye on the Cabinet Room door.

Visitors are shepherded into a gloomy waiting room off the lobby, suggestive of a grand but slightly shabby medical practice – even down to the out-of-date magazines piled neatly on the table. The bookcases are full of books provided by Cabinet Ministers, each of whom, by convention, donates one on appointment – and a curious collection they are. Curiouser still is the other room in this corner: the Gents.

Jonathan recalls Norma Major's amused reaction to the place when she was on a tour around the building checking access for disabled people. This scruffy, tiled urinal struck her as extraordinarily basic, suitable for little boys rather than great men. But it is where many crucial conversations and deals take place.[2]

The Political Secretary's office lies between the waiting room and the Cabinet Room itself, although the inter-connecting door to the Cabinet Room is now locked. Once Walpole's dressing-room, it is an office that captures the two sides of Downing Street life. High-ceilinged, with a fine cornice, a marble fireplace and some distinguished paintings, in the early 1990s it also boasted a chipboard bookcase, battered metal filing cabinet and an armchair with the springs hanging out of the bottom.[3] When Jonathan inherited this office, early in 1992, he found it perfectly placed to monitor the comings and goings of the Prime Minister's life, for by then John Major had set up office in the Cabinet Room. He had virtually abandoned the first-floor study, alienated both by its style and distance from his staff – even the acquisition of a portrait of the cricketer W.G. Grace could not make him feel comfortable there.

[2]In one of his TV dramas, Michael Dobbs only slightly stretches the truth by arranging for Prime Minister Urquhart to sack his Environment Secretary in the Gents. Not, however, in anything as shabby as the real thing. The scene was set in a marbled mini-palace, furnished with ivory hairbrushes and all the other trappings of the grandest London club. On the first floor of Number 10 there is a Ladies much more in line with this image: a fearfully grand little temple of gilt and mirrors.
[3]Margaret Thatcher recalls in her autobiography how, when she arrived, the whole building shared this seedy appearance of a 'furnished house to let'.

With its chintzes, cabinets of silver and curious lack of bookshelves, it could not have been more different from the severe, book-lined elegance of the study in Number 11.

Working in the Cabinet Room had much more of the feel of the kind of departmental office to which he had become accustomed over the years. Most importantly, it followed the departmental style of having a Private Office of officials next door to shout to, chivvy and consult. John Major always liked to work off his restlessness by wandering the building, picking through people's in-trays, discovering for himself what his staff were up to. The Private Office is too crowded to aspire to a gracious reflection of its history: its inhabitants work long hours in cramped conditions which would be furiously rejected by the average district auditor. These rooms are connected with the basement filing clerks and 'Garden Room Girls' by the kind of creaking dumb waiter that used to fuel the dining-rooms of Edwardian London. The battered 'in' and 'out' trays look as if they went through the Blitz, which they probably did: you can see identical ones in the carefully-preserved Cabinet War Rooms under Great George Street.

But the Cabinet Room itself, enlarged from the original library of the house, is a fine room, light and well-proportioned – though the new security windows require muscle and persistence to open. French windows lead on to the terrace; steps lead down to a spacious, if slightly bleak, garden. Walpole presides over meetings from behind the Prime Minister's chair; those on the Prime Minister's side of the table can enjoy an eighteenth-century view of the green fields of St James's, painted by George Lambert from the Downing Street terrace – only a few feet from where they are sitting. Otherwise the walls are bare, allegedly to minimise distractions and prevent ministerial minds from wandering.

There are two fine clocks, with an unfortunate tendency to tell different times. One is on the mantelpiece behind the Prime Minister, the other on a small table opposite him, which now also carries an offensive weapon – the gold-cased sword presented to John Major by the Saudis after the Gulf War. The brown baize-covered table is adorned by some historic pieces of silver (and some distinctly unhistoric water carafes).

To the right of the Cabinet Room – looking from the Downing Street end – you reach the main staircase of Number 10. Down in the stairwell is the globe presented by President Mitterrand to Margaret Thatcher, so large it had to be split in two to get it through the front door. There may be another reason why it lurks in the bowels of the building: below the reference to the Falklands Islands is the unfortunate legend 'Islas Malvinas'. But there is no reason to look down. Your eye is led firmly upwards by the black-and-white prints and photographs of past Prime Ministers that line the stairs.

At the top, in the 1980s, there was a temporary change: a colour photograph of James Callaghan was added. But when Margaret Thatcher's picture was put up after her departure, the opportunity was taken to restore the black-and-white uniformity of history.

It is at the top of the staircase, in the three state drawing rooms, that the grandeur of the building really breaks out; much enhanced in Margaret Thatcher's later years, by Quinlan Terry's redecoration. Corinthian touches to the White Drawing Room, Doric to the Green, Ionic to the Pillared Room – all combine to make an impressive statement of prime ministerial power.

The White Drawing Room is rich in elaborate but delicate plasterwork, its four corners decorated with the national emblems of the rose, thistle, daffodil and shamrock; it is furnished for the stateliest of conversations between international leaders. Traditionally, it has also been used for television interviews, giving the Prime Minister full benefit of the gilt of office, but John Major came to prefer less frothy backgrounds.

The Green Drawing Room – once the dining room at Number 10 – contains the desk at which William Pitt worked through the Napoleonic wars. Like the other state rooms it is hung with a fine collection of paintings, predominantly eighteenth and early nineteenth century. One of these occasionally gives rise to mis-understandings – most notably at the London Group of Seven summit in 1991. One of the Private Secretaries, hastening to the Green Drawing Room to look after President Mitterrand, found the French President serenading the painting in the corner, by George Romney, of a beautiful creature with long fair hair and a long dress. President Mitterrand was giving a spirited rendering of 'Auprès de ma blonde'. Pausing diplomatically on the threshold, this official had his reward. The solo became a duet as the Group of Seven's other French speaker, Brian Mulroney of Canada, arrived and joined in. Neither, clearly, had studied the inscription, which reveals that the portrait is of one Thomas Fane, dressed as 'unbreeched' little boys traditionally were, right up to the beginning of the twentieth century.

Through the double doors is the Pillared Room. The biggest of the three, it is used for everything from parties to speech practice. In the far left-hand corner, beyond the pillars from which the room takes its name, is the doorway that leads to the hidden beauty of Downing Street, the panelled dining rooms created by Sir John Soane in the early nineteenth century.

The Small Dining Room has enormous charm – though when the modern works sponsored by the Silver Trust[4] are added to the combination of scientific busts and portraits chosen by Margaret Thatcher, it can look slightly like an upmarket junk shop. The Large Dining Room has more space to display the vast Silver Trust salts and peppers and other creations. It is now sadly darkened by the heavy metal grilles constructed to protect the windows after the IRA mortar attack. But it is still a room of great beauty, in which up to sixty people can dine. It is also used for press conferences, though it is far from ideal for that. The combination of panelling and television lights can raise the temperature to tropical levels. But unless it is warm enough to use the garden, there is nowhere else suitable.

[4]Downing Street was, as Margaret Thatcher discovered, singularly lacking in silver. She was lent a fine collection by Lord Brownlow, whose great house, Belton, is very close to her Grantham birthplace, but this was hardly a permanent solution. The Silver Trust was set up, and raised money to commission some work for Downing Street by modern silversmiths. One of its most imaginative ventures was a series of silver plates by different designers, each sponsored by an individual or company, whose name is engraved on the back. When it came to the presentation party at Number 10, however, there were some official raised eyebrows at one of the names, who had recently finished a prison sentence. The Prime Minister, however, was firm. The man concerned had paid his debt to society – and what's more, the Silver Trust had allowed him to pay for a plate. He was entitled to come to the party with all the other sponsors.

Number 10 is not the very model of a modern government office. There is no briefing suite, White House style: lobby journalists crowd into the Press Secretary's office. There is no nineties-style fitness room, not even a fifties-style canteen (staff have to foray into the Cabinet Office for sandwiches). When, in 1990, Sarah asked for a laptop, this caused some consternation: although secretaries and the 'Garden Room Girls' – whose nickname reflects the location of their office – worked on screen, senior officials did not. Whitehall business was heavily paper-based. By 1995, with a Principal Private Secretary[5] who is a serious computer expert, Number 10 was properly interactive and on the way to being connected to the Internet.

Number 10 is, in short, a converted house. Over the years, Prime Ministers have surrendered living space to offices. The flat used by present-day Prime Ministers was created in the 1930s, and it is markedly less grand than either the Chancellor's living quarters next door, or the Defence Secretary's flat in the Admiralty. Offices are shoe-horned into every corner of the building, from basement to attics. Sarah's office, as head of the Policy Unit, was once not so much part of the 'kitchen cabinet' as the nursery region of Number 10, inhabited by the children and grandchildren of Prime Ministers.[6]

The staff crammed into these offices are a mixture of civil service 'insiders' and political 'outsiders'. The Prime Minister's six Private Secretaries are career civil servants, who work for whomever happens to be in office. They handle the day-to-day flow of business from departments, fix meetings for the Prime Minister, take the minutes of such meetings, put together his briefings and transmit his wishes around Whitehall.

A still grander civil servant sits at the Prime Minister's right hand

[5]Alex Allan, the Treasury official who took on the job after the general election in 1992.
[6]Lady Elliot of Harwood, born in 1903 into the Tennant tribe which produced Asquith's wife, once came with Elinor Goodman of ITN to recall her memories of Number 10 for television. Gazing out of Sarah's office window, which gives a bird's eye view of the street theatre of Downing Street, she related how she had once thrown her teddy bear down into a crowd of suffragettes who had assembled below.

at Cabinet, big ministerial meetings and weekly meetings on the management of government business: the Cabinet Secretary, alias the Head of the Home Civil Service. He can always been found in the Private Office or the Cabinet Room when the Government's alarm bells have started ringing. But his office is not in Number 10:[7] the personification of permanence in British administration lives next door, in the Cabinet Office.

The Political Secretary and the Parliamentary Private Secretary are not civil servants, and are appointed personally by the Prime Minister. The Political Secretary is responsible for links with Conservative Central Office and the party in the country, acts as secretary to Political Cabinet (when the official Cabinet Secretary and his team discreetly leave the room), accompanies the Prime Minister on his political tours, prepares material with which he can attack the Opposition, and deals with the most sensitive of the letters which require an overtly party political reply. His overall role is to ensure that while the Prime Minister is busy being Prime Minister, he does not forget that he is also the leader of a political party in whose name he stands for office.

The Parliamentary Private Secretary is – like the PPS to any other Minister – a backbench MP. He is the Prime Minister's eyes and ears in the House of Commons and the House of Lords. He provides his boss with an alternative stream of knowledge about MPs to that flowing from the Whips' Office in Number 12.

The Press Secretary is normally but not necessarily a civil servant, from either the civil service information service (which supplies his staff), or the mainstream of the mandarinate. His job is to brief the lobby correspondents for the Prime Minister (on everything but strictly party matters) and to co-ordinate the Whitehall media machine.

The Policy Unit is the lineal descendant of the Central Policy Review Staff, which was established in the Cabinet Office in the

---

[7]The Cabinet Office lives the other side of the back door to Number 10, made famous by the episode in *Yes, Prime Minister* in which Prime Minister Jim Hacker locks his intrusive Cabinet Secretary, Sir Humphrey, out of the centre of power. Real life's smarter civil servants have ensured that access is governed by a smart card.

1970s under Lord Rothschild. But the CPRS, or 'think-tank', was responsible to the Cabinet, not solely to the Prime Minister. James Callaghan added a small Number 10 Policy Unit, and Margaret Thatcher continued this tradition. In 1983, she finally abolished the CPRS and enlarged the Policy Unit to take up the slack. This history explains the traditional mixture of Policy Unit staff. While Secretaries of State can appoint one, or at most two Special Advisers, the Prime Minister can choose a Policy Unit of seven or eight. Normally, however, a couple of these are permanent civil servants on secondment from their departments, the kind of high-flyers who would previously have joined the CPRS.

The Policy Unit's job is to keep the Prime Minister in touch with outside thinking, to work on his own ideas and to act as a sounding board for Ministers, advising on the flow of proposals and counter-proposals that pour in continuously from all around Whitehall. The Prime Minister can use his unit as storm troops, invading the complacent hinterland of Whitehall; or as peacemakers, building bridges between warring departments and Ministers. In practice, the Unit tries to do a bit of both: to be both grit and oil in the government machine.

These four elements – private, political, press and policy – make up virtually the entirety of the Prime Minister's department. In pockets around the building can be found other essential and traditional elements of office, such as the Appointments Secretary and his staff, who diligently select bishops and lord lieutenants for the Prime Minister to recommend to Her Majesty. But at the rough end of the business, dealing with high policy, low politics or the real-life mixture of the two, the heart of government is small. Compared with any Whitehall department, or the offices of heads of government anywhere else in the western world, it is tiny. The sheer size of ministerial departments, compared with the Prime Minister's office, creates a healthy pluralism at the centre, but it also puts enormous pressure on Number 10 staff.

Margaret Thatcher's Private Secretaries became, overnight, John Major's. They were led by Andrew Turnbull, the Principal Private

Secretary, a role that carries a bizarre range of responsibilities stretching from royal affairs to the rewiring of Downing Street, taking in all the Prime Minister's most sensitive meetings on the way. The job is traditionally filled by a Treasury civil servant marked out for the top.[8]

The other inhabitant of the inner Private Office is the Private Secretary for Foreign Affairs, an overloaded job made even more burdensome by the fact that everything to do with Ireland – Northern or Republic – also lands on this desk. Charles Powell, who was knighted in Margaret Thatcher's resignation honours, was irreplaceable with the Gulf War looming. It was therefore not until March that Stephen Wall, who had run John Major's Private Office during his brief stay at the Foreign Office, took over.[9]

Graham Bright, MP for Luton South, was the Prime Minister's Parliamentary Private Secretary. He shared the office the other side of the Cabinet Room with John Major's first Political Secretary, Judith Chaplin, who had been one of his Special Advisers in the Treasury.

There is a crucial difference between the Political Secretary and the other outsiders working in the Prime Minister's Policy Unit. Like the Special Advisers in other departments, these are temporary civil servants, paid for by the taxpayer. It is accepted that they may behave differently from 'established' (or permanent) civil servants,

---

[8]Of Margaret Thatcher's Principal Private Secretaries, by 1995 one – Sir Kenneth Stowe – had retired after becoming Permanent Secretary at the DHSS; another – Sir Clive Whitmore – had just retired from the job of Permanent Secretary at the Home Office; a third – Sir Robin Butler – was Cabinet Secretary; a fourth – Sir Nigel Wicks – had become Second Permanent Secretary at the Treasury. Andrew Turnbull became Permanent Secretary at the Department of the Environment in 1994.

[9]The other members of the Private Office team were Barry Potter (who dealt with economic policy), Dominic Morris (parliamentary affairs), Caroline Slocock, succeeded by William Chapman, who took over Dominic Morris's job shortly before the election, and Sandra Phillips, the Diary Secretary. In 1993, Dominic Morris returned to Number 10 as a member of the Policy Unit, and the Private Office team was enlarged by the addition of an Assistant Private Secretary for Foreign Affairs.

but there are still limitations, carefully policed by the Cabinet Secretary.[10]

The Prime Minister's other import from the Treasury was his Press Secretary. A South Londoner like the Prime Minister, an economist with a strong academic background, Gus O'Donnell was much liked by the lobby[11], who found his easy manner a perfect reflection of the Prime Minister's. Chris Patten, who understood how important Gus's role was, once described him as 'a younger brother ready to behave like an older brother'. He was certainly obliged to share the contents of his suitcase like a brother, digging into it on foreign trips for the shirts and sweaters the Prime Minister had forgotten to pack.

For the Policy Unit, the Prime Minister looked further afield. Sarah was sitting in the *Daily Telegraph* office one evening of his first week in office, pounding through a piece for the centre pages, eye on the clock, mind on her promise not to be late – not again, not this time – for an evening helping her husband Douglas do his stuff as a Foreign Office Minister, entertaining the President of the Gambia at the theatre. The phone rang. It was Andrew Turnbull. Could Sarah 'pop in' for a word with the Prime Minister?

She knew such journalistic opportunities often came at short notice, but she had to explain her date with Douglas, assorted Gambians and Sondheim's *Into the Woods*.

---

[10]One rule is rigidly enforced: Special Advisers may not become parliamentary candidates. If they do, they have to resign straight away. So Judith Chaplin had had to resign as John Major's Special Adviser in the Treasury when in 1990 she was adopted as Conservative candidate for Newbury. But since the Political Secretary is paid for by the party, the Prime Minister was able to bring her back on to his staff in that capacity. Tragically, Judith Chaplin died in 1993, less than a year after being elected member for Newbury.

[11]The lobby is a self-policing group of parliamentary journalists who attend twice-daily background briefings by the Prime Minister's Press Secretary. Their group name comes from the ante-chamber to the House of Commons, to which they have access, and from which they pick up the rest of their daily diet of information. By 1990, some national newspapers had withdrawn from the lobby system, refusing any longer to abide by the conventions of the unattributable briefing. In Gus O'Donnell's time, they returned, but the convention that Number 10 briefings should not be sourced was frequently broken.

'Could you come in the interval?' said Andrew.

That was difficult. She didn't know when the interval was, how long, how easy it would be to leave . . .

'Er, fine,' Sarah said.

'Could you come in the side way?' added Andrew.

That would make any journalist suspicious.

In Number 10, Sarah found the Prime Minister flanked by the Cabinet Secretary and the Chief Economic Adviser. He came straight to the point. Would Sarah become head of the Policy Unit? An evening of pure Whitehall farce followed, as she went back and forth – *Into the Woods*, then into Number 10 – dragging Douglas into the corner for advice and the editor of the *Daily Telegraph* from his watering-hole in St James's for permission to break her contract. By midnight, she had abandoned twenty years of journalism for life on the inside. She was to work in Number 10 for more than four years.

The Prime Minister needed a full Policy Unit quickly. He wanted to bring in Nick True, whose skills he had come to value when he was a junior Minister at the Department of Social Security, and Nick was a Special Adviser there.

The two civil servants in the unit, Carolyn Sinclair and John Mills, agreed to stay on until the election; so did Howell Harris Hughes, who filled the City slot, a vital listening-post in the Unit.[12] That left two posts to fill. Alan Rosling, who joined from Courtaulds, supplemented the unit's business skills. The final member of the Policy Unit was Jonathan.

Jonathan had for several years been Kenneth Clarke's Special Adviser. He worked with him in three departments – Employment, Trade and Industry, and Health. Then in 1989 he decided that he wanted a change, and left Whitehall – he thought for good. But he found that he couldn't shake off the political bug. Just before Christmas 1990, Sarah contacted him and asked if he would like to talk about working for John Major. He joined in early February,

[12]Sir Percy Cradock, the Prime Minister's Foreign Affairs Adviser – who reported directly to him, and also carried Cabinet Office responsibilities as the Chairman of the Joint Intelligence Committee – had already agreed to stay.

and the Prime Minister asked him to take over as Political Secretary when Judith Chaplin finally left to work full time as candidate for Newbury. Having taken up the reins the day the election was called, he stayed in Number 10 until the end of 1994.

It was Andrew Turnbull's job to 'settle the Prime Minister in'. Small matters loomed large to begin with. The Prime Minister wanted to go back to his Huntingdon home – and constituency – as much as possible, and Norma decided to keep that as her base. So his house, The Finings, had to be brought within the communications and security net. Meanwhile, Margaret Thatcher's personal support team had naturally disappeared from Number 10, so one of Andrew's first tasks was to find someone to shop and cook for the Prime Minister.

John Major had been camping in Number 11, and showed signs of following the same unsettled habits in Number 10. Never much interested in food, he was inclined not to eat at all when under pressure; once the critical meeting or statement was over, however, he would then urgently need refuelling. This caused a security panic in his first week, when the Prime Minister went missing. Although 'Switch', Number 10's peerless telephone switchboard team, soon developed an uncanny ability to track him down, at that time the system was unused to John Major's habit of wandering around the building. Since he had already forbidden his Principal Private Secretary to operate the buzzer system which is supposed to tell his Private Office when he enters or leaves the building, it was some time before the detectives realised he had gone AWOL. He wasn't anywhere in Number 10. His car was still in the street. He hadn't walked out the front door. Where could he be?

They were saved from heart failure by the discovery that the Prime Minister had gone out through Number 12 with a colleague to McDonald's in Victoria Street.

Eventually, it was arranged that someone from Chequers, tra-ditionally staffed by the Royal Navy and WRNS, would come up to Number 10 on rotation. One after another, they brought a characteristic breezy Naval cheerfulness to the Downing Street flat, coupled with a readiness to whip up a bacon sandwich at short notice. The personal back-up for Britain's Prime Minister has certainly improved since the days when poor Ramsay MacDonald found he had to complete the furnishings himself. But compared with the circumstances of any other western leader, it is not generous. Historically, this derives from the Prime Minister's position as a mere servant of the Crown; even his formal rights of precedence were not established until Arthur Balfour became fed up with following the younger sons of peers in to dinner, and got himself jacked up to just behind the Archbishop of York. Not for Prime Ministers the comfort of a Civil List salary, large state-financed household and right to accept presents from foreign dignitaries. The Prime Minister is paid less than the Cabinet Secretary, and in real terms, the salary has declined dramatically since the nineteenth century.

The rules against personal use of official services are such that if he uses his official car to drive to the shops in Huntingdon – something his security advisers will insist on – he will get a bill for mileage. If he receives any presents worth over £125, he has to pay for them, hand them over, or leave them in the building. In 1991, he was particularly sad to part with a piece of Lalique presented to him at the launch of the European Bank for Reconstruction and Development. At Christmas, the Policy Unit had a whip-round in Number 10, and bought it for him. There was something peculiarly British about a collection of public servants buying something from the state for which it had not paid in the first place.

Other, tedious aspects of the settling-in process fell to Gus O'Donnell to deal with. There were seemingly-endless photographs for one purpose or another (it took months to get the Prime Minister to agree to one for distribution to the Tory faithful), and a session modelling for Madame Tussaud's. There was a rush of instant books, and an insatiable press interest in the precise details of his early life, his exams, jobs and time on the dole. The Labour MP Jack Cunningham even seemed to think it worth questioning whether a particular film (*The Flame and the Arrow*) the Prime Minister said he had seen while he was unemployed had actually been on release at that time. The media fuss seemed ludicrous, particularly when it became clear that Cunningham was wrong.

The press also made a meal out of the Prime Minister's O-levels, taken after he had left school. He could not remember exactly what he had taken, nor when; nor did he think it the press's business. Norma did not see why she should spend her time searching through the attics at Huntingdon for certificates just to satisfy the tabloids. Eventually, however, she found them, Gus got a grip on the Prime Minister's *curriculum vitae*, and interest in his personal history subsided.

But Andrew Turnbull nearly lost his grip when an admirer of the Prime Minister wrote offering him a Dalmatian puppy. The Prime Minister was tempted – he could get some exercise while taking it for walks. Finally, however, Andrew – not a dog-lover – managed to dissuade him. Humphrey the cat continued 'his' (actually her) reign over Downing Street – and a career as a serial duckling killer in St James's Park.[13] As for the walks, they had to wait until a medical peer, Ian McColl, joined the Downing Street team in 1994. Determined to make sure the Prime Minister had fresh air and exercise, even in London, he would do everything but wear a collar and lead himself in order to get John Major out of Number 10.

According to Harold Macmillan, events are the enemies of Prime Ministers. But routine is a killer, too. Before he had appointed his personal staff, even before he had finished appointing his Government, the Prime Minister had to face the most relentless and public element of his routine. On Thursday 29 November, he had to go to the Commons for Prime Minister's Questions. Unless he was unavoidably occupied elsewhere – and nothing much less than absence overseas would count – he would have to answer questions every Tuesday and Thursday throughout the parliamentary year.

In Canberra in 1994, Sarah went to watch the Australian Prime Minister, Paul Keating, handle his equivalent parliamentary occasion. Everyone told her that it would be a shock to her English sensitivities; in truth, compared with the House of Commons, it was a picnic. Questions ambled on for an hour; other Ministers gave some of the answers; no one was allowed a come-back question, or

---

[13]When, in 1994, some nestlings were found dead in the Downing Street garden, suspicion naturally fell on Humphrey. The Prime Minister defended the cat on prime-time television. An excess of human attention probably did for these baby birds, but given Humphrey's previous, a verdict of 'not proven' would be safer than 'not guilty'.

'supplementary'. At Westminster, Prime Minister's Questions only run for quarter of an hour, but this brevity heightens the tension. By convention, the Leader of the Opposition may have three bites at the cherry – a question and two come-backs. The Prime Minister and the Leader of the Opposition are struggling both to win this strange parliamentary tennis-match, and to make their point briefly for the early evening news – not quite the same thing. The form of Prime Minister's Questions has evolved in the post-war years, and perhaps not entirely for the better. In the early 1950s, for example, there was no fixed time for 'PMQs'. The batting did not pass automatically to the Prime Minister at 3.15 p.m., as it does today, but rather when the previous questions on the order paper, put down for other Ministers, had been dealt with. If the first Question to the Prime Minister was not reached by 3.30 p.m., that was it.

Sarah's father, who was a very new junior Treasury Minister at the time, recalls the hazards of answering questions ahead of Winston Churchill in the early 1950s. The Whips, by then uneasy about Churchill's forensic skills, would encourage those before him to bore on as long as possible. But Sir Winston adored his parliamentary outing, and would get extremely restless as 3.30 p.m. approached. Ministers performed at the Despatch Box to a background of conflicting stage whispers.

'Keep it up,' the Whips would mutter.

'Don't answer that – sit down!' the Prime Minister would growl.

This system was changed in the 1960s; and then in the 1980s Margaret Thatcher ended the practice of 'referring' detailed questions to the relevant Minister. The subject of most questions is concealed beneath the cover of an anodyne inquiry about the Prime Minister's engagements. This allows for a supplementary on whatever issue the backbencher wants to raise, so the range of subjects the Prime Minister has to be prepared to cover is enormous. PMQs were therefore completely different from the questions sessions John Major had experienced before, even as Chancellor of the Exchequer.

Margaret Thatcher had prepared for questions with what was known as the 'Plastic Fantastic' – a folder which contained key topical briefings at the front, followed by pages of 'killer facts' on the main topics. So, if she did not have anything at the front that dealt specifically with the issue raised, she could flip quickly to the back and reel off one of her trademark lists of statistics.

On his first day as Prime Minister, there was no time for the Number 10 team to find out if John Major wanted to work the same way. He had to make do with the Plastic Fantastic. He looked at it doubtfully. He had clearly been expecting something a bit more, well, substantial. A bit more information. He had got used to lots of detail at the Treasury. But there was nothing anyone could do about it in the time available.

Questions came. He survived. But some of his answers were, to be honest, a bit thin.

One of Margaret Thatcher's team had come to operate on the principle that the worse she had done at Questions, the more she would need reassurance afterwards. After John Major's first Questions, when they all went back to his room in the Commons, the official in question therefore went into overdrive. 'Fantastic, Prime Minister – you did marvellously. Absolutely terrific.'

John Major looked at him in astonishment. 'No, I didn't', he said. 'It really wasn't very good at all. And I'd much rather you told me the truth. There were lots of things I could have done better. What we need to do next time is this, this and this . . .'

'Whoops,' the adviser said to himself. 'Sycophancy is out.'

One of the problems of the Prime Minister's life is that people he meets tend to tell him what they think he wants to hear. One of the least agreeable features of an adviser's life is to listen to 'friends' ladling out praise for some speech or announcement to the Prime Minister's face, only moments after the very same people have taken you aside to hiss in your ear how disastrous it has been. It isn't, however, always easy to be the one who delivers the message. After speeches, or interviews, the Prime Minister would always ask what his team thought. Jonathan, Sarah and Gus O'Donnell developed the kind of code which is part of an adviser's toolkit, and which caused the Prime Minister some considerable amusement as he watched them wriggle their way round the truth.

'That was . . . (pause) . . . fine, Prime Minister,' meant it was not a great success. '*Really* fine' meant better than that. 'Great' meant just that. On the other hand, 'Umm . . . not the best I've heard you give,' meant: don't expect any bouquets. And 'Well, you certainly gave them their money's worth,' meant: thank heavens, we wondered if you were ever going to stop.

After a year or two, the Prime Minister had learnt to handle PMQs with a professionalism that more than once dispelled the fractious turbulence of his own backbenchers. He could use the occasion to steady his party's nerve. He could even – in a victory for common sense – refuse to answer ridiculously detailed questions of which he had been given no warning. But at the beginning, the onus was on him to demonstrate the necessary confidence and omniscience, and he had to absorb a massive amount of information on subjects which he had never before had to deal with.

The basic routine he settled to was much as in Margaret Thatcher's day. At nine o'clock each Questions morning, he would work through a note prepared overnight by one of his Private Secretaries, then the media summary prepared by the Press Secretary. At that stage, he liked all of his key staff there, and anybody could pitch in – so long as they didn't waste his time. During the morning, the lines he wanted to take on particular issues would be worked up for him. Sometimes that would involve some sharp arguments with departments. What were they doing about X? The Prime Minister wasn't happy with the line on Y. Where had they got to with his questions on Z? And so on.

Since the Prime Minister himself will have meetings all morning, he has to spend lunchtime reading the results of his parliamentary team's work, in John Major's case alone except for his Private Secretary for Parliamentary Affairs and Political Secretary. This represented a change of routine – where Margaret Thatcher had liked to have another Private Secretary or two at hand, John Major preferred to work with a smaller team, get comfortable with the line he was going to take, think it through for himself. Although, as time went on, he too developed a mental lists of 'killer facts', he never quite cured himself of a desire to answer the question.

Just before 3.00 p.m., the rest of the Questions team gathers in the hall – the other Private Secretaries, Parliamentary Private Secretary and Press Secretary. There follows that scene familiar from a thousand television news clips, as the Prime Minister and his team head out of the door for his car ('Forget the cameras, Prime Minister, don't look, don't smile, don't look worried, don't look too cheerful. *Smile*.'). His PPS joins him, while the others scramble into the back-up vehicles.

They re-group in his room in the Commons, behind the Speaker's chair, for any last queries the Prime Minister may have. He paces up and down while practice questions are fired at him. Just before 3.15, the Prime Minister enters the chamber, to backbench 'Hear, hears' whose strength is a first indication of the political climate. The Press Secretary heads for his seat in the gallery. The rest of the Number 10 team do their best to get quickly into the officials' box in the corner of the chamber, as the team supporting the previous Ministers at the Despatch Box is summarily ejected the minute the Prime Minister gets up.

However awful Prime Minister's Questions may look on tele-vision, with the protagonists shouting over the noise of baying parliamentary opponents, it serves two vital functions. First, it gets the Prime Minister out of the Downing Street bunker, and into the cockpit of politics. Sir Gordon Reece, who was generous in his advice to Sarah when she started in Number 10, urged her to dissuade the Prime Minister from spending too much time in the 'convent calm' of Number 10. As Gordon Reece used to tell Margaret Thatcher, it was just too cosy. Everyone bustles around to do the leader's business ('Yes, Reverend Mother, no, Reverend Mother.'). Outside, in the raucous real world, things are different.

Secondly, it obliges Prime Ministers to keep the whole gamut of government activity constantly in view, since at any moment they may be obliged to answer questions on it. Of course, the kind of review that can take place in a few hurried moments on Questions day can only be superficial. But it operates as a warning system. Those who served both Margaret Thatcher and John Major can testify to occasions when the threat of a question has changed policy.

Even after his first PMQs, the Prime Minister could not relax. He had insisted on honouring his commitment to speak at an MP's annual dinner, way up in the north-west of England, that very evening. The Private Office were appalled. Was this going to be the pattern? How many was he going to do? What else in a Prime Minister's crowded life would have to give?

The sharpest battles among the Number 10 staff are over rival claims for the Prime Minister's time. His Parliamentary Private Secretary wants him to spend time in the Commons tea-room. His Appointments Secretary wants him to see museums and holy men. His Press Secretary wants him to give interviews. His Political Office wants him to remember he is leader of the Conservative Party, and tries to keep days clear for him to stomp the country. His Private Office struggles to schedule committee meetings. His Policy Unit wants to carve out thinking time. The Diary Secretary does her level best to keep five minutes free for the Prime Minister to see his family or drop in at a cricket match. But at the periodic diary meetings, umpired by the Principal Private Secretary, the heaviest fire is exchanged between the 'foreigners' and the rest.

Keeping international relationships, 'special' or otherwise, in working order requires a great deal of telephone communication. Britain's much-prized overlapping circles of world influence – through membership of the Group of Seven, NATO, the UN Security Council, the European Union, and the Commonwealth – generate a continuous stream of international meetings. Face-to-face 'bilaterals' with other statesmen, both home and away fixtures, add to the diary overload.

The pressure is increased by the fact that the British constitution offers no presidential alternative to the Prime Minister. There is no superannuated politician to share the task of receiving the great and good of other countries. These eminent persons love to stay with the Queen, and roll back into Buckingham Palace for a full-dress state banquet. But for affairs of state, there is no substitute for the Prime Minister. Unfortunately, London is a popular port of call. It is not only 'State Visitors' (the top category) and 'Guests of Government' (the next grandest) but also foreign leaders on 'private' (i.e., shopping) trips who want to call in on their friend John Major.

The Foreign Office man in Number 10 is therefore subjected to a flow of requests from his department. These requests always tend to take the same form: His Excellency Mr X is the up-and-coming member of government Y, where Britain has important interests and excellent export prospects. Mr X has not yet met the Prime Minister, and his office is pressing for a 'very brief' meeting/ handshake/photo-call.

The brevity has almost always turned out to be an illusion, existing only in the mind of the Foreign Office. Preparation time was needed; John Major hated being under-briefed. Then, a combination of his ineradicable politeness and tendency to get interested in whomever he met would always tend to turn a fifteen-minute courtesy call into a forty-five-minute meeting. To the Foreign Office, the Prime Minister's time was a precious commodity to be traded with other governments, a card to play in the endless round of who-sees-whom. To his political staff, it was a resource needed to win him the right to be in Downing Street in the first place.

Having fought off 90 per cent of Foreign Office requests, Charles Powell or Stephen Wall would then fight like demons to insert the remaining 10 per cent into the diary. Yet, as every political strategist has reminded every Prime Minister, electoral mandates are rarely won abroad. So, as the election approached, the battle for the diary became ever more intense. As late as the end of January 1992, Sarah had a despairing note from Jonathan. Fresh from trench warfare at a diary meeting intended to clear time for the Manifesto, he reported glumly that a crucial planning day still contained two bishops and the inevitable 'Dr Apfelstrudel'.

But at the end of 1990, with a new European treaty looming and the still more immediate prospect of war in the Gulf, no one could quarrel with the dominance of international affairs in the Prime Minister's diary. The world was all too much with us. His priority was to make foreign friends – and deal with foreign devils.

3

Foreign Devils and
American Friends

The last hurrah in the global game.
The Hon. Raymond Seitz, American Ambassador to the
Court of St James's, on the Gulf War

The Gulf crisis had been building up steadily all through Margaret Thatcher's last months. Soon after Kuwait was invaded on 2 August 1990, the United States and Britain announced troop deployments. In London, Parliament was recalled for a special two-day session at the beginning of September. The War Cabinet began meeting – only the fourth time since 1945 that ominous label had been given to a Cabinet committee.

The week before the new Prime Minister took office, the Defence Secretary, Tom King, had announced the formation and deployment of a British armoured division. Then, on the day of John Major's first Cabinet, the UN Security Council had passed Resolution 678. This set the deadline – 15 January – for Iraq to withdraw from Kuwait, and authorised the use of 'all necessary force' to compel obedience. John Major had inherited an international policy, but now the national responsibility for carrying it out was his.

The imminence of war had made it urgent for the Prime Minister to build contact with other world leaders; above all, with President

Bush. On 21 December 1990, John Major was in Washington, ready to go to Camp David for his first prime ministerial tête-à-tête with the President. With the winter weather closing in, it was thought too dangerous to travel there from Washington by helicopter, so George Bush and John Major drove together along the snowy roads to the presidential holiday camp, with their advisers, Brent Scowcroft and Charles Powell, jammed into the front seat.

George Bush, at that time, lacked wholehearted congressional support for war. But John Major was convinced from the beginning that Bush would go ahead with military action whatever the opposition. The President knew he could count on the support of the new Prime Minister; and as they drove to Camp David, neither believed that Iraq would give way. In that hour-and-a-half, John Major and George Bush settled almost all the outstanding details, when and how to move from jaw-jaw to air war to land war. What's more, they developed an ease in communication that was to survive their rare differences over policy. Neither the disagreement over the safe havens for the Kurds the following spring, nor the strains of European–American trade disputes, ever seriously threatened their trust in each other.

The story of the friendship between John Major and George Bush is historically important. It had substantial results. It also demonstrated that the inevitably unbalanced 'special relationship' can still be made to work to the satisfaction of both sides; but it requires both sides to want it to work. Above all, it needs a genuine trust between two people; without that, when put under pressure, all the ties of history, interest, language and diplomatic networking can unravel from the top.

On the day John Major launched his election campaign in 1992, George Bush was asked his view of John Major. With the polls telling him the Prime Minister was a risky bet, the President could have been forgiven for backing off. Instead, having made all the necessary disclaimers of any right to interfere in another country's politics, he gave a warm endorsement of the Prime Minister's leadership qualities in the Gulf War.

If the Prime Minister had inherited a policy, he had also inherited the task of uniting the people of Britain behind it. It was not easy. In the Falklands, we had been fighting for 'our people'; in Kuwait, we would be fighting for something more abstract: the maintenance of international order in a sensitive region of importance to Britain. Public opinion was broadly behind the war, but it was not rock-solid. As late as 11 January, an ITN/Harris poll indicated that while 58 per cent backed military action, 38 per cent thought sanctions should be given more time to work. The Labour Party were equivocal. In early January, their foreign affairs spokesman, Gerald Kaufman, said they would not support the early use of force.

John Major built unity, brick by brick. He took time and trouble to talk to Church leaders, convincing Archbishop Runcie and Cardinal Hume of the justice of the cause. Early in January, he went to the Gulf, to tell the troops to their face that they would soon be at war. The news bulletins were full of shots of John Major 'at ease with himself': relaxed, informal, casual, listening. A sweater-clad Prime Minister went from unit to unit in the desert, chatting to the soldiers clustered round him.[1] Robin Oakley – then working for *The Times* – reported from Dhahran that his style was, 'more fireside chat than Henry V . . . unscripted, direct and unvarnished, it was all the more effective for its lack of artifice'. This, he concluded, was 'a Prime Minister who pays audiences the compliment of listening to them rather than to the world outside'.

Robin Oakley noted only one, highly uncharacteristic failing: the Prime Minister forgot to tell the troops the latest cricket score.

Right through the Gulf War, the Prime Minister was to prove his popularity as a national leader – and his obvious ability to communicate with the people of Britain. Politically, this increased the pressures on him, leading his party to depend more and more

[1]He ignored the advice given in a briefing note – which had emerged from somewhere in the bowels of the Ministry of Defence – attempting to indicate the correct response by 'non-military personnel' to a salute. Britain has no equivalent of the American President's hand-slapped-on-heart. The MoD seemed to be advocating a physical movement somewhere between the royal wave and a Hitler arm-jerk.

on him to carry the load of winning them votes. At the time, however, it was the cement holding the country together, as it embarked on what was seen to be a highly dangerous national enterprise.

For the Prime Minister the Gulf was a baptism of fire. Chairing a War Cabinet, in a building which had survived the Blitz, would bring the weight of history down on anyone's shoulders. There were huge uncertainties. The War Cabinet was braced for chemical or biological attack – intelligence reports indicated either was possible. Estimates of casualties ran into five figures, and throughout Britain, hospitals were on standby, with wards set aside for the wounded, burned and gassed. Many doctors and nurses volunteered to serve in the Gulf. At home, there were all sorts of bureaucratic glitches to be sorted out in advance, to ensure that both casualties and their families were given the help they needed.

The massive media coverage expected raised further difficult issues.[2] In the Gulf, unlike the Falklands, the war would be covered from both sides. Crews could beam back pictures from anywhere, and would no longer be so reliant on official help to get footage back to London. On the home front, there were such grisly questions to answer as how close the cameras should be allowed to get to body bags coming off the planes.

Margaret Thatcher had already set up a liaison committee, chaired by John Wakeham, then Energy Secretary, to handle the news management of the war. In theory, he had had overall responsibility for presentation for some time, but in practice this had involved little more than the occasional chairing of the weekly meeting of departmental heads of information. The role was more an excuse for Margaret Thatcher to put him on any Cabinet committee where she felt she needed eyes, ears or a voice. John Wakeham's new committee brought together Number 10,

[2]At one stage, the BBC was offering as much as fifteen hours of news coverage a day on the Gulf. They suffered a backlash among viewers, sated with coverage of the war.

the press officers of the Ministry of Defence and the Foreign Office, and the political machine. Right through the Gulf crisis, it met daily, to back up the global, strategic decisions taken by the War Cabinet.[3]

Learning the lessons of the Falklands War, the committee wrestled with the question of government spokesmen. It would not be comfortable to have British casualties announced by American military commanders in the Gulf, so the MoD would have to carry a big briefing role. But the committee wanted to avoid the Falklands experience of a single civil servant becoming 'the voice of the war', so the task was shared between Sir David Craig, the Chief of the Defence Staff, and press officers in London, though the arrangements still came in for criticism. Commanders on the ground, notably Sir Peter de la Billière, proved better communicators.

On 14 January, in the very last days before the war, the Prime Minister flew to Paris for special talks with our nearest neighbour, military ally and ancient rival. An elderly Frenchman of the left and a middle-aged Englishman of the right were never going to be soul-mates. Presidential socialism and down-to-earth Conservatism could hardly be more different – in style as well as substance. Still, the meeting, with President Mitterrand, seemed to go well enough. By tea-time, John Major was back in London, positively cheerful; he sat down with Barry Potter and Sarah to work through some new poll tax papers.

Then, on the early evening news, he learned that the French had launched a last-minute Gulf peace initiative – a move they had not even mentioned that morning. The Prime Minister was, understandably, furious.

Admittedly, the mood in France was equivocal about the war, and François Mitterrand may have thought he needed to demonstrate independence from the Anglo–American lead. But his little flicker of a peace initiative blew away, unnoticed and unsuccessful, dispersed

[3]The War Cabinet was known officially as OPD(G) – for Overseas Policy and Defence (Gulf); John Wakeham's committee was known by an even longer set of initials, OPDG(MH) – for 'media handling'.

by the winds of war. All it left were the ashes of mistrust in the Prime Minister's mind.[4]

The final pre-war skirmish in Britain was a parliamentary debate on 15 January. A total of 534 MPs voted in favour of military action. Neil Kinnock supported the Government, but 55 Labour MPs rebelled, including two of the Labour front bench. Even some Labour elder statesmen were critical: Denis Healey described the war as a 'dreadful gamble'.

Operation Desert Storm began at 11.36 p.m. the next day. The details of the first strike were a closely guarded secret. Once Charles Powell heard from Brent Scowcroft that the missiles were on their way, he rang Douglas Hurd, Tom King, Neil Kinnock, Paddy Ashdown, and Margaret Thatcher. If Defence Secretary Tom King already knew from his own military sources, he was not so tactless as to say so. After the first attack, the Prime Minister went to bed, to be briefed on the results at 6.00 a.m. the following morning. He had a long day ahead.

It began with a War Cabinet at 7.00 a.m. Then the Prime Minister stepped out into Downing Street to make a brief announcement to the battery of television cameras that had been there since dawn. He had to prepare for the usual Thursday Questions, make a parliamentary statement, go to see the Queen, and give confidential briefings to senior politicians outside the Government. On top of all that, he had decided to do a prime ministerial broadcast, 'straight to camera', from Number 10 that evening.

It was a clear mark of his own, different style. Margaret Thatcher had never made this kind of broadcast in eleven years of office – not even at the start of the Falklands War. Using television to speak directly to the people of Britain was an essential element in his strategy, but it was a gamble.

Speaking to camera is a difficult art. Most people's eyes begin to glaze after a minute or two of reading from an autocue. Their

[4]Major and Mitterrand had to go on working together for another four years, until the President's final departure from the Elysée in May 1995. While they were never close, there were moments when the French President was generous in his support; for his part, the Prime Minister greatly admired Mitterrand's courageous struggle with illness during his final years in office.

expression becomes strained with the effort of avoiding a stumble – which will require the whole thing to be recorded all over again. A package of the kind familiar from all news programmes – in which the speaker is off-camera for a time, 'talking over picture' – is much easier, since the voice tape can be cut and edited. The Gulf broadcast would have to be a long statement, over six minutes, without editing – and the Prime Minister had very little time to prepare or record.

For Gus O'Donnell and Sarah, it was an early lesson in the relentless pressure of the timetable in Number 10. During the afternoon, an official draft emerged, which covered all the issues but was too cold and convoluted for television delivery. It had to be redrafted – but with no Prime Minister on hand, Gus and Sarah could get no guidance. They beavered away, cutting and weaving the heavy language of UN resolutions into – they hoped – a simpler message.

When the Prime Minister returned, there was little time to spare. The BBC team was looking nervously at the clock. Fortunately, he wanted only a few changes. He went up to record with only minutes to spare – and just let it flow. He had time to make a second recording, just for safety, but Gus and Sarah could breathe again. It was done. It was well done. And it was warmly-received, nationwide.[5]

Very early on Friday 18 January came the first blast of the most dangerous news of all: Saddam Hussein had started bombing Israel. This might be the torch that ignited world war. Charles Powell had just headed home to his flat in south-west London when, at 1.00 a.m., the call came from Brent Scowcroft in the White

[5]The broadcast was one of three pieces of prime ministerial television which Central Office subjected to an analysis technique which involves a group of people constantly pressing reaction buttons while they watch. Their combined reactions are then turned into a graph overlaid on the broadcast film, so that you can watch what is happening to their reactions while reviewing the tape. All through the Gulf broadcast, the reaction line was extremely positive; however, it plunged in another piece which was tested – an interview with the Prime Minister, in which the economic jargon familiar to a former Chancellor crept into his answers.

House, letting him know that Iraq had launched Scud missiles. With chemical and germ warheads very much in both their minds, Charles asked:

'What's on the end of them?'

'We don't know,' Brent replied.

Charles rushed back into his car and broke every speed limit to get back to Number 10. He was at his desk before the missiles, damaging but 'conventional', landed on Israeli soil.

Almost every day of the campaign brought new points of pressure. Our losses of Tornado aircraft mounted through January. British prisoners of war were put on parade in Baghdad. There were threats and phony peace offers from Saddam. As a result of Iraqi sabotage, oil was pouring into the Gulf. Attempts were made to bomb Saddam's bunker. His excursions into Saudi territory were repelled; but the real trial of strength was to come.

Before the ground campaign began, the Prime Minister was to have his own reminder of mortality. On a snowy day in February, the IRA landed a mortar bomb in the garden of Number 10, destroying a cherry tree only about a hundred feet from where he was sitting. Right round the building, windows were crazed by the blast, or – where they were not made of toughened glass – blown in altogether. There was a good deal more damage in Downing Street than appeared from the outside. In the Chancellor's flat in Number 11, Rosemary Lamont was just unpacking her daughter's things, only to have them covered by shattered glass. Number 12 had also taken some of the force of the blast. Neither area, at the time, had shatter-proof windows.

But as in most sensitive public institutions, the windows of Downing Street were draped with hideous, metal-reinforced, grubby-looking, loose 'net' curtains. Sarah confessed afterwards that she had always been convinced they were useless, just a security officer's placebo; she had grumbled when forced to put them up at home, when her husband Douglas was appointed a Home Office Minister. But in the attack on Downing Street they proved extraordinarily effective, catching the flying shards of glass and saving many people from serious injury.

The War Cabinet had just started – in advance of Thursday's full Cabinet – and, with economic Ministers added to the regulars, was talking about how to pay for the war. The only senior Ministers not present were Ken Baker, still in the Home Office, and Michael Heseltine, who had just gone upstairs to Sarah's office to talk about the poll tax.

A splendid Boy's Own story emerged at the time, of Ministers regrouping instantly in COBRA, Downing Street's underground control centre. Real life, however, is always a bit more confused. The Private Secretary at the Prime Minister's side, Charles Powell, remembers that his mind was full of Iraqis, not Irishmen: he assumed it was a car bomb on Horse Guards Parade. As befitted the Defence Secretary, Tom King got it right: 'That's a mortar,' he said. Charles Powell grabbed the Prime Minister by the shoulder and shoved him down; other Ministers followed him, scrambling under the table. When they all came to their feet again, John Major simply remarked: 'I think we'd better start again somewhere else.'

But there was still some delay. Outside the Cabinet Room, armed police were braced for further attack. Charles Powell paused to think where to take the Prime Minister. His civil service instincts came to his rescue. Used to locking up secret papers, he applied the same principle to the Prime Minister, taking him to a huge, indestructible walk-in safe used for confidential material. He tried to persuade John Major into it, while he found out what had been happening. But the Prime Minister was not much amused. He wasn't going to stay locked up with the files. Hearing there was damage to the top of the building, he was particularly worried about 'Switch', keeping the telephones working up there under the eaves of the building. Keen to find out what had happened in the rest of Number 10, he managed to escape from his cubby-hole. Finally, he and his Cabinet did regroup in COBRA.

At that time – and for long after – life in Downing Street had been made hideous by the noise of repairs to the façade of the Foreign Office, which overlooks Number 10. The Policy Unit, with offices at the front of the building, had grown only too accustomed to the sound of scaffolding poles crashing down from a great height. When the bomb went off, Sarah supposed that it was merely an extra large pole hitting the ground. Michael Heseltine, like Tom King, knew better.

'I didn't think the poll tax was quite such an explosive subject,' he said.

Along the corridor, they soon discovered the damage. The offices were littered with broken glass.

Sarah ran down the stairs and through to Number 12. There, standing close to the window, she could see the still-smouldering case of a second bomb on the little green by Ambassadors' entrance to the Foreign Office. Idiotically, she stood gawping at it, waiting for it to explode.

The Chief Whip's office was a shambles. Richard Ryder himself was on the phone to the police. 'There's something nasty smoking on the ground outside my window,' he said. 'Could someone put it out?'

Gradually, the police emptied the building of junior staff, out into the strange world of a snow-covered, traffic-free Whitehall. The area was cleared – even Cabinet Ministers found themselves briskly turned away from buildings for which they lacked the relevant passes.[6]

Inside Number 10, no one was permitted to go back above ground level for fear of further attacks. Sarah went up briefly to collect things for the secretaries from what she supposed would be an empty Policy Unit. Wrong again. Undeterred, Michael Heseltine had returned to her office, and was now demanding briskly to get on with their meeting. Weakly, Sarah asked if she could come across to the Department of the Environment later.

The mortar attack did at least still the silly spiteful voices who had accused Margaret Thatcher of misplaced grandeur when the

[6]Whitehall departments are very possessive about 'their' passes. A Number 10 pass, which one might suppose to trump all others, is treated with firm indifference by the security staff in all other government departments – and with disdain by the police guarding the Palace of Westminster.

Downing Street gates were installed. Later in 1991, bombs placed in taxis, whose drivers were then forced to take them to Whitehall, made the point equally forcibly. The IRA mainland campaign continued through 1991, with bombs at Paddington and Victoria stations less than two weeks later.

There had, however, been plenty of evidence of danger before that. Terrorist violence had been accelerating throughout 1990, causing seventy-six deaths in Northern Ireland and six outside it. The Prime Minister's visits to Northern Ireland were always kept extremely secret, until he was actually on his way, and never even featured in the internal Number 10 diary. Jonathan recalls Stephen Wall's alarm when the Prime Minister began talking about a forthcoming trip, even though only his closest staff were in the room.

The guardians of the Downing Street buildings themselves were not exactly swift in their reactions to the bomb. Any private company would have pulled out all the stops to repair the chief executive's office; John Major, however, had to live with the damage. And every visitor to Number 10 was given visible evidence of how close the IRA had come to killing the Prime Minister of the United Kingdom. When, a month later, Jacques Delors gazed disapprovingly at the hole left unrepaired in the State Room ceiling, Sarah fumed with secret shame.

Perhaps there was some excuse for delay in installing the heavy, new, purpose-made bomb-proof windows – an extraordinarily lengthy business, which forced the Prime Minister to decamp to Admiralty House in the summer of 1992, and greatly complicated the management of government during the critical weeks surrounding Black Wednesday. But there was no excuse at all for leaving the sitting room in the Prime Minister's flat with a hole in the ceiling and curtains torn by the blast.

But there was little time for reflection after the IRA attack. Only three weeks later, the Gulf crisis culminated in the ground campaign. It lasted only four days. In all, twenty-four members of Britain's armed forces were killed in action.[7] These, however, included the nine tragic victims of American 'friendly fire', close to the very end of the war. To learn that some of them were barely older than his own schoolboy son[8] hit the Prime Minister hard. Down outside the Private Office in Number 10, Sarah found him standing, quite still, unlike his usual restless self. He told her what had happened. The following day was the only time during the Gulf War that he confessed to sleeping badly.

Saddam Hussein had boasted that he had sixty divisions ready for 'the mother of all battles'. The Ministry of Defence could only guess at the quality of his Revolutionary Guard, but they had reckoned it was good. They were not to know that when the allied offensive came, he would sacrifice untried troops rather than risk his elite divisions. The western military machine found itself engaged in a 'turkey shoot' – the very American image of wholesale slaughter – and were glad to stop. It was all over by 28 February. Cease-fire followed three days later. It was frustrating to see Saddam still in command, and venting his spite on the Kurds of northern Iraq. But the war aims had been achieved. Saddam had been driven out of Kuwait, which was what there had been – and all that there had been – international agreement to do. A week later, the British army was on its way home.

On 6 March, the Prime Minister went to Kuwait to see for himself the mixture of the destruction Saddam had created and the wealth he had been forced to abandon. Kuwait was still a chaotic combination of money and muddle, of which several members of the British party remember the same trivial but vivid example. There was no running water in which they could clean up before the meeting with Sheikh Sa'ad. Oil money could not magically undo the total destruction of the country's services . . . but it could pay for Perrier water, in which they were all invited to wash.

[7] The final British death toll from the Gulf War was put at forty-seven, including all those killed in accidents in the preparations for war, or in the Gulf but outside the field of battle.
[8] James Major had had his sixteenth birthday the day that Desert Storm was launched.

★   ★   ★

John Major's relationship with George Bush did not fade after the Gulf War. It was to grow stronger through the summer. For, on top of everything else that year, the Prime Minister was chairman of the Group of Seven. Since 1975, when President Giscard d'Estaing of France got world leaders together in Rambouillet to forswear protectionism, the leaders of the United States, Japan, Germany, France, the United Kingdom, Italy and Canada have taken it in turn to play host to the others every summer. Sometimes these so-called 'economic summits' are just empty charades. Sometimes they do real business – as they were to, for example, in Tokyo in 1993, when the Group of Seven finally unblocked the GATT round of trade talks. Sometimes they are more of a political stock-taking – as they were, after the Gulf War and before the break-up of the Soviet Union, in London in 1991. Whatever the substance, for the host country concerned, a meeting of the leaders of the world's most powerful economies always involves an enormous amount of national prestige.

The year before, in Houston, President Bush had put on a fabulous summit show for the seven government delegations and thousands of camp-followers, ending with a Texan rodeo. As George Jones and Sarah, there for the Telegraph Group, sat waiting for the show, George had reflected gloomily that next year's London summit was bound to make the British look like shabby old relations. They both recalled the seedy chaos of the previous London Economic Summit, in 1984. Remembering this conversation in early 1991, Sarah talked to Stephen Wall, who sent up warning signals. It wasn't necessary to spend on the Houston scale, since London's traditional assets could be mobilised to great effect. But it was important to remember that events would be reported by journalists – or rather, that they wouldn't be reported if the facilities for journalists were inadequate or they were excluded from all the smart events.

The summit was managed with great professionalism, which was to pay off again in Edinburgh, for Britain's European Summit the following year.[9] Heads of government dined at the Queen's House in the Tower of London, and lunched at Spencer House, just a stone's throw from the meetings in Lancaster House. Norma Major took the other spouses down the river to Kew – providing the best picture opportunities of all. Journalists were invited to the courtyard of Buckingham Palace to watch the finale, a cleverly-designed *son et lumière*. The official guests enjoyed themselves. The media coverage was excellent.

But the spectre at the feast was Mikhail Gorbachev; and the main issue of the meeting was how to respond to his calls for assistance. For the Prime Minister as chairman, the critical task was reconciling American and German views. The newspapers made much of Mikhail Gorbachev's lonely arrival in London at a time when the leaders of the west were thronging the Buckingham Palace balconies. Nor, when the huge but tatty motorcade of specially-imported Zils finally swept up to Lancaster House, wire coat hangers waving from their aerial slots, was the Russian leader promised much in the way of western aid. But the Prime Minister avoided dangerous humiliation of his guest.

Both Margaret Thatcher and her successor had a good relationship with Mikhail Gorbachev. John Major had talked to him a good deal before and during the Gulf War, and visited him immediately afterwards. He respected the Russian leader's forward-thinking realism about reform and western help. And both clearly enjoyed the final, informal evening of the summit, when John Major invited the Russian leader to dinner at Number 10 with the G7 leaders.

Mikhail Gorbachev arrived in cheerful form, and spent most of the evening telling jokes against himself. His favourite was the one about Russian queues.

[9]One of the side-shows of economic summits is the sparring between the British and Italians – who vie for fifth place in the economic pecking order, now Italy is deemed to have a bigger economy. When, therefore, the electricity failed on the first night of the Naples economic summit in 1994, leaving John Major and Bill Clinton sweltering in the gloom, Foreign Office facilitators could barely suppress a smirk. Hadn't the Italians realised what demands the world's press would make on a city's energy capacity?

One man in the queue says: 'I've had enough. I'm going. I'm off to shoot Gorbachev.'

When he comes back, half an hour later, the next person in the queue asks: 'Did you do it?'

'No,' says the would-be assassin. 'There was a queue ahead of me.'

That joke was to turn sour barely a month later. The Prime Minister had come back to Number 10 from Huntingdon on the evening of 18 August. At 6.00 a.m. on the 19th, Stephen Wall told him of the coup against Gorbachev.

The next two days were spent in a whirl of global telephonics – John Major was still chairman of the Group of Seven – a succession of meetings and doorstep announcements. There were calls from President Bush, who came out strongly for Gorbachev, from President Mitterrand, Chancellor Kohl, the Japanese, Dutch, Canadian, and Polish Prime Ministers, and also Václav Havel of Czechoslovakia. Each was hungry for information from or about the others, as well as about events in Moscow.

The Cabinet's main foreign affairs committee met on the 19th. The next day, just after half-past three on the afternoon of the 20th, John Major spoke to Boris Yeltsin in the Russian White House, while the tanks of the would-be military dictators rolled towards the building. He was the first western leader to get through. Yeltsin, perhaps over-dramatising, said that this might be the last call that he was able to make. The tanks were certainly rolling towards him, but not that close. Still, it was a tense moment. It was another two days before the Prime Minister was able to talk to Mikhail Gorbachev himself.

This was an occasion when the Prime Minister's instincts came strongly to his rescue. Despite some official caution at first, he came out firmly for Gorbachev. He had to make that decision without waiting for the products of our vast intelligence machine; as so often when events are breaking fast in distant places, Number 10 was reduced to relying for news like everybody else largely on Reuters and CNN.

Barely two weeks later, the Prime Minister was off on his travels again. George and Barbara Bush had invited John Major and Norma

– of whom they were particularly fond – plus their children, Elizabeth and James, to stay at Kennebunkport, the President's holiday home on the New England coast. Sir Robin Renwick, who had arrived as ambassador to Washington that summer, came with his wife Annie. Stephen Wall, Gus O'Donnell and Sarah came out with the Majors from London.

There was huge British media interest in the meeting. Did the President have any use for his friend John, the journalists wanted to know, now the Gulf War was over? Above all, in the minds of the British media, there was a consuming interest in the personal relationship between the two leaders. While Margaret Thatcher had got on famously well with Ronald Reagan, she had never seemed so comfortable with George Bush. She may well, as she clearly believes, have stiffened his resolve to fight in the Gulf, but that had not led to easy friendship. Close observers reflected that she was too formal with him. If a relaxed visit to Maine in sweatshirt and sneakers would not have been her scene, it suited the Majors down to the ground – although, as usual, the Prime Minister came under-equipped and was reduced to raiding Gus's suitcase. Norma's sense of style had to do for both of them.

There was time for a bit of fishing before the inevitable press conference. While the Prime Minister and Stephen Wall were on the boat with the President, Gus and Sarah cobbled together a draft of some opening remarks. A light touch was needed. They added some extraordinarily feeble jokes. When he returned and read it, the Prime Minister grinned. He turned to them. 'How,' he inquired with dangerous politeness, 'did you know I wouldn't catch any fish?'

The President had said he wanted to make the press conference 'John's show'. Privately, Sarah doubted if he would; experience had taught her that most statesmen, once confronted with the camera, simply cannot help competing for the limelight, particularly on home ground. But George Bush was as good as his word. For the benefit of the cameras, he spent much more time admiring his present of the inevitable cricket bat than the Prime Minister spent on the reciprocal baseball bat. More importantly, he allowed the Prime Minister the lion's share of the strategic comments to the press:

on Iraq, on the international trade deadlock, on other Group of Seven business. Given a lift back by the President in his golf buggy, Sarah plucked up her courage to thank him; remembering the Prime Minister's role in the Gulf War, George Bush said, he was only too glad to help.

At that time, the President was riding sky-high in the opinion polls; the Prime Minister looked unlikely to win a general election. With all too accurate foresight, George Bush reassured him. 'Just you wait,' he said, 'next year you'll have that five year feeling. I'll be the one who's haunted.'

The Prime Minister and his team were to pay George Bush two visits in 1992, after the pendulum of power had swung John Major's way: one after the Prime Minister had won his national election, the other after George Bush had lost his. The Prime Minister had done his best to try to help the President achieve one last-minute triumph he had much desired: a conclusion to the GATT negotiations on world trade. But the gap between American and European trade positions had been just too wide to bridge in time. At the end of the year, the time came to say farewell.

With Kennebunkport damaged by storms, both visits were to Camp David – also a sporty place, even in the snow and sadness of a farewell party. Fortunately Gus O'Donnell, a favourite of George Bush's, was there to defend Britain's honour at volleyball against the President's men. Stephen Wall whizzed along the paths in the woods on one of the bicycles provided, while wimps like Sarah huddled over the fires.[10] Then they went to the chapel at the centre of the log cabins, snow once more on the ground, to sing carols. There was a valedictory song for George and Barbara Bush, who sat smiling, relaxed and grateful. British minds flashed back to the

---

[10]One of the pleasures of Camp David the Prime Minister shared with President Bush was putting aside the boxes of official papers and putting his feet up to watch a video. On the first 1992 visit, the video shown for the benefit of the British team was *Patriot Games* – apparently an excellent choice, since it gave a more accurate view of Irish terrorism than most of what was seen on American screens. But so far as Stephen and Gus were concerned, it had certain defects. The Private Secretary turns out to be a traitor, and the terrorist's name is – O'Donnell.

tragic face of Margaret Thatcher, imprinted with the shock of the brutal speed at which she had been forced from Number 10. The American system, with its fixed terms and transition periods, deals more gently with its ex-leaders.

For George Bush, the Gulf War came too soon in his presidency to help him win an election. But for John Major, the successful prosecution of the war offered the possibility of a 'khaki campaign'. The liberation of Kuwait did drive up the British Government's standing. A Conservative lead in the opinion polls opened up between the middle of February and the second week of March. But the Prime Minister was never keen on a khaki election, and the poll lead soon melted away again.

There was, in any case, a little local obstacle to an early general election. While the battle for Kuwait went on, the internal battle over the poll tax had hung fire. In the political jungle, the natives were getting restless. *The Times* had already portentously pronounced that poll tax reform was 'set to be John Major's first substantial domestic fiasco'.

It was time to attend to the home front.

4

Launching Big Bertha

To tax and to please, no more than to love and to be wise, is not given to men.

Edmund Burke

If it was Europe that broke up Margaret Thatcher's Cabinet, it was the poll tax that lost her the loyalty of her parliamentary party. When John Major took her place in Number 10, something – it was clear – had to be done. Quite what that something was took five months to sort out.

The Prime Minister, Chris Patten and Michael Heseltine knew that before a general election could be called they would have to have answers to the question: what comes after the poll tax? But there was no chance of bringing a new local tax actually into operation before polling day. There was no way that a new system could be designed, consulted upon, taken through the House of Commons and the House of Lords and – most time-consuming of all – implemented by thousands of local authorities around the country by election day. In the meantime, people would still be paying the poll tax, so that had to be made electorally palatable, too.

The Community Charge – as the Government had doggedly continued to call the poll tax – had only come into effect in April 1990. It had replaced that bugbear of Conservative conferences, the rates – a tax levied by local councils based on the notional, and often highly artificial, rental values of domestic properties. The White

Paper published before the 1987 election by Nicholas Ridley, then Secretary of State for the Environment, made it clear what he and Margaret Thatcher thought was the root of the trouble with the rates: too few people paying too much tax. Only 16 million householders got a rates bill from their local authority. Perhaps only 12 million had to pay the full charge. Why should so many people escape local taxes? In particular, Tory MPs complained, why should little old ladies living alone on their pensions pay the same tax as bulging households of young, working adults? Only seventeen Tories voted against the Community Charge on the second reading of the parliamentary bill. Most were keen to see the cost of paying for local government spread much more widely, and about 37 million people would be expected to pay the new tax. The 21 million extra taxpayers were, however, less than delighted at the prospect. In the spring of 1990, the introduction of the Community Charge led to riots in Trafalgar Square.

But Margaret Thatcher had survived and even thrived on controversy before. Indeed, the violence of the anti-poll tax demonstrators did more than anything to make her Government determined to persevere. Much more dangerous to her was the mood in the Conservative constituency associations, and the spread of resistance to the new tax indicated by MPs' postbags. The problem was that the charge was much higher than expected. At £363 per person, the average in 1990 was more than double the figure forecast. Some local authorities had clearly taken advantage of the change to jack up revenue, while blaming the Government. Meanwhile, the Treasury – which under Nigel Lawson had robustly opposed the creation of the Community Charge – had proved extremely reluctant to ease its introduction with higher local government subsidies. Finally, and perhaps fatally, the new tax hit the rural areas hard. Even today, the anger of the shires is a signal Tory governments ignore at their peril.

From the fourteenth century onwards, poll taxes have always run into the same difficulty. Flat-rate taxes can only be imposed at levels everyone can pay, which limits the amount of money they yield. You may be able to finance the BBC that way, but local government is on a quite different scale. Attempts to raise poll taxes to higher, more cost-effective, levels have always led to riots, and in the end such taxes have always had to be turned into graduated taxes, more sensitive to people's ability to pay.

On his first full working week in Number 10, the Prime Minister got down to the job of overhauling the Community Charge. There was no consensus on a successor. Michael Heseltine, who had been out of the Government when the Community Charge was introduced, simply wanted to get back as quickly and smoothly as possible to the rates. But to the parliamentary party, the rates were still anathema; the idea of a personal local tax still important; and Michael Heseltine still the assassin of Margaret Thatcher. It might be poetic justice for him to have been given the task of dealing with the Community Charge. It did not mean the party would trust him. His colleagues had spent years attacking the system of local government rates as unfair, unrelated to ability to pay, and open to exploitation by left-wing councils, since so few voters felt the full burden. MPs were not at all keen to re-create such a system.

Replacing the Community Charge was a consummate test of the Prime Minister's skill in holding the ring between different elements in the party, and – equally importantly – between Michael Heseltine and the Treasury. This time, the Treasury had to be bound into the negotiations – and not merely for reasons of Whitehall politics. The Department of the Environment on its own did not have sufficient tax expertise for the Prime Minister to be sure it would get the detail right.

There was plenty of research on the stocks. The Green Paper[1] *Alternatives to Domestic Rates* had been published as long ago as 1981. Michael Heseltine considered that exercise a triumph, since it had come full circle back to the rates again. But now the other options had to be taken more seriously. Local sales taxes, local income taxes, mixed taxes – all had their advocates, armed with parallels from other

---

[1]In theory, governments publish 'White Papers' when putting forward specific plans which will be shortly translated into bills, or proposed pieces of legislation; 'Green Papers' when they are simply testing the water or airing a variety of views. But this rule is often breached, or at least the colour code has been abandoned now that departments have a taste for publishing much fancier-looking documents.

countries. Little old ladies in large houses – the hard cases that had told so heavily against the rates – would do better under almost any of these than under property taxes.

But none of these options attracted much parliamentary support. All presented difficulties in a small, crowded country, where people often live in one local authority area, but work or shop in another. If voting was based on residence but tax on something else, local accountability would become even weaker. MPs became more and more certain about what they didn't want, less and less clear about what they did.

Some Ministers' minds were moving in a different direction altogether. By December 1990, many – not only Margaret Thatcher – were exasperated with local government, and not just because of the level of domestic rates. Businessmen had complained furiously about high city rates on commercial property, on which they had no say at local elections: so at the same time as introducing the poll tax, the Government had imposed a single, national, Uniform Business Rate. This 'nationalisation' of local business taxes, however, meant that local councils were now directly responsible for raising only about a quarter of what they spent.[2] More and more Tory MPs thought the logical solution was for central government to take over completely.

It looked for a time as if local authorities might be cut right back to rubbish collection and street lights – the kind of services they could reasonably be expected to provide out of money they could raise themselves. After all, their biggest responsibility – for education – was already being trimmed. Polytechnics had been taken out of local authority hands; soon, colleges of further education would follow. Individual schools were choosing to assume greater management responsibility, or even opt out of local authority control altogether, becoming 'grant-maintained' by the Department for Education. Some Ministers now wanted

[2]The new Uniform Business Rate also proved deeply unpopular in those parts of the country where the simultaneous revaluation of commercial property led to steep increases in the rates levied. Chris Patten ascribed his defeat at Bath to a combination of the poll tax and the UBR.

to transfer all education – and perhaps police and fire services too
– to central government.

There was a still wider consensus among Ministers and MPs that
local spending and tax-raising should be 'capped'.[3] Meanwhile, if
local government was to raise less money and have responsibility
for fewer services, did it make sense to maintain both district and
county councils? Finally, Michael Heseltine wanted radical change
of another kind: he expressed his long-standing enthusiasm for a
system of directly-elected mayors.

The Prime Minister was not, however, carried away by the mood
of the times. He did agree to a review of local government structure
with a bias towards new, unitary councils – but balanced by a strong
feeling for local wishes. And none of this, he insisted, should be
allowed to delay the solution of the poll tax problem.

It was, however, this debate that set the scene for the discussion
of what Chris Patten privately christened 'Big Bertha'. The basic
proposition was that the only way to take the heat out of the
Community Charge was to find a lot of money from somewhere
to cut the headline figure. The alternative approach was known as
the 'salami slicer' – chipping away at the tax with more and more
special relief schemes designed to help selected individuals. Either
Big Bertha or the salami slicer would, a gloomy Treasury could
foresee, prove extremely expensive.

In early December 1990, the Cabinet endorsed a 'comprehensive
review' of the Community Charge to decide what should replace
it in the long term. At the same time, the Prime Minister quietly
asked Norman Lamont what would have to be done – immediately
– to cut the poll tax in half. This would be a very big 'Bertha'.
The Treasury provided calculations. The costs, of various options,
ranged up to £8 billion.

The Treasury, however, was not very keen. How could such

[3]This centralising tide ebbed once the poll tax problem was solved. In 1992,
the Government actually gave more responsibility to local authorities, with
the transfer from Whitehall of community care. Capping lasted longer. But by
1995, many Tory MPs were arguing for greater freedom, on the grounds that
Labour councils should be given more rope with which to hang themselves
electorally by over-spending and over-taxing.

a huge increase in public spending be sold to the markets? The Government would have to say where the money was coming from. The Budget would have to be brought forward – and it was not ready. Moreover, the Treasury feared that if councils were handed a huge extra dollop of cash, they would simply spend it – leaving Community Charges as high as ever, central government's coffers emptier than ever, and the Chancellor with the unpopular job of raising income tax to foot the bill.

The Treasury insisted that the long-term problem – what should replace the Community Charge – must be sorted out before they coughed up. In mid-January, at a small meeting in the Prime Minister's study, Big Bertha was rolled back into the bomb shelter, and hard pounding began on the structure of a future tax.

The scaffolding of reform consisted of two special Cabinet committees: 'GEN 8', including a number of senior Cabinet Ministers and chaired by the Prime Minister, and 'GEN 14', the back-up group. The work of departmental officials was to be co-ordinated by Peter Owen, the senior civil servant on the domestic side of the Cabinet Office.

The Cabinet Office is the back office of government. Ministers and officials working there inhabit a strange jumble of Whitehall buildings, a kind of junk-yard of constitutional history. There is the old Treasury, with its green and gold Treasury boardroom, still used for Cabinet committees. There is the Cabinet Secretary's fine panelled office. There are the remains of Henry VIII's tennis court, and more of the old Palace of Whitehall, as you pass through Cockpit Passage to the offices facing on to the more modern stretch of Whitehall. Above, in the attics, is an object mysteriously described as Queen Anne's bath; below are the dark subterranean tunnels that provide a second route to the emergency control centre. COBRA itself is something of a period piece, circa *Dr Strangelove*, with its computer screens quaintly encased in pine.

The Cabinet Office services a part of the system which has been in long-term decline: the system of Cabinet committees. It has been said that 'procedure is all the constitution the poor Briton has'. If so, the bits of procedure which require Ministers to put their policy proposals to Cabinet committees for clearance are amongst the most important. Cabinet committees are the unseen sinews of the body politic.[4]

Some have associated the decline in Cabinet committee work with Margaret Thatcher, but it began decades before her premiership. As the pace of government speeded up, Prime Ministers became impatient with the ponderous processes of committee work, so Cabinet committees came to be used as a kind of back burner for policy, where it could be left to simmer unattended. Over the past few years, however, they have begun to come back into their own again – perhaps the most significant constitutional development of the 1990s.

There are usually about twenty-five committees in all. The Prime Minister chairs perhaps half a dozen himself, such as the main Overseas Policy and Defence Committee, identified by the initials OPD, or the catch-all Economic and Domestic Policy Committee, EDP. The Prime Minister allots the remaining big committees to senior Ministers who have few or no departmental responsibilities (the Deputy Prime Minister or the Lord President, for instance). Special committees can be created at will.[5]

The advantage of Cabinet committees is that they provide a relatively low-key way of resolving ministerial differences. Failure to reach agreement in full Cabinet is always a bit of a crisis, meat and drink to the media (who usually find out the results of a Thursday Cabinet in comfortable time for that day's lunchtime news). In Cabinet committees, Ministers can knock the subject – and each other – around for quite a bit without reaching crisis point. And on the whole, perhaps because fewer people are involved, they leak less, too. So Prime Ministers can use them to ensure that any proposal enjoys the support of a reasonably solid body of ministerial opinion before it is brought to Cabinet itself. On occasion, the final committee has been held only minutes before the actual

[4]In his 1992 Election Manifesto, the Prime Minister committed himself to publishing something akin to an anatomical guide to the committees and their membership.

[5]There is a special code for these, which changes with Prime Minister. Such special committees began in Margaret Thatcher's day with MISC – for miscellaneous; in John Major's time, they begin with GEN – for general.

Cabinet itself; the advantage being that if the committee revealed a continuing dispute, the issue need not be forced to a conclusion on the more open ground of Cabinet.

Devising a replacement for the Community Charge was classically a case for careful Cabinet committee treatment; and GEN 8, the key committee, was a rare example of a special one-off Cabinet committee chaired by the Prime Minister himself. But while committees deliberated on a future replacement, the Community Charge was causing more and more trouble in action.

The Audit Commission reported that it was costing twice as much to collect as the rates. In some inner cities, collection rates were as low as 60 per cent. Magistrates' courts were getting clogged up with non-payers. Such problems threatened to become cumulative, since councils would have to raise the following year's charge still higher to recoup their losses.

Politically, there was a silver lining to this cloud: where local councils had managed to hold down the charge, the voters had responded positively. But there were too few Wandsworths or Westminsters. Some Conservative Party associations noted that people wishing to be sure of avoiding the charge altogether were keeping themselves off the electoral register – and that these did not tend to be card-carrying Conservatives.[6] But in March, the Tories' thirteenth safest seat – Ribble Valley, from which David Waddington had been elevated to the Lords, causing a by-election – was roundly lost to the Liberal Democrats. Everyone who went there reported two words of complaint on the doorstep: poll tax.

Ribble Valley is the kind of area that was precision-bombed by the poll tax. Raising money from people irrespective of the value of their property meant increasing taxes in the north and west of the country. In Ribble Valley, families who had been paying a couple of hundred in rates suddenly found themselves facing bills of £800 or more. Sometimes this was only the notional bill, reduced

[6]However, post-election research suggests it was not a significant factor. Non-registration was less than one percentage point higher in 1991 than in 1981. While it shot up in inner London (perhaps as high as 20 per cent), the effect was concentrated in seats which were Labour strongholds, anyway.

in practice by special 'relief' or income support, but that did little to blunt voters' anger.

When Big Bertha was packed away in January 1991, the salami slicer had been taken out again. Back in 1990, the Treasury had conceded a modest 'transitional relief' scheme, intended to damp down the effect of the introduction of the poll tax in hard-hit areas. Now this was boosted by £1 billion, and renamed a 'reduction scheme'. Theoretically, this approach had many attractions; at one stage, it even seemed possible that it might provide a way of solving the long-term problem, too, without a big-bang reform. Perhaps, it was argued, with more and more 'reduction' schemes the flat-rate Community Charge could be turned into a tax which varied according to people's ability to pay. Already, by the spring of 1991, special schemes had reduced the number of people expected to pay the full whack by over half.

But these hopes faded. Although special schemes helped individuals, they had little political impact because they made no difference to the headline figure. A tax which looked high but yielded little was both politically and fiscally unappealing, and annoyingly it was the headline figure   now looming close to a national average of £400 per person – that the Central Statistical Office insisted on putting into the basket of prices that made up the Retail Price Index.

The poll tax was clearly disintegrating. But in GEN 8, let alone the House of Commons, there was still no agreement on what should take its place. The Prime Minister stuck doggedly to the line that 'nothing was ruled in, nothing was ruled out'. The party and the press were becoming impatient, complaining that his inability to say more looked indecisive. They made little allowance for the fact that he was, at the time, preoccupied by war. It was not that the Gulf crisis made petty questions of local taxation seem irrelevant to the Prime Minister (indeed, one of the vexed early questions was whether those fighting in the Gulf should be exempt from the Community Charge, and for how long). It was more that he was, at this period, very short of time for any domestic issues.

The Government now faced a pretty stark choice. Either it could carry on with the salami slicer – or it had to do something dramatic. The Budget was the only real opportunity. But time was running short.

On Saturday 2 March, the Prime Minister had been at the Queen Elizabeth II centre in London to speak to the Conservative Local Government Conference; after that, he headed to Huntingdon for the rest of the weekend. That day, Sarah rang Andrew Turnbull. Because of the Gulf War, she felt the Prime Minister had not had all the meetings to discuss the Budget with the Chancellor that he should have had. The Department of the Environment were now pressing for extra help from the Treasury to be made available after the Budget, perhaps in June, but another fiscal package only three months after the Budget would smack of panic. Shouldn't they look, one final time, at Big Bertha?

Andrew agreed: they should talk to the Prime Minister. When Sarah rang him, she found she was knocking at an open door. He had already come to the same conclusion. He asked Andrew to fix a meeting with the Chancellor in the flat at Number 10 on Sunday evening. Sir Peter Middleton, the Permanent Secretary to the Treasury, Terry Burns and John Gieve, the official most closely involved, came too.

Norman Lamont was however very worried about changing the Budget with only two weeks to go. Some taxes can be tinkered with up to the last minute, but changing something like the Community Charge, which would affect everything from public spending to the Retail Price Index, would be pretty devastating. He offered to produce a couple of Big Bertha scenarios, but the decision would have to be taken within forty-eight hours, at the very most. This was awkward. It had been announced that the Prime Minister was going to Moscow on Monday morning, but the rest of his trip had been kept very secret: not even the Chancellor knew that on Tuesday, John Major would be in the Gulf. The Prime Minister got rid of officials, and explained the difficulty. Nothing could be settled before Thursday.

In his absence, there was much to-ing and fro-ing between Number 10 and the Treasury. The Prime Minister got back from Saudi Arabia at 2.00 a.m. on the morning of Thursday 7 March. At 8.00 a.m., Barry Potter, Andrew and Sarah briefed him on the Treasury's proposals. He saw the Chancellor shortly before 10.00 a.m., and again shortly before mid-day. At those meetings, Big Bertha was – finally – cleared for take-off.

VAT was to go up by two and a half percentage points; the money would go to local authorities so that they could bring the Community Charge down by £140 per person, to a headline rate of only just over £250. The Treasury had two conditions. One, that they could be sure councils could not use the money to increase spending, rather than cut the Community Charge. This was easier to prevent, now they had actually fixed their budgets for the coming year, though all kinds of legal nooks and crannies had to be investigated before the Government could be sure the switch could safely go ahead. Two, that when – as everyone foresaw – this switch had taken the heat out of the issue, the Government should still go ahead and put a new, durable local tax in place. The Treasury suspected that if this didn't happen, the Department of the Environment would be back for more, and that local taxation, already terribly eroded, would simply wither away. In other words, Big Bertha had to be an alternative to the salami slicer, not just the first of a series of very thick slices.[7]

The tax switch was generally applauded. An effective performer in the House of Commons, the Chancellor won plaudits for his delivery, and overall, the Budget had a fairly good reception. The *Daily Telegraph* commented that it 'skilfully reconciled a number of conflicting objectives', although it also noted that, 'the denial of Mrs Thatcher's personal economic credo is also clear in Mr Lamont's very definite commitment to the ERM'.

Then, two days after the Budget, Michael Heseltine made a parliamentary statement on the principles of the new tax that

---

[7]Afterwards, many friends of Margaret Thatcher's were to argue that if only the money had been put in earlier, the poll tax could have been saved. Her own reactions at the time were rather different. She criticised the first salami slice in January, saying it ruined public spending control. She had a point: though the cause was, of course, the unworkable Community Charge itself. By the end of its short life, local councils were raising only an average of 15 per cent of the money they spent, and some of the subsidies that had to be paid out to protect the poor from the Community Charge could never be clawed back.

would replace the Community Charge: accountability, fairness, ease of collection, and some contribution from 'most people'. But he offered no concrete proposals. The press and parliamentary party became restless. Suddenly, the clouds gathered. The political climate took a sharp turn for the worse. At the Conservative Central Council[8] meeting in Southport that weekend, Michael Heseltine's speech was ill-received. The Prime Minister got a better reception, but his delivery was criticised. He was all too clearly exhausted.

Under the cumulative impact of general tiredness, things began to go wrong. The Prime Minister's schedule had become impossibly overloaded in March. The day after he returned from the Gulf and agreed the Budget, he had gone off to Scotland; on his return, on Saturday 9 March, he had done a full day's constituency work. On the Monday, he went to Bonn to deliver his 'Heart of Europe' speech; the following Friday, he left London again to meet President Bush in Bermuda, getting back in time for the Budget four days later. He admitted to the journalists accompanying him that he was weary. The vultures had begun to close in, with speculation as to whether he was 'up to the job'.

Criticism of his handling of the poll tax increased. The unkindest cut of all came from Nigel Lawson in the House of Commons, quoting Mendès-France to the effect that 'to govern is to choose'. Understandably, but unwisely, the Prime Minister hit back with a list of things Nigel Lawson had not 'chosen' to do as Chancellor. Then on Wednesday 27 March, he came very close to parliamentary disaster.

The Opposition had put down a motion of 'No Confidence' in the Government. Given the size of the Tory majority, Labour had not a hope of winning the vote. But the debate would be an important test of the new Prime Minister; a big occasion, his first extended head-to-head with Neil Kinnock. A good performance was vital to his own and his party's morale.

The Whips' office had told Number 10 that the motion would be 'widely drawn' – in other words, the Speaker would allow all

[8]The Central Council meeting is the second most important conference in the Conservative Party's calendar.

aspects of the Government's policies to be discussed. In Number 10, a wide-ranging speech was therefore prepared. Virtually Charles Powell's last act before Stephen Wall took over the foreign affairs seat in the Private Office was to contribute a sparkling overview of the Gulf War. The speech dwelt on the economy, education, the Citizen's Charter. It dealt only briefly with the Community Charge. By the morning of 27 March, the Prime Minister felt quite pleased with it.

At 12.30 p.m., bad news came from the Chief Whip. The Speaker had agreed with the Labour Party that the debate on their motion should be 'narrowly drawn', focusing entirely on local government finance. The draft speech was therefore completely useless. In three hours, the Prime Minister would have to get up in the House of Commons and give the best performance of his life. But he had no text; nothing prepared to say.

He remained extraordinarily calm, blaming no one. The parliamentary team started again from scratch. Dominic Morris sent out distress signals to Barry Potter and Sarah, asking them to put as much flesh as possible on the bare bones of the new local government tax. Jonathan was also hastily co-opted in. Everyone drafted frantically, while the Prime Minister shredded, assembled, questioned, rejected and rewrote what was produced.

Sarah learned a hard lesson that day about life in Number 10. In quieter times, she had arranged to have lunch with her old boss Max Hastings, the editor of the *Daily Telegraph*. He was not amused when she arrived appallingly late – not, admittedly, for the first time. She then had to listen to a lecture on poor Number 10 organisation, biting her too-ready tongue, since she could not tell him the reason without alerting him to the potential disaster looming ahead.

In the event, the media judged the debate a draw. Neil Kinnock was not on top form, but the Tory benches listened in polite silence; when it was the Prime Minister's turn to speak, the Labour benches did their best to rattle him with distracting chatter and interruptions. Not for the first or last time, Labour's backbench auxiliaries were more effective than the Tories'. And John Major's speech was, not surprisingly, somewhat jerky.

At any rate, the debate was over. The poll tax saga, however, was not.

Before the Budget, Michael Heseltine and Norman Lamont had agreed that the new tax should include a property 'element' – something the Secretary of State for the Environment had wanted from the start. The Chancellor was cautious, but his interests lay in getting a tax in place which was durable and reliable – and that, the Treasury was convinced, meant a property tax. Still the party was uneasy. Little old ladies haunted MPs' dreams again. Scotland had had the poll tax for a year more than England; past and present Scottish Secretaries – who had had to defend a personal tax most robustly to voters who resented being used as a laboratory for English experiments – were anxious that it should not now be swept away. And no one outside the Department of the Environment had much faith in the self-restraint of local councils. Was the property-owning democracy going to be ripped off again?

For a time it was thought that the only answer would be a national property tax, set by the Treasury. In the end, however, a scheme was designed which it was thought safe to allow local authorities to operate, involving a limited range of tax bands. These would be based on real property values, unlike the rates, which depended on highly notional rental values.

Since the beginning of March, work on what was still variously called the 'Local Tax' or 'Household Tax' had accelerated. But the first scheme to emerge from departmental work did not find favour with GEN 8. It was a highly complicated double tax with separate personal and property elements. The tax bands rose steeply, evoking memories of high rates bills. It was proposed to vary the tax between regions, which meant that people would find themselves paying very different taxes on properties of the same value. And the personal element of the tax – a separate charge for each person in the household – would mean keeping the Community Charge register, while deriving even less money from it. With two registers – for property and people – the new tax would be even more expensive to collect than the old. The Prime Minister was not happy. He asked the Policy Unit to drop everything else, to engage the Treasury, and to try to help Environment come up with better answers.

The breakthrough came when the Policy Unit finally established how few households contained more than two adults likely to be eligible for any new tax – it had already been decided to exempt students, while many elderly people would also be protected. This clinched the argument against hugely complicated registers of both properties and people and in favour of a simpler tax charged at only two 'personal' rates: one for households with more than one adult, another for people living alone.

By mid-April, officials were ready to put the final version of the tax to GEN 8, and then to full Cabinet. Every household would be expected to pay a two-person tax based on the value of the property, unless they could show that there was only one adult in the house – in which case there would be a 25 per cent discount. (If the house was empty, there would be a 50 per cent discount – or, looked at another way, no 'personal element' at all.) There would be seven bands of property tax; the inhabitants of properties in the top band (those valued at over £160,000) could not however be charged more than two and a half times the tax on the cheapest, thus restraining councils from imposing penal rates on the few.

The Inland Revenue had gloomily reported that it might take up to five years to introduce even this simpler tax – advice Michael Heseltine robustly refused to accept. All that was left to do now was ensure that the new tax was clearly and persuasively presented.

Number 10 geared up for the full announcement, in a way which was to be replicated on future occasions. There was, at last, a name for the new tax: the 'Household Tax' or 'Local Tax' had finally become the 'Council Tax'. In Number 10, Jonathan took responsibility for monitoring the launch arrangements, working closely with Michael Portillo, who was to write the foreword to the White Paper.

Number 10 went into the Department of the Environment like rats into cheese: Sir Terry Heiser, its Permanent Secretary, helped promote teamwork, overcoming territorial pride. Gus O'Donnell got the Treasury and Environment press machines working in harmony. Jonathan turned the opening summary into English. Backbenchers were briefed, constituency chairmen mailed, the media taken through the detail with immense care. Michael Heseltine gave a bravura Commons performance.

There was a long parliamentary process to be gone through before the Council Tax became law, and this was to have important conscquences for election timing. There would be mild tweaking of the tax on the way – most notably, Michael Heseltine added an eighth band, requiring people whose properties were valued at over £320,000 to pay a higher rate of tax. Yet, even before the dust had settled on 23 April, it was clear that the biggest burden of the Prime Minister's inheritance had been cleared.

Five months might in retrospect seem a very short time in which to design a new local government tax which would prove to be robust and electorally saleable. It was what Chris Patten later described as 'the most brilliant piece of government I ever saw'. The Council Tax never became an issue in the General Election. But no government can expect applause for solving a problem that the public considered to be of its own making.

Moreover, safe exit from the poll tax had not come cheap. It very nearly spelt the end of local government. And it cost the Prime Minister time and energy. Five months had been spent on the essentially negative task of undoing his predecessor's biggest mistake.

It was time to tackle the Conservatives' biggest problem.

5

Europe: Hearts and Minds

My political generation . . . did not have to take up arms in a European war. We grew up in the armed peace that followed. Now we have the chance to re-create more of the European family. To build on those post-war structures. To construct a safe and prosperous home for European generations to come. It is a chance that we must not miss.

John Major, Bonn, 11 March 1991

Early in 1990, European leaders had agreed to work towards two new treaties on monetary and political union. In October, Margaret Thatcher went to Rome for what turned out to be her final European Council, where they started to talk detail. It had been an explosive occasion – on which her comments had prompted Sir Geoffrey Howe's resignation, and precipitated the sequence of events that led to Michael Heseltine's challenge for the party leadership.

Only days after John Major succeeded Margaret Thatcher, he had to go to Rome for another European Council meeting – his first as Prime Minister. At this Rome Council, Europe set its deadline for treaty negotiations: the Maastricht Council at the end of 1991. Before they left London, Sir John Kerr, Britain's Ambassador to the European Community, painted an alarming picture of the ambushes that might be waiting. 'UKREP',[1] as his job is known in Whitehall

[1]United Kingdom Permanent Representative to the European Community, a job to which Stephen Wall was appointed in 1995, when John Kerr became British Ambassador to the United States.

5

jargon, 'Machiavelli', as the Prime Minister called him, John Kerr was to play a crucial part in the Maastricht story. He warned the Prime Minister that other heads of government might try to bounce a rookie Prime Minister into commitments on the contents of the treaties.

The second Rome Council, however, went more peacefully than John Kerr had feared. On John Major's debut, the other European leaders were at their most Anglo-friendly. Surely the new Prime Minister would understand that any previous differences had been all Margaret Thatcher's fault? Charles Powell, still in the Prime Minister's Private Office at the time, remembers the expression of horror on the face of Giulio Andreotti's aides when he turned up in Rome in John Major's wake – at least, they had assumed, we will be getting rid of that Signor Powell along with la Signora Thatcher.

But even at Rome, rocks showed through the calm waters. The longest-running argument with Britain had been over Jacques Delors' dream of a single currency. Back in 1988, Jacques Delors had persuaded Europe's central bankers – including Britain's Governor of the Bank of England, Robin Leigh-Pemberton – into designing a blueprint for monetary union. These money men envisaged the Community moving to a single currency in three stages. In the first, all countries would demolish controls on capital flows and join the European Exchange Rate Mechanism, which meant limiting movements between their national currencies. In the second, Europe would create institutions and rules for managing a single currency. In the third stage, the Deutschmark, franc, pound and lira would be merged. There would be no greater difference between them than between English and Scottish banknotes.

As Chancellor, John Major had tried to persuade other governments to go down a different road: to develop a 'common' or 'parallel' currency, one which people could use in any country of the Community, but which did not automatically replace their own national banknotes and coinage, as a single currency would. Treasury officials had flown from capital to capital, doggedly advancing detailed technical arguments for this approach. It was not a new idea, though still perhaps ahead of its time. The initiative failed, but the effort was not entirely wasted. It convinced the rest of Europe that we were serious about the argument.

The other decision Britain had taken was, of course, to join the Exchange Rate Mechanism (ERM). This meant agreeing a 'central rate' for the pound against all other European currencies, and undertaking to keep its market exchange rates within defined limits, either by intervening to manipulate the price, or by moving interest rates up or down to make it more or less attractive to hold sterling assets.

Since 1979, Margaret Thatcher's Government had been saying it would enter the ERM 'when the time is ripe'. This expression had been intended to demonstrate the new Tory Government's confidence that – unlike its Labour predecessor – it could get inflation down to the low levels enjoyed elsewhere in Europe. With British inflation under control, the implication was, industry would no longer need a falling exchange rate to keep it competitive. But through the 1980s, another argument for the ERM grew stronger, as one domestic monetary discipline after another collapsed, and inflation crept up again. A stable pound would not just be the jewel in the crown of success in the fight against inflation, it would be a weapon for achieving this success. With the pound linked to the German mark inside the ERM, British industry would have to practice German-style cost control in order to stay competitive.

When John Major became Chancellor in 1989, after Nigel Lawson's resignation, his own deep-seated hatred of inflation was reinforced by the experience of the past five years. The failure of previous policies made ERM membership both more attractive and more difficult. A clear discipline was needed, one which could not be tossed aside as easily as a broken monetary target; the clearer and more credible, the quicker inflation could be destroyed and interest rates – now 15 per cent – could be brought down again. On the other hand, with inflation approaching double figures – way out of line with Germany or France, the principal ERM members – entry into the system might be a bumpy ride.

Through the summer of 1990, inflation went on rising. But it was reckoned to be close to its peak. Meanwhile, 'Will she, won't she?' speculation was making the financial markets extremely jumpy, and delaying any cut in interest rates. So in September, Margaret Thatcher agreed that Britain should enter the ERM before the autumn political season really got under way.

The original plan was to announce this in her party conference speech in early October. But as Chancellor and Prime Minister discussed the issue in the week before the conference, they began to fear the timing would look too political – particularly since it had been agreed that interest rates would be cut at the same time. It was thought better to go ahead straight away. Britain entered the ERM on 8 October 1990, at a central rate of 2.95 Deutschmarks to the pound – close to its market rate before entry – and with 6 per cent fluctuation margins either side.

It went extraordinarily – perhaps deceptively – smoothly, despite mutterings from some parts of Europe that there had not been proper consultation on the rate. After a brief surge, which made it look as if the Government might have to cut interest rates again, sooner than it wished, the pound settled down. When John Major became Prime Minister, it was trading at around its central rate; and its stability through the turmoil of the leadership election campaign was considered a feather in the ERM's cap.

After all the wild swings in exchange rates – which had taken the pound up close to five Deutschmarks in the early 1980s, bankrupting British exporters by the score – industry liked the stability of the ERM. It also increased Britain's credibility in international financial markets. This meant that the margin Britain had to maintain over German interest rates – the price of our inflationary reputation – narrowed steadily. Between 1989 and 1991, the gap between the two countries' three-month rates shrank from just under seven points to just over two.

British interest rates, which were cut on the day Britain entered, were cut again, twice, in February 1991, and again in March, April and May. This caused no problems with sterling. During the spring of 1991, the pound fell against the dollar, which helped exporters, but actually rose against the Deutschmark. There was widespread support for membership. Even one of the most Euro-sceptical newspaper proprietors, Conrad Black of the Telegraph Group, told an audience assembled by the Coningsby Club that the Prime Minister had won his ERM gamble.

Full monetary union was, however, a very different matter. It would mean that no country could ever realign its currency, because national currencies would have ceased to exist. The Prime Minister was always sceptical, questioning whether this would make sense for the rest of Europe, let alone for Britain. But he was determined to keep Britain's options open, and to be involved in discussions on a project which could affect the British economy in general and the City of London in particular.

A single currency would be managed by powerful new institutions. There would be a European Central Bank, independent of governments. And the European Commission would monitor national budgets – leading Jacques Delors to forecast that up to 80 per cent of all economic decisions would eventually be taken in Brussels.

Most other governments liked the idea of full monetary union. Paris saw it as a way of gaining some control over decisions taken by the German Bundesbank, which in practice settled French interest rates. Bonn reckoned it a price which had to be paid to the French for progress on political union, Helmut Kohl's passion, and acceptance of German unification. The Mediterranean countries saw it as a test of their economic virility. Most of the smaller northern countries saw monetary union as a *fait accompli*. They had little effective independence from the mighty Deutschmark, anyway. Only the Danish Government really shared Britain's hesitation. In the last few weeks before Maastricht, there were some rumblings of unease in the German press; but in no other European country were the issues aired in political debate to the extent they were in Britain.

Monetary union was by no means the only troublesome issue on Europe's agenda. There was the problem of the treaty on political union, too. Many other members of the European Community were using it as an opportunity to press for a federalism which was quite alien to the Prime Minister's vision.

To get a handle on these negotiations, John Major decided he needed to do two things. First, he needed to build some alliances for Britain in the Community. Second, he needed to make some no-go areas clear to those allies, well in advance of Maastricht itself.

Hope springs eternal in some Foreign Office breasts of a *grande alliance* with France; at every change of power in Paris, a new effort is suggested. There is some logic, not merely romance, in this: the French ̇share with the British a suspicion of Brussels power-mongering, and a scepticism about the role of the European Parliament – both issues on which Chancellor Kohl's attachment to the idea of political union were going to give Britain trouble. But a 'French strategy' was never going to work in 1991. The French were, for a start, hell-bent on a single currency. And besides, François Mitterrand was an unlikely deal-broker for the British; indeed, at Maastricht itself, he played only a small part in the final argument.

Fortunately, John Major had built, day by day, a powerful alliance for Britain through his personal relationship with the leader of a newly-unified Germany, Helmut Kohl. Throughout the spring and summer they met frequently, in Bonn, London – and on one notable occasion, at Chequers.

Some of the Prime Minister's advisers remained deeply suspicious of the German Chancellery, believing – with reason – that when forced to choose, Helmut Kohl would always desert the British camp for the French. On his visits to Bonn to discuss Maastricht with Kohl's advisers, Charles Powell's successor as Private Secretary for Foreign Affairs, Stephen Wall, was only faintly surprised to find Mitterrand's adviser sitting in. But John Major's particular gift in foreign affairs is to get the best out of his partners; and in 1991, he got the best out of the German Chancellor.

Helmut Kohl is a child of war, who as a fifteen-year-old boy spent VE-Day trudging in his hot winter Hitler Youth uniform back along the railway tracks from the anti-aircraft battery to which he had been assigned. His commitment to the ideal of European union is rooted in his own experience. The Prime Minister saw the need to convince him that Britain was not in the Community simply to wreck the European idea – but to argue for its own idea of Europe. Early on, he looked for an opportunity to make his kind of Europe clear.

John Major went to Bonn in February for talks with the German Chancellor, and a formal reception. He reviewed a German guard of honour – generating the first of many photographs in which his silhouette contrasted hilariously with Kohl's bulk.[2] But these talks were overshadowed by the Gulf War. It was not really until a day-trip to the Rhine on 11 March that the two leaders sealed their relationship.

John Major and a number of his ministerial colleagues enjoyed a kind of government-*fest* in the Federal Chancellery, with lunch in the gleaming Palais Schaumburg. As the British delegation walked into this smooth, curiously antiseptic building, Sarah recalled John le Carré's description of Bonn as a city washed in milk. To Chris Patten, the impression was of the very best kind of building society.

It was a day of courtesies and political alliances. This time the Prime Minister had not gone just for the talks. He was to make his first speech as Prime Minister outside the United Kingdom. In the afternoon, to an Anglo-German audience assembled in the dark conference room of the Konrad Adenauer House, the headquarters of the ruling Christian Democrats (CDU), he delivered his speech on 'The Evolution of Europe'.

It was a political occasion, as well as a foreign policy milestone. The CDU were not entirely soul-mates of the British Conservative Party – which owed, as the Prime Minister delicately expressed it, rather less to the concept of 'solidarity'. But they shared a belief in 'the great Conservative values – stability, opportunity, community, identity'. They believed in 'individualism and the obligations that flow from responsibility to others'. They were, in short, the political underpinning of the alliance he was forming with Helmut Kohl – and they were given a reminder of the Conservative

[2] This visit also accelerated the spirited flow of letters to Number 10 on the Prime Minister's schoolboy habit of standing with hands behind his back or in his pockets; surprisingly, the defenders of this unsoldierly stance were nearly as numerous as the curmudgeonly critics.

Party's strength as 'the oldest organised political party in any free society'.[3]

What became known as his 'Heart of Europe' speech repays study. It put down markers not just for Maastricht, but for the years ahead. It spelt out – not in detail, but in outline – his vision of a free-market Europe, based on nation states, open to the new democracies of the east, a bulwark of peace as well as an engine of prosperity.

Europe, John Major said, should develop by evolution, not some treaty-based revolution provoking disunity in the cause of unity. It must keep its Atlantic ties strong. Britain had not, by playing its part in the transformation of Europe, 'abandoned our history or our ties with the Commonwealth and the United States'. But there were limits to the notion of a common foreign and security policy for European countries; NATO must remain paramount. So far as monetary union was concerned, 'we think it best to reserve judgement', and 'we cannot accept its imposition'. Co-operation – already an important code-word for a way of doing business outside the straitjacket of the Brussels institutions – was the way forward for members of the European Community. Above all:

> Europe is made up of nation states: their vitality and diversity are sources of strength. The important thing is to strike the right balance between closer co-operation and a proper respect for national institutions and traditions.

It was clear from the beginning that this speech was going to be compared with Margaret Thatcher's speech on Europe at Bruges in 1988. As Charles Powell – working in Number 10 before both Bruges and Bonn – said at the time, there was nothing of substance in the speech that could not have been said by Margaret Thatcher.

[3]The CDU was much the most important stop on the Party Chairman's tour that year of centre-right Europe, endeavouring to support his Prime Minister with Europe-wide political alliances. It was a journey that took Chris Patten from rooms over bicycle sheds in Belgium to marble palaces in Rome (where he met a string of people who would soon be fully occupied helping the police with their inquiries), pointing out with some irritation that the Conservative Party had a rather longer democratic pedigree than any of them.

Even the *Independent*, one of her harshest critics, detected 'no substantial shift in policy', although the Prime Minister and the Foreign Secretary had 'steered British policy on to a more sensible course'.

But according to most of the newspapers, the tone was profoundly different. The *Daily Mail* concluded that 'the carping has stopped'. Britain, said its leader column, 'is where it belongs: at the centre of Europe'.

That almost exactly reflected the phrase the Prime Minister had written, in his own hand, on the draft that had been winging its way around Whitehall:

My aims for Britain in the Community can be simply stated. I want us to be where we belong. At the very heart of Europe. Working with our partners in building the future.

The message of the 'Heart of Europe' speech has been misrepresented since. It was never code for a federalist agenda. It was a signal that Britain was going to play an active part in the Maastricht negotiations. In the velvet glove of European sentiment, there were some iron messages. Accurately forecasting the year ahead, John Major warned that, 'Britain will relish the debate and the argument. That is the essence of doing business in today's Community.'

The first bit of business was to come to the boil well before Maastricht itself. In June 1991, the Westminster air had become thick with demands that the Prime Minister should declare for or against a single currency. As many who have tried to bounce John Major on this issue have found, he would not be budged. He stuck firmly to his view that he should not tie Britain's hands for the future. But he felt it necessary to devote much of his speech to the Welsh party conference on 14 June to laying out his position.

Just before a key European Council meeting was not the easiest moment to have to do so. In London that Friday morning, Sarah scurried between Treasury and Foreign Office, getting the Prime Minister's speech text bomb-proofed by the experts while he waited impatiently in Swansea. The Manifesto trailers on domestic policy, to which Nick True had devoted his speech-writing skills, had to be swept aside. The assembled Tory workers in the Brangwyn Hall were to be the recipients of the Prime Minister's historic pledge that he would accept no coercion on this issue at Maastricht. Any future move to a single currency would require separate, specific endorsement by Parliament at the time.

John Major's predecessors now entered the debate. Margaret Thatcher attacked the Government's position from the other side of the Atlantic – seemingly unaware that her speech would be picked up by the British media. Edward Heath had already attacked her, and the legacy she had left John Major. The row between them escalated. They reminded Jonathan of the two grannies in Laurie Lee's *Cider with Rosie*, kept alive by their loathing of each other.

Back in Britain, Margaret Thatcher gave her support to John Major in the House of Commons. The polls, in any case, suggested that the row between them was not doing the Prime Minister much damage. A Gallup survey confirmed that voters thought he was the best person to handle Europe; and that Margaret Thatcher should recognise she was no longer Prime Minister.[4] But it was an uncomfortable backdrop to a key European Council – the last staging-post on the road to Maastricht.

The lead in European negotiations is in the hands of whichever member of the European Community is in the presidency chair. Each country gets a six-month turn, and each turn ends with a meeting of heads of government, part business, part bean-feast. It has become fashionable to stage these Councils in fancy locations: Corfu in 1994, Cannes in 1995. Often there is also a mid-term Council, usually held somewhere rather less agreeable. But the Euro-tiddlers do not have so much choice of location, and in the first half of 1991 the presidency was in the hands of the smallest of all, Luxembourg, in the person of a future President of the European Commission, Jacques Santer.

Luxembourg's first Council, that April, had done little Maastricht business. The burning issue of the time was the fate of the

[4]At the end of June, Margaret Thatcher announced that she would be leaving the Commons. Edward Heath was to outlast her, in Parliament if not in influence, to become 'Father of the House' – the longest-serving MP – in 1992.

Kurds, victimised by Saddam Hussein, scattered starving across the mountains of northern Iraq. On the plane to Luxembourg the Prime Minister had put together a plan for safe havens, which he forced to the top of the council agenda; he won early support from President Mitterrand, and the Europeans showed a more united front on this issue than they had managed during the Gulf War itself. At the June Council, however, it was back to a good old European wrangle.

Brussels had been busy designing the European equivalent of the tower block. On this plan, more and more power would be added to the existing institutions, notably the Commission and the European Court. But Britain did not want a treaty on political union that would give the European Commission lots more 'competence' – a polite Euro word for power – over such key national policies as defence and immigration.

So the British had begun to design a different piece of European architecture. They argued that the European Union should develop other, separate 'pillars' of direct co-operation between national governments – that is, independent of Community machinery. This 'pillared structure' first appeared on a British blueprint for co-operation in defence and foreign affairs. Then John Kerr canvassed support for a 'third pillar' to cover law and order issues, keeping them away from the existing Brussels structure, too.

At the June Council, however, Europe was not sold on pillars. The French were persuadable – though their notion of a European defence strategy differed from that of the British. Luxembourg, punching above its natural weight from the presidency chair, was also on the British side. But the Germans and Italians were hostile, as well as the Belgians and – more importantly – also the Dutch.

With so much unsettled, the conclusions were kept deliberately low-key. That suited the Prime Minister, for several reasons. Firstly, while he had agreement in principle to some kind of opt-out from monetary union for Britain, he was reluctant to try to clinch a deal on that too soon. There was too much detail to be checked. He wanted to make absolutely sure that Britain remained free to take its own decision not just when, but whether, to join in a single currency. The Treasury also wanted time to make sure that the intermediate stages of monetary union – to which our opt-out would not apply – were swept clean of Brussels bugs.

Secondly, at the Luxembourg Council the Prime Minister still had his own election options open. He had put down markers, particularly on monetary union, but also against political federalism; and he had plunged into the centre of the negotiation battle. He had not lost – but he had not won. He was not so far down the treaty track that he would have to conclude a deal before calling an election. He could afford to pause. In June 1991, he had not yet decided whether to take the Maastricht gamble before the election.

His instincts, already, were to 'do Maastricht first': that summer he reflected, with a bombast so unlike his usual style that it stuck in the minds of his Number 10 staff, that only the Conservative Party could get the right result for Britain, and that only he could do it for the Conservative Party. But politically, he was not committed. At Luxembourg, everything was still in play.

There is one image of uncertainty recalled by many at Luxembourg. True to form, the Prime Minister had merely picked at Mr Santer's lavish cuisine, while his officials had snatched food when and where they could. At the end of a long series of meetings, a tired and hungry John Major sent Stephen Wall out for the familiar energy boost: a round of Big Macs.

This time, however, it was not a success. At the heart of Europe, they put in a sight too much mayonnaise for the Prime Minister's taste. And, not for the first or last time, he found his Foreign Secretary yearning for more traditional fare. The Luxembourg Council ended with Douglas Hurd standing by the window, peering doubtfully into the entrails of his bun.

Back home there was hunger for food of a different kind. Distracted by Europe, the Prime Minister was under increasing pressure to outline his political philosophy and define his domestic agenda. Journalists who had resiled from the gamey taste of late Thatcherism now complained that they were being offered a vegetarian diet.

They wanted to know: where's the beef?

6

Where's the Beef?

We cannot revive old factions,
We cannot restore old policies,
Or follow an antique drum.
      T. S. Eliot, *Little Gidding*

From the moment he arrived in Number 10, John Major was pestered for his 'Big Idea'. His personal popularity showed up in every poll. In Chris Patten's phrase, people 'like what they see, and want to like what they haven't yet seen'. But that did not save him from the inquisition Where was 'the vision thing'? What was 'Majorism'?

The new Prime Minister was not a single issue politician. He was, in the deepest sense of the word, a conservative, not fond of change for its own sake. His 1992 general election Manifesto has subsequently been described as highly radical: but he would not necessarily consider that a compliment. He disliked 'isms'. He liked people. He did not want to make a cult of his own ideas; he believed in the traditional values of his party.

The journey from Brixton to Huntingdon had left him with strong convictions about the dignity of personal ownership, and a desire to give people more direct control over bureaucracy. These instincts underlay his hatred of inflation, his commitment to privatisation, to open markets. He shared these with his predecessor. They also led him to develop an approach to public services which did not contradict what had gone before – but filled a clear gap in 1980s Conservatism.

John Major was sensitive to misfortune, tolerant of diversity, and a living example of the 'Britain without barriers', the 'classless society', the 'country at ease with itself' that he wished to create. When he talked of 'the power to choose, and the right to own', these ideals reflected his own aspirations. He spoke of bringing income tax down to 20p on his very first evening as Prime Minister, and talked early of lifting the shadow of inheritance tax from middle-class families.

He had strong, down-to-earth Tory views on crime and punishment and the value of the 3Rs. Again, this insistence on getting 'back to basics' – long before the 1993 Party Conference – did not go against the grain of his predecessor's attitudes. But – particularly at the Home Office and the Department for Education – it did require changes in policy.

In Europe, he followed the course which – with so much greater consistency than their Labour opponents – Conservative Prime Ministers had followed from Harold Macmillan to Edward Heath to Margaret Thatcher. He believed there was a way forward for Britain in the Community. He fought hard both for the development of 'our kind of Europe', and for the right to stand aside from developments in which Britain did not want to share.

However, journalists, reasonably enough, wanted to know whether to tick the box marked 'continuity', or the one marked 'change'. Was Margaret Thatcher the back-seat driver of the new Government? Or was the new Prime Minister not only from a different generation, but a different kind of Tory?

Civil servants were asking the same question. From all over Whitehall, they called up the Policy Unit, asking for 'a steer' as to the new Prime Minister's views on everything and anything, down to the most ludicrous points of detail. It was liking sitting in the *Mastermind* chair, answering questions on 'John Major's views on 25,000 things you never knew about government'. Filtering some of these messages back to the Prime Minister, the Policy Unit encountered his highly rational exasperation. He wasn't going to tick the 'yes' or 'no' box lightly – or, in civil service parlance, signal he was or was not 'content'. Instead, notes would come back with the scribble 'Please refer' in the top right-hand corner, which meant his advisers would be in for a detailed cross-examination before he would go nap.

Neither the media not the mandarins were, of course, wholly disinterested. Journalists need political 'big ideas' to write about. Whitehall is, as ever, more subtle than Grub Street. As Sarah worked her way round the official circuit, taking coffee with one courteous Permanent Secretary after another, she met a genuine spirit of inquiry – and just the occasional display of the time-honoured techniques of the departmental 'bounce'. Civil servants instinctively see the opportunity of a change of Prime Minister to do a bit of steering themselves. A conversation that may afterwards permit them to claim a proposal had been given a fair wind by Number 10 is always useful.

'Policy' is an overworked word. Not surprising, perhaps, since it has a pretty loose history: early English derivations relate it to anything from commonwealth to cunning. Governments are expected to have policies on far too many things. On the other hand, both journalists and civil servants had a point. People do have a right to get on with their lives in reasonable understanding of what the Prime Minister is trying to do – and to vote in reasonably clear anticipation of what would-be Prime Ministers will at least try to do. Without policy, the diffuse business of government easily becomes confused and self-contradictory. Decision-makers fall over each other's feet. Ministers plough their own furrows – until another one arrives, and ploughs everything up again.

Once a policy has been enunciated, however, the media's main interest is in a deviation from it: in failure or 'U-turn'; in a contradiction between colleagues, or – better still – between present and past Prime Ministers. In 1991, John Major knew, the task of recalibrating policy was a particularly delicate one.

Plainly he did not start with a clean slate. He had been in the Government for seven years, and in the Cabinet for three. He had the slightly equivocal support of his predecessor, sensitive to anything her 'friends' might tell her was a deviation from the path she had followed.

When Chris Patten re-selected Saatchi & Saatchi as the party's advertising agency in the spring of 1991, their advice was unequivo-cal. The Prime Minister should be asking for his own first term, not for Margaret Thatcher's fourth. His novelty was an advantage. His difference from her – as the opinion polls continued to show – was an electoral asset. But John Major was instinctively hostile to attempts to personalise politics – or indeed policy. From the very beginning, he resisted any talk of 'Majorism'. His team knew they could expect a Prime Ministerial talking-to if he saw it creeping into the newspapers.

Like Baldwin, with whom he was increasingly compared, John Major liked plain English, simple images rooted in tradition and love of country, down-to-earth objectives and practical policies. He hated pretension and prejudice, knew from experience what life was like inside a struggling city heap, and wanted to widen the channels of opportunity which Thatcherism had opened up for the toughest and most able. 'A hand up, not a hand out' is a phrase credited (with much applause) to Tony Blair. It is actually a very typical John Major phrase, used by him frequently from 1991 onwards and featuring widely in 1992 Tory election literature.

These instincts led naturally towards the first area the Prime Minister singled out for attention: education.

It was new policy territory for him. As a local councillor in south London, he had been most concerned with housing; in national government, the only department he had served in before the Treasury (briefly interrupted by the Foreign Office), had been Social Security. But education was, self-evidently, the key to opportunity. And it was bubbling with live issues. The school reforms were reaching a crucial stage. Not until the new tests were in place would there be the full, damning evidence of differing standards in schools, which deprived cohorts of city children of a fair crack at life. But with a third of those entering further education needing remedial help with basic English and mathematics, no one could pretend all was well. In speech after speech in early 1991, the Prime Minister put education at the top of his personal agenda for Government.

Politically, it was an ambitious choice. The conventional wisdom is that parties should stick to their home territory, because it is easier to raise the 'salience' of an issue than to alter perceptions of who handles it best. On this theory, the Labour Party should do everything it can to raise the salience of health, welfare and unemployment (conventionally seen as their territory), while Tories should stick to inflation, defence, and law and order.

Education was battleground territory – though traditionally more Labour than Tory. And it was a battleground in another sense: Ken Clarke was having to fight reform through, in the teeth of opposition from the teachers' unions. The conflict was made worse by the fact that the bodies set up to organise the new curriculum and tests allowed the process to become increasingly bureaucratic – overloading teachers with paper, and then infuriating them further when they had to reform the reforms. The fact that the teachers' unions themselves contributed to the paper chase, by pressing for teacher-controlled assessment rather than simple classroom tests, passed almost everyone by. It was the Government that took the flak.

On 29 January 1991, the Prime Minister had a working supper with the Policy Unit. The team was still far from complete. Neither Nick True nor Jonathan were there. But John Mills, the civil servant on secondment from the Department of Trade and Industry, spoke with fire and force on education – and, most particularly, on the need to sort out the tangle of education for the over-sixteens. Ken Clarke and Michael Howard, Secretaries of State for Education and Employment respectively, were both reviewing their departments' policies. The decision was taken to work for a joint White Paper, to be launched by the Prime Minister himself.

Before then, however, the Prime Minister was to have his first general review of policy, in a style which would become established practice. Late on Saturday 23 March, he arrived at Chequers, the country retreat of Prime Ministers, for a series of meetings with Ministers and advisers which were to run on into Monday afternoon. Coming at the end of a particularly busy month, the timing was not ideal. But it might be the only chance he had to catch up on what his Ministers were up to, get up to speed on unfamiliar issues, clear the decks and set the course for the election Manifesto.

On Sunday morning, he reviewed the first themes on which the

Policy Unit[1] had been focusing: choice, opportunity, responsibility and ownership. Then, when his Ministers arrived, he began a series of meetings whose chief purpose was to identify policy priorities for further work.

Set in the Buckinghamshire countryside, Chequers has great advantages for such meetings. There are fewer distractions than in Number 10, where all the different communications channels are pulsing with news, queries, and emergencies competing for the Prime Minister's attention. When all these have to be filtered through one Garden Room girl stationed in the little front-hall lobby at Chequers, some of them magically disappear, while others lose their urgency. The Great Parlour is bigger than the Cabinet Room at Number 10, and less stuffy. The park at Chequers provides the Prime Minister with a rare opportunity to mix work with a breath of fresh air, even a walk – local people using the ancient rights of way may suddenly find themselves confronted by half the Cabinet and a few discreet Special Branch security men. But Chequers has certain peculiarities, as Sarah was to find out that evening.

Jane Uff, the Chequers guardian, asked Sarah if she would mind sleeping in the Prison Room. 'How wonderful,' she said innocently.

Up in the second-floor corner of the building, half-hidden and half-timbered, this is the room in which Lady Jane Grey's sister, Lady Mary, was kept a prisoner by Elizabeth I. She had committed the opposite mistake to Lady Jane, who had married so dangerously well: Lady Mary – from her portrait, clearly not the family beauty – had married beneath her. All she seems to have wanted to do was to be allowed to live free and far from the court with her husband. But her life, too, ended sadly – if

[1]Within the policy unit, Nick True ranged widely, drafting most of the Prime Minister's key speeches; John Mills worked on education, local government and European issues; Carolyn Sinclair on health, environment, and law and order; Howell Harris Hughes on industry, finance and Wales; Alan Rosling on employment, Scotland and defence; Jonathan began by dealing with housing and transport, but pretty soon became the unit's cross-departmental trouble-shooter.

not so abruptly as Lady Jane's – and there is a melancholy feel to the room.

Sarah went sleepily to the Prison Room at 2.00 a.m., having messed around with papers for the morning session and written up some fairly incoherent minutes. She looked at the spot where the prisoner had covered the walls with her sad graffiti. The wind rattled the window-frames; perhaps, after all, she should have opted for a downstairs room. But the discovery of a bathroom to the side of the room added a reassuringly modern note. It was really just another bedroom. Wasn't it?

Sarah opened what she thought was the clothes cupboard. No such thing. Down at her feet began a secret, spiral staircase.

She looked at the door, hoping to lock off this alarming exit . . . or entrance. No lock. She knew she couldn't sleep without finding out where this staircase led to – or rather, led from. Feeling remarkably foolish, Sarah crept down one flight, and found a door. She touched the handle, then hesitated at the thought of what other sixteenth-century horrors might lurk there. So she crept further down, to ground-floor level. Another door. She tried the handle; there was a menacing growl the other side.

The alsatians that patrol the Chequers grounds do so, Sarah knew, only in the company of armed policemen. But she didn't fancy disturbing dog or gun at that hour. She crept back upstairs and tried not to think of ghosts.

In the morning, the 'Wren' who brought her a cup of tea was highly amused. 'Oh, sorry,' she said. 'We forgot to tell you. I'll show you where it comes out.' Behind the side-table in the Great Parlour, where the Prime Minister held meetings, was a door disguised as a piece of panelling – securely locked.

The policy review started again at breakfast in the Great Parlour, with the arrival of Ken Clarke and Michael Howard. It was then that they agreed the bones of the education and training White Paper, which was fleshed out and published in less than two months.

This White Paper – John Major's first domestic policy initiative – went with the grain of his own experience of leaving school with no qualifications and finding himself on the wrong side of the education tracks. Its theme was the need to break down artificial barriers in education and boost the quality of the 'second-class' vocational route. The old binary line, which permitted third-rate universities to look down on first-rate polytechnics, was to be abolished: all were to be able to compete for reputation and funds on grounds of quality. On the training side, the main announcement was a pilot scheme for a system of training credits, fought for determinedly by Michael Howard, which would give greater choice of opportunities for sixteen- and seventeen-year-old school-leavers.

When launch day – 20 May – arrived, Number 10 staff learned some important lessons, not least about the Prime Minister. Jonathan, Barry Potter and Sarah were called in to tell him about the arrangements for the press conference in the Queen Elizabeth II centre that afternoon. They got an earful. The briefing was not full enough. What was the answer to this, that and the other? Their answers would not do. He simply wasn't going to take part in the launch on that basis.

With alarming visions of the afternoon's arrangements going up in smoke, Sarah began to blather. The Prime Minister only had to set the scene, the parliamentary statement was going to be made by Ken Clarke, who would be there with Michael Howard, flanking the Prime Minister at the press conference, anxious to deal with the detail . . . No dice.

Officials were hauled over from Education and Employment to brief the Prime Minister at length, and were grilled until he felt fully in command of the subject. At the press conference, he ignored all advice to farm the difficult questions out, and answered them himself.

It was a pattern repeated many times. During the general election campaign, Chris Patten reminded the Prime Minister over and over again that the Party Chairman was there to act as first line of defence, flinging himself into the breach or 'falling on his sword' if press conferences became tricky. And over and over again the Prime Minister ignored this advice.

Preparation of the White Paper had thrown the overlap between Education and Employment into sharp relief. This hotted up an internal argument, not finally resolved for another four years: should the Departments of Education and Employment simply be merged?

Many senior officials, including the Cabinet Secretary, were keen. The Permanent Secretary at Employment, Sir Geoffrey Holland, was about to be promoted to the bigger job at Education, so from the mandarins' point of view it looked like a good moment for the change.

But when the Prime Minister came to review the Whitehall maze in preparation for the Manifesto, there was one overwhelming political argument against a merger. At a time of rising unemployment, it would have been politically inept to abolish the Cabinet job of Secretary of State for Employment. So the change had to wait until 1995.

In the meantime, there was no shortage of work for the Secretary of State for Education. The national curriculum was going off the rails. Forms were in, facts were out. The history curriculum became a bone of contention when it became clear the extent to which the acquisition of knowledge about the past had been abandoned. Only the tests for seven-year-olds were under way before the election. The target was to introduce tests for fourteen-year-olds and eleven-year-olds by 1994. And it was already clear that this deadline was under pressure.

On 3 July, in a speech to the Centre for Policy Studies, the Prime Minister tackled some of these issues. In the somewhat incongruous environment of the Café Royale, he put down more 'back to basics' markers. He spoke of the 'mania that undermined common sense values in schools, rejected proven teaching methods, debased standards – or disposed of them altogether'. It was, he said, 'a canker in our education system which spread from the sixties on'.

The speech drew together two themes: the economic need to raise education standards, and the personal need for educational values. 'A Conservative society is one that knows about and respects its roots, while having the self-confidence to embrace new ideas.' The Prime Minister signalled some changes designed to put the reforms back on track. 'We need to shift the emphasis towards shorter, standardised tests, which the whole class can take at one time.' The proportion of GCSE marks given for coursework should be limited, and the exams must be set in ways which challenged the most able – a pointer to the introduction of the A★ grade. And the Prime Minister announced legislation to smooth schools' path to grant-maintained status, preventing local authorities from selling off their assets, spending huge sums on anti-opt-out propaganda, or refusing to supply details of grant-maintained choices in primary 'feeder' schools.

Keen to offer the carrot as well as the stick, the Prime Minister had meanwhile agreed, after long debate with the Treasury, to Ken Clarke's request to set up a pay review body for teachers. This recognition of their status did not save him from what became one of Downing Street's epic exchanges of correspondence.

Fred Jarvis, former General Secretary of the National Union of Teachers, took exception to what the Prime Minister had to say – hardly surprisingly, since the speech struck at many of the fashionable educational theories to which Fred Jarvis had been committed. He wrote to the Prime Minister setting out, very cogently and lucidly, why he believed the Government's view was wrong. It was a detailed and serious letter which merited a detailed and serious reply.

In the sometimes random way in which the Number 10 letter-sorting process works, this letter was deemed to be 'political' – and was therefore passed not to the Private Office but to the Political Office. A junior member of staff unfortunately sent back the bog-standard 'political' reply, thanking him for his views – and suggesting that he took them up with his local Conservative political centre.

This did not go down well.

Exchanges were still going on when Jonathan took over as Political Secretary, eight months later. They were still going strong over two years after that. The whole correspondence was reproduced in full in a pamphlet published by Fred Jarvis. It featured regularly in the *Times Educational Supplement* – and even in leaders in *The Times* itself. Thus began – as so often, by accident – a guerrilla war between two utterly conflicting views of how the educational system should be run.[2]

But the education debate was only a rehearsal for the Prime

---

[2]If by any chance Fred Jarvis should read this, Jonathan says please – please – do not bother to write.

Minister's broader agenda. He and Chris Patten saw how badly the Tories needed a language in which they could talk not only about privatisation, but also about those public services which were going to remain the responsibility of government. In Number 10, Jonathan, in particular, also saw an opportunity for the Conservatives to put Labour on the defensive. By standing up for the little man against the big public sector battalions, he argued, the Prime Minister could wrong-foot the Opposition, defenders of the vested interests of the trade unions, shattering the illusion that Labour were the party of good public services.

Just as the Conservatives had dominated the agenda in the 1980s with privatisation, so, Sarah and Nick True believed, in the 1990s they could drive it forward with public service reform, developing a toolkit of ideas that would apply market stimuli and private sector skills to the task of raising public sector standards. Competition in a free market creates 'people power'. It forces producers to listen to consumers, to raise the quality of their service – or lose sales, money, jobs. So many practical improvements cost thought, not money – active management of waiting lists, response targets, published information. Public monopoly providers, with their bottoms parked comfortably on the Consolidated Fund, face no real pressures to make these bothersome changes, to look outwards, to listen to the people who use their services. The pressures are all inward instead: to listen to the powerful monopoly trade unions.

Both the departments and the Treasury tended to shy away from talk about standards or quality. The departmental view would be that if they were to be asked to do better, they should simply be given more money. And the Treasury did not want them to be asked to do better, for fear that the end result would be them getting more money to do it. The Citizen's Charter, as it came to be called, was an explicit effort to break out of this trap: to stimulate public services to use public money better.

The Policy Unit had started work on these ideas right back in February 1991. Their starting-point was some words the Prime Minister had used in a speech made to the Audit Commission in June 1989, when he was Chief Secretary to the Treasury:

'Shoddy public services should not be an option. Nor should they be tolerated.' Coming from a Treasury Minister, this mild expression of concern for standards was almost revolutionary. But the whole Charter approach had much deeper roots in his experience of life without privilege: a first-hand knowledge, denied to the children of the chattering classes, of the indifference of bureaucracy to the powerless individual.

By early March, Sarah, Nick and Jonathan had made some progress with the work on principles – but the Prime Minister's baby was still unchristened. What should it be called? Suffering from a surfeit of Cabinet Office sandwiches, they one day decided to take themselves to the Indian restaurant in Horseferry Road, to see if a curry would stimulate their imaginations. The Kundan is just sufficiently far from Whitehall to reduce the probability that they would find ourselves elbow to elbow with Permanent Secretaries and lobby correspondents.

Jonathan had been attracted by the idea of a 'contract' between government and people, but preferred the word 'charter', which was less legalistic, to describe it. Sarah and Nick agreed. By the end of the chicken tikka, the Policy Unit group had dismissed 'customer' and 'consumer' as narrow, econo-cratic words. They plumped for 'citizen'. But would the Prime Minister like it? He did. The working title 'Citizen's Charter'[3] was launched in his Central Council speech at Southport on 23 March.

But the real work had yet to begin. At the Chequers meeting in late March, the Prime Minister took the ideas further – particularly with Malcolm Rifkind. The Prime Minister confirmed his determination to privatise British Rail, but asked also for plans to raise service standards in the meantime. He canvassed ideas for the Charter with Ken Clarke, with Michael Howard, and most of all with Chris Patten.

Early the following week, Andrew Turnbull sent a letter, drafted

[3]For some time the apostrophe was a movable feast, as the Policy Unit debated the merits of 'Citizen's' as against 'Citizens''. With the logo, it became fixed in the singular position. A Conservative Government should, the Unit argued, be focused on the individual rather than the collective.

by Nick True, round the 'Private Secretaries' net' linking all the departments of Whitehall.

Ministers rarely write directly to each other. Instead, their Private Secretaries launch missives at each other, purporting to pass on messages from 'my' Secretary of State to 'yours'. Their political masters, referred to in the third person, tend to feature as a species of unruly pet, for whose behaviour their Private Secretaries are personally responsible. This system enables Ministers to be much ruder to each other than they would be in person, a tendency over-encouraged by some Private Secretaries, so that correspondence may escalate offensively to the point where neither can back down. But it is a vital, even essential network, without which government would grind to a halt.

So far as the Prime Minister is concerned, it is a usefully impersonal way of delivering firm instructions to departments. And that is precisely what, in the week of 25 March, Andrew did. All Secretaries of State were told to report back with proposals for the Charter by 30 April.

Asking is one thing. Getting, another. At the end of April, it became clear that what departments would deliver spontaneously would be quite insufficient for a successful launch. Newspapers began to carry reports that the Policy Unit was not satisfied with the first results of its trawl through departments. This time, the papers were right.

The essence of the Charter was its diversity. It was not just a matter of the Prime Minister laying down the law. He needed departments to use their initiative. It was clear that a piece of machinery was going to be needed to pump policy out of Whitehall. The Prime Minister spoke to Robin Butler, and the Cabinet Secretary did the best thing he conceivably could have done: he put Andrew Whetnall, a senior official in the Cabinet Office, on the job. Andrew chaired the group of officials working on the White Paper launching the Citizen's Charter, with total command of the mysteries of Whitehall process. He and a Cabinet Office colleague, Diana Goldsworthy, saw the document right through to the printers, hammering home the last detail.

In Number 10, Nick True – who sat on Andrew Whetnall's

group – was the powerhouse for Charter ideas. In early May, another salvo was fired off to all departments by Number 10, in the form of a series of 'challenge questions' drafted by Nick. At much the same time, the Prime Minister provided himself with another weapon – this time, in the Treasury itself.

The Prime Minister needed a Minister to help launch the Charter, give it political momentum, and to nag colleagues. He also needed to engage the Treasury, which was bristling with suspicion. A certain not-invented-here grumpiness threatened to lose the Treasury the chance to shape the Charter initiative. The answer to both problems was, however, already in the Treasury building, in the shape of the Financial Secretary, Francis Maude.

Following the Chequers meeting in March, Norman Lamont had been encouraged by the Prime Minister to launch Francis Maude on a campaign to kick-start the privatisation programme. Now the Prime Minister asked the Chancellor to broaden these 'bilaterals' with Ministers to cover other Charter policies – such as information, inspection and redress – as well. Armed with the Prime Minister's authority, Francis pounded round Whitehall, filling in the Charter scorecard. Nick, then Jonathan, went with him, riding shotgun. The Treasury, finding one of their Ministers almost totally absorbed by Charter business, became slightly grumpier. But Francis Maude steamed ahead, lugging the Treasury in his wake.

To raise the profile of the Charter, and bring in outside ideas, the Prime Minister held a seminar at Chequers on 3 June, inviting an eclectic mixture of industrialists (Sir Richard Greenbury, John Allan), service providers (Gordon Lister, Sir Bob Reid), regulators (Sir Bryan Carsberg, William Reid), inspectors (Judge Tumim, Howard Davies), and think-tankers (Graham Mather, David Willetts). From Government, he invited two junior Ministers, John Redwood (a former head of the Policy Unit in Margaret Thatcher's day), and of course Francis Maude. Sarah, Nick and Andrew Turnbull were there from Number 10.

The Great Parlour at Chequers resounded with some incongruously modern arguments about competition, contracting-out, standards, tests, performance pay, quality measurement, compensation, complaint and redress. Stephen Tumim's advocacy of independent inspection particularly impressed the Prime Minister. After all, if the prison system could be opened up, surely other public services could face the same challenge? Ideas sparked. The programme took a step forward. So did Francis Maude.

This happened almost by accident. Come the day of the Chequers seminar, Gus O'Donnell wanted to know who could go on the airwaves. Francis Maude was the obvious answer. The Prime Minister's 'fifth columnist', as the newspapers called him, was now publicly declared to be the 'Minister for the Citizen's Charter'. The Treasury became even more grumpy. But Francis wasn't bothered. And he was greatly helped by his Private Secretary, Philip Rutnam, a terrier who dived down one Whitehall rat-hole after another.

The Policy Unit took stock in the middle of June. Nick had deliberately played a double game, helping Andrew Whetnall to extract as much new policy as he could from the official machine, then coming back himself to ask for more. Now, however, time was running out if the Charter was to be launched before the summer break. Sarah asked everyone in the Policy Unit to drop all other work and pitch in. The White Paper had deliberately been designed as only a first step on the Charter ladder, but it would have to be sufficiently far off the ground to carry conviction. She now went on a trouble-shooting (or trouble-making) circuit of departments.

To anyone in a private sector company, it may seem strange that the whole exercise was so difficult. But Whitehall is not like a centrally-driven business – or even the Roman army: when Number 10 says go, it is not always the case that the system goeth. Of course, if the Prime Minister pushes a Minister into a corner, he or she will normally concede. But wise Prime Ministers do not do that too often, particularly on matters of detail. And with the Charter, the devil was all in the detail. It was the Policy Unit's job to keep the number of fights the Prime Minister had to have to a minimum.

Departments are large, heavyweight institutions, with a very big turning circle and infinite capacity for obstruction and delay. It is a rare policy that succeeds without the momentum of one of these institutional tankers behind it. Yet the essence of the Charter was that it was non-departmental. The miracle is that it managed to turn the public-sector fleet as far as it did.

The Prime Minister had the advantage of the active involvement of a tough, experienced Principal Private Secretary – and even more importantly, of the Cabinet Secretary. The civil service machine therefore received two important signals: that whatever the Prime Minister's political enemies might be saying outside, this was not a frivolous political add-on – yet another of those barmy ideas that politicians hire advisers to waste their time on – but a serious review of the aims and methods of government. Careful to balance an attack on bureaucracy with respect for those who wanted to provide good quality public service, on the day of the Charter launch the Prime Minister sent a letter explaining his aims and intentions to every civil servant.

An early Charter battle was over the principle that public servants dealing with the public should be ready to identify themselves. This met with strong resistance from some quarters. It was argued that it would make staff more 'vulnerable'. In fact, there was evidence pointing in quite the opposite direction: angry clients or claimants were more inclined to treat faceless bureaucrats as human beings if they could put a name to them. To the Prime Minister's delight, the Cabinet Secretary turned up for the Number 10 launch wearing a name badge prepared by his secretary. It read: 'I'm Robin – can I help you?'

To succeed, the Charter approach had to make an impact on the lives of patients, parents and passengers. So three departments were obviously crucial to the programme: Health, Education and Transport.

At Education, Nick True found an open door at ministerial level. Ken Clarke used the Charter White Paper as an extra lever in his own battles for reform with his officials. At Transport, Jonathan found it harder going. But Sir Bob Reid offered to come in to Number 10 to talk about what British Rail could do. Sarah and Jonathan began by asking him what kind of training programmes BR had to encourage their staff to respond to passengers. 'Oh,' said Bob, 'we certainly teach them how to deal with difficult passengers.' Clearly the Charter approach still had some way to go . . .

Just before she left Downing Street and he left BR, Sarah went to lunch with Bob Reid in his office, and reminded him of this moment. He was generous enough to say that the Charter had been a catalyst, transforming attitudes inside BR. Sarah wasn't so ungenerous as to say that she still hoped for more.

At the Department of Health, Nick True and Carolyn Sinclair – the Policy Unit member who 'shadowed' health – reported running into serious difficulties. Again, the Secretary of State, William Waldegrave,[4] was responsive, but the Charter approach came up hard against the nanny instinct. The system was being asked to deliver choice, convenience and shorter waiting-times for operations; but it was far happier setting targets for other people – what to eat and drink, when to exercise, how to give up smoking. However, Duncan Nichol, the Chief Executive of the National Health Service Management Executive, was an early and important convert. He saw that the initiative came at the right moment in the wider reform of the health service, when it was important to break up the language of the market by injecting an emphasis on quality.

But it was the involvement of nurses in the Charter programme that was critical, since they carry responsibility for most of the day-to-day care of patients. The Charter proposal that there should be a named nurse with special responsibility for each patient came directly from the Royal College of Nursing. Four years later, the impact of the Charter is generally seen to have been greatest in health – and education.

But at Health, the Charter also ran into the first sign of a perennial problem: differences with the 'territorials'. The Scottish Office was roaring ahead with limits on waiting times for common operations, such as hip replacements. In the Department of Health, civil servants were wary. They grumbled that it was all very well for the Scots: they were rolling in public money.[5] In the English

---

[4]After the general election, William Waldegrave became the first Cabinet Minister with responsibility for the Citizen's Charter.

[5]On every public service issue, English departments grumble about Scottish money. This is because public expenditure is apportioned according to a formula which automatically gives the Scots – and the Welsh – more per head than the English – part of the delicate balance of advantage in the Union that would never survive devolution. Measuring the performance of public services tends to throw this difference into sharp relief.

regions, there were not so certain that even long limits on waiting times would hold.

The Charter was a supreme example of another peculiar Whitehall phenomenon: long battles between entrenched positions, followed by a quick skirmish, very close to the deadline, that suddenly ends the war. On 28 June, Nick True set out the final timetable for the Prime Minister. A paper on the Citizen's Charter would have to be circulated to Cabinet on 8 July. But the most important departments were all still in dispute with both the Cabinet Office and Number 10.

At Education, there was still no agreement, even at the end of June, on the publication of a Parent's Charter, or of school results and reports in a format that would permit people to make real comparisons. Nor was there full agreement on reform of the schools inspectorate. This was clinched at a meeting on 1 July between Ken Clarke, Francis Maude and Nick True. That same day, the Prime Minister himself secured Ken Baker's agreement to the publication of performance tables for police forces. He also personally settled the outstanding Charter points on housing with Michael Heseltine on 2 July. And in that same, final week, Francis Maude secured Peter Lilley's commitment to greater competition in postal services.

Now the pace was hotting up, with everyone adding their twopenny-worth as the White Paper ground its way through the printers. Andrew Whetnall, official guardian of the text, displayed endless patience as Sarah reported news from the battlefront. At Health, Carolyn Sinclair eventually secured agreement to limits on waiting times for operations in England that could at least compare with what was to be offered in Scotland. A final breakthrough was agreement to publish comparative information on hospitals.

Jonathan battled on with Transport. British Rail had by now agreed to the publication of its first Passengers' Charter. But couldn't the department offer some liberalisation of its own? Make some people-friendly contribution? Even a gesture, to show willing? How about making it easier for people at work to take driving tests, by allowing them in the evenings and on Saturdays? No demand, they were told. Eventually, Nick and Jonathan secured

Transport's agreement to test public opinion – which, strangely enough, indicated that there was 'demand'.

Finally, the last piece of the White Paper jigsaw was in place, the Cabinet was agreed, the Government's press machine ready to roll. But there were still last-minute hitches. The business managers sought to persuade the Prime Minister to delay the announcement until the recess: the Charter did not, strictly speaking, have to be announced to Parliament – and they were being inundated with demands from departments for parliamentary time for tedious announcements that did have to be made in the House of Commons. But Number 10 stuck to its guns – and its schedule.

On 27 July, the Prime Minister launched the Charter, first in the Commons, then at a press conference, with most of his ministerial team present, at the Queen Elizabeth II centre. The Charter logo, filling the background behind him at the press conference, had been through several incarnations before acquiring its final simplicity. The design of the White Paper itself had driven the Policy Unit nuts. Anything but white, it was a singularly unsuccessful example of contracting-out. Jonathan managed to tone down some of the over-use of colour and seemingly random use of photography by the designers hired for the job, but it still displayed such tedious design tricks as a summary shaded from cerulean to cerise, for all the world like a paint manufacturer's colour chart.

However, the contents were a respectable start to the Charter programme. The summary list of more than a hundred announce-ments ranged from sophisticated management mechanisms to down-to-earth changes in services to citizens.

The paper was organised thematically. It committed the Govern-ment to more privatisation (railways and buses in particular), but also wider competition in the delivery of public services, further contracting-out, more performance-related pay; it introduced pub-lication of performance targets, at both local and national level, and of information on standards achieved; it instituted more effective complaints procedures, independent inspection, and better systems of redress.

In education, the Charter stressed the importance of independent inspection, and the provision of information: school reports for parents, the publication of school results – not just for exams, but on other measures such as truancy levels. In the National Health Service, agreement on waiting-time limits for operations had an almost instant effect: the number of people waiting over two years for admission to hospital in England came down from 43,517 in September 1991 to 336 in September 1993. Appointment systems, and a check on the hideous practice of last-minute cancellation of operations, also came in under the Charter.

In transport, the Charter required published information on standards set and met, particularly for punctuality. British Rail had also committed itself to a new system of compensation for grossly unpunctual or cancelled services.

Standards of performance were to be published right across the public services, from the courts to the Post Office. League tables, vigorously contested in the pre-publication negotiations but now widely taken for granted as an information service provided by government, were another breakthrough announced in the Charter White Paper.

There had still been disappointments. An important Charter principle was to empower independent inspectors to speak out openly about the standards they found. In education, change in the system of inspection was already under way. Number 10 had secured Home Office agreement to open up the Inspectorate of Constabulary, and two 'lay inspectors' were appointed in late 1993. But the words on the Social Services Inspectorate were depressingly cautious.

The 'right to repair', giving council tenants the freedom to get on with urgent small repairs, had been watered down – though it was enshrined in legislation in 1993. But it took until 1994 for regulations to be implemented giving tenants the right to manage their own estates. On motorways, the White Paper included a commitment to step up 'lane rental' – which provided direct incentives to contractors to close off carriageways for as short a time as possible. But it would take years to loosen the Department of Transport's regulatory grip on motorway service areas.

Number 10 staff had learnt the lesson of the Education White Paper: there was enough time in the Prime Minister's diary to cross-examine his team on the final detail. He was on good form at the press conference; and the Charter was well-received. 'Power to the People' was the *Daily Express* headline; 'Major plans curbs on faceless giants' said the *Sun*; '"Consumer rights" to be central theme of the 1990s' was the rather more downbeat verdict of the *Independent*. The *Daily Telegraph* concluded that it was not 'dramatic or profound', but 'sensible, serious and public spirited'.

'Broad sweep to value-for-money Citizen's Charter' was *The Times*'s catch-all headline. Its leader, entitled 'Mimicking the Market', concluded that 'The package exudes the regard for courtesy and probity which Mr Major has made his hallmark.'

It also gave the Charter some remarkable antecedents:

Despite its noble ambitions Mr Major's charter is pragmatic, drawing inspiration from classical liberalism, from American consumerism and from the public service idealism of school inspectors such as Matthew Arnold or popular judges such as Lord Denning.

Well, maybe. It's a wise child that knows its own parents, and on 23 July 1991 the Charter seemed to have plenty. The Institute for Economic Affairs traced Charter ancestry to a Hobart Paper they had published in the 1980s, on the notion of government by contract. Madsen Pirie, of the Adam Smith Institute, pronounced it in tune with the arguments the ASI had been advancing. The Centre for Policy Studies noted that their director, David Willetts, had been a speaker at the June Chequers seminar. The National Consumers' Council traced ideas back to one of their publications.

The Charter came to be attacked by the far right as a retreat from privatisation, by the left as hostile to public sector unions. The Labour Party alternately claimed it as 'their idea' and condemned it as a 'Tory gimmick'. There was some predictable tut-tutting over the use of the word 'Citizen' in a monarchy, though no one quite had the nerve to suggest it should have been called the 'Subject's Charter' instead. A huge programme, it scored, over time, many unsung successes in improving the quality and efficiency of public services — as well, inevitably, as one or two exasperating failures.[6]

From the very beginning, however, the Charter was almost too successful in attracting imitators. Every public service now wanted to introduce its own Charter, and many private-sector companies rushed to replicate the idea. Internationally, it attracted a great deal of attention in other governments and political parties which were struggling with the same problems of inward-looking, quality-indifferent public services.

Within the next six months, fifteen charters had been published. One million copies of the Patient's Charter had been ordered; four million of the Parent's Charter, to be distributed through schools. A unit had been set up in the Cabinet Office, under a senior civil servant, Brian Hilton, to co-ordinate this wave of enthusiasm. The Prime Minister had his own panel of outside advisers, under the chairmanship of Sir James Blyth.[7] Chairman of Boots, and former head of sales at the Ministry of Defence, Blyth was a blunt Scotsman who was to fight many Charter battles. Another stalwart member of the panel was Madsen Pirie.

The Charter was a statement of hard policy principle, about the application of market disciplines — information, competition, direct accountability to consumers, reward for performance — to public services. It was, in that sense, the lineal descendant of privatisation. It was not just a string of bright ideas for improving services. But there is never anything wrong with a few bright ideas, for which the Charter provided a new stimulus. And the ideas that found favour resonated in some surprising

[6]The most infuriating of these was the infamous 'Motorway Cones Hotline', which came to haunt tabloid coverage of the Charter. In 1993, the Prime Minister had hauled in a team from the Department of Transport to review their distinctly patchy delivery of Charter principles. The offer of a hotline was produced for him, a rabbit out of the departmental hat, in an effort to distract him from other failures. It sounded good — a real service to the motorist. But, almost unbelievably, Transport launched this service simply by feeding the hotline into the departmental switchboard. Frustrated drivers could expect to get no more informative answer than from any other busy telephone operator.
[7]Now Lord Blyth of Rowington.

quarters – as Number 10 found when Saatchi & Saatchi's were let loose on it.

Conservative Central Office had decided to follow up the launch of the Charter by featuring it in a party political broadcast. This caused a flurry of the kind with which Number 10 was becoming familiar. The Prime Minister was pressed to take part. His contribution was filmed – at the last minute – in Deputy Chief Whip Alastair Goodlad's house nearby in Westminster. The overall package then had to be checked well past the last minute by Jonathan and Sarah. In this broadcast, however, the high spot was not so much the Prime Minister's own piece to camera as a *jeu d'esprit* by Saatchi's, who filmed – from above – a small hospital waiting room filling up with extremely pregnant ladies. All of them had been given the same appointment time, a well-known hospital trick condemned in the Patient's Charter.

This struck a chord with at least one pregnant lady – Julia Langdon, of the *Sunday Telegraph*:

> An average visit to the ante-natal clinic at Queen Charlotte's Hospital in West London calls for similar preparations to those needed for a long journey. You need to take newspapers, a book, and probably something to drink.

She compared her experience unfavourably with a train journey from London to Newcastle.

On 24 July, Chris Patten sent a letter to all Tory constituency chairmen. The Citizen's Charter, he wrote, had been a 'terrific success . . . It gives us a key theme for our future campaigning.' It was a reminder that, however exhilarating the business of Government might be, the business of politics could not be long delayed. Seen from Conservative Central Office in Smith Square, the Charter had been part of John Major's 'summer offensive'.

Would it now be followed by an autumn election?

7

Long Cold Summer

Oh, the grand old Duke of York,
He had ten thousand men;
He marched them up to the top of the hill,
And he marched them down again.
And when they were up they were up,
And when they were down they were down,
And when they were only half way up,
They were neither up nor down.

Traditional

Had Michael Heseltine won the leadership election in 1990, he would have had to go for a quick election, before Thatcher diehards could launch a revenge attack. But John Major came to power with support from the old regime. For better, or perhaps worse, that allowed him to wait.

At the end of January 1991, Chris Patten sent the Prime Minister a paper rehearsing the arguments for going to the polls early or late. This narrowed the field to just twelve possible Thursdays. The latest was 18 June 1992, although in theory the election could be delayed even longer, to 9 July.[1] The earliest date was 2 May 1991.

[1]The five-year limit on the life of the 1987 Parliament ran to 16 June 1992 – after which a new election would have to be called.

Economic forecasts suggested it would be better to 'go long'. According to the Chancellor, wrote Chris Patten somewhat sceptically, by the spring of 1992 we should be seeing 'pearly-fingered dawn breaking over a night sky'. However, his note argued, there was something to be said for the Prime Minister seizing the initiative, and (like Anthony Eden in 1955) going to the country early to secure his own 'mandate'.

The January paper also summed up the evidence on 'target groups'. The latest polls suggested that the main shift in votes since the last general election had been a switch from Liberal Democrat to Labour. This would make it harder to win a sizeable majority, since the anti-Tory vote was less evenly split. In 1983, the share of the vote secured by the Liberals and SDP shot up to 25.4 per cent – just two points behind Labour, at 27.6 per cent. In 1987, the Liberal–SDP Alliance had won 22.6 per cent, against Labour's 30.8 per cent. But in January 1991, the Liberal Democrats appeared to have dropped to below 10 per cent of the vote, while Labour was bowling along at over 40 per cent.

In the polls taken since John Major had become leader, the Conservative Party seemed to be doing better amongst women than in 1987; and also amongst the managerial, professional and clerical groups (socio-economic groups ABC1). Former Lib Dems in these categories seemed to have been switching back to the Tories, as well as to Labour. But the Tories were doing worse amongst the famous C2s – skilled manual workers – and the less skilled. Central Office had concluded that the party should aim to build strength among the under-thirties, women and C2s: a pretty broad target. Language, the research paper added helpfully, should be 'inspirational, visionary, confident'.

Much of this advice flowed from a meeting the Chairman had convened in January in the stately surroundings of Hever Castle, arranged long before as a brain-storming session to prepare for Margaret Thatcher's fourth campaign. Judith Chaplin, Nick True and Sarah went from Number 10. A great deal of even more expensive research on 'values' was presented, concluding – as such research always seems to – that the Conservative Party's strategy should be based on offering people 'hope' and 'peace of mind'.

By the spring, Chris Patten had reappointed Maurice Saatchi's agency to run the party's campaign for the next election.[2] Saatchi's concluded – equally true to form – in favour of a quite different strategy. The campaign should concentrate on destroying any peace of mind voters might have acquired about the Labour Party.

These two different strategy tunes were to be played, energetically if not always in harmony, right through 1991.

What the polls most clearly confirmed was that John Major's personal stock was very high, and had been rising through January. In March, Central Office had carried out its own private exploration of attitudes to Neil Kinnock and John Major. It used the technique of protracted discussion with carefully-selected groups of 'floating' voters.

Central Office found that these groups saw John Major as sensible, likeable, confident and approachable. Neil Kinnock was seen as rather more 'in touch', but long-winded, waffly, and not as likeable or sensible. John Major's 'quietness' was seen as 'effective'; he was 'straight'; he 'lets everyone else do the shouting'. This survey seemed to confirm the huge impact of the scenes on television news showing the Prime Minister standing among the troops in the desert.

By the summer, however, these images were fading. John Major's approval rating was still high – 59 per cent in April, according to MORI, barely down from the 63 per cent peak achieved in February – and he would continue to be more popular than his party. But the proportion of voters telling Gallup they thought he was 'firmly in charge' had fallen from 65 per cent to 45 per cent over the same period. The time taken to deal with the poll tax was clearly taking its toll, and there had been very little else happening to cheer voters up.

The Budget was hardly a classic pre-election sweetener. There was some applause from women's groups for the increase in Child

[2]Central Office had been resistant to reappointing Saatchi's, since Margaret Thatcher had lost confidence in the agency during the final days of the 1987 campaign – a campaign which had been characterised by a good deal of bad blood between her and the Party Chairman, Norman Tebbit.

Benefit. Business was pleased with the cut in corporation tax. But the main Budget headline had been the hefty increase in VAT, levied to take the heat out of the poll tax. And for another month, the story of a replacement for the poll tax dragged on – ruling out that first, early May, election date on Chris Patten's list.

June, however, was still a possibility. On Monday 22 April – the day before the Council Tax announcement – the Prime Minister had a meeting to discuss the June option with the Party Chairman and the Chief Whip. Sarah prepared a note for him beforehand on the policy issues that would have to be resolved. None of it looked impossible, but it would be a scramble. So far as the campaign itself was concerned, John Major was far from ready. He had not, at that stage, even met the campaign team at Saatchi's.

There was very little speculation in the press about a June election. The Government had been motoring happily along with the line that Labour were only anxious for an early trip to the polls because they knew the economy, and hence the Government's fortunes, were going to get better. The Conservative Parliamentary Party was not exactly raring to go. The Prime Minister told the meeting he was not keen on an early election; nor, however, was he persuaded by the Chancellor's arguments for waiting to the bitter end. Late June was not ruled out – at least until the Prime Minister saw the results of the local elections on 2 May.

These were not encouraging. Since the Conservatives were starting from a high base – the gains secured in the late 1980s, when these council seats were last contested – Central Office expected to lose perhaps 400 of the 12,000-plus seats up for grabs to Labour. In the event, they lost more than twice as many, more than half of them to the Liberal Democrats. It was the Conservative Party's biggest local election rout since the early 1980s.

Although the voting figures still suggested that the Tories were only just behind Labour, the Prime Minister was alarmed that the Lib Dems' advance had taken the party unawares. In one sense, it was good news: Labour were not, after all, going to be able to corner all the anti-Tory vote. What was bad news was that Liberal Democrat gains were concentrated, raising the spectre which had haunted the Tories right through the 1980s: of a pincer movement against them, with Labour hordes coming down from the north and the Lib Dems sweeping up from the west. In fact, the Lib Dem advance in the West Country was restrained by a Labour revival there, too. But that left the Tory local election campaign looking pretty battered all round.

On 16 May, the Monmouth by-election ended any hopes that the Government's worries might be over with settlement of the poll tax issue. The health service had become the new focus of controversy. Scare stories about privatisation had been spread assiduously by the Opposition. Some of the jargon of the health service reforms, which separated the 'purchasers' of health care (the health authorities, acting on behalf of the government) from the 'providers' (the hospitals delivering the care) was used to create a fear in the minds of voters that it would be the patient who would have to make the 'purchase', with his or her own money.

William Waldegrave, the Health Secretary, tried to nail what he called the 'Six Labour Lies', but with little success. Labour won Monmouth with a 13 per swing from the Tories. An early general election was clearly off. The Prime Minister and his Chairman began to prepare for the long haul.

That month, the Chief Whip had written round to say that the Prime Minister had asked him to reconstitute the kind of handling committee that had met every morning during the Gulf crisis. This time, he, rather than John Wakeham, would be in the chair of what came to be known simply as the 'Number 12 Committee'. The first meeting was scheduled for 16 May 1991 – the day of the Monmouth by-election.

As well as Richard Ryder, his deputy, Alastair Goodlad, and John Wakeham, the committee included the Leaders of the Lords and Commons, David Waddington and John MacGregor. Chris Patten or, in his absence, John Cope or Gillian Shephard represented the party, accompanied by Shaun Woodward (a former producer of *That's Life* whom Chris Patten had recently appointed Director of Communications) and Andrew Lansley (Director of the Conservative Research Department). Sarah, Nick True or Jonathan went from the Policy Unit, and Judith Chaplin and Graham Bright from the Political Office. Gus O'Donnell represented the

Government press machine; after a time, one or more of the Prime Minister's Private Secretaries began to come along too.[3]

The Committee met around the long table in the Whips' meeting room. Its remit was 'to improve the co-ordination and presentation of Government policy' – i.e., to spot promotional opportunities and banana skins.

This involved a fair amount of chivvying of Ministers, which did not make either the Chief Whip or his committee very popular with colleagues – particularly the Chancellor, the Number 12 Committee's most frequent target. The Committee lacked its own machinery, which sometimes led to buck-passing; but Richard Ryder's dogged chairmanship did much to put the Government on a political war footing, and the Number 12 Committee survived the election as a feature of the government landscape.[4]

The meeting would start with Gus's summary of the morning's news. Other members soon learnt to interpret the O'Donnell language, in giving what was in effect a report on the results of the Committee's efforts. 'Pretty mixed' meant 'pretty awful'. 'Good coverage on page five' meant a signal failure to generate a front-page story. 'Hard one to get across' meant a bog-up or plain bad news.

News management is not as easy as armchair strategists suppose. It is not merely that the media obviously do not want to be managed: departments do not, either. Even the most obvious, and apparently simple, objective of preventing clashes in ministerial announcements is quite difficult to achieve in practice. Minister A will be addressing a conference that day, and 'must say something'. Minister B has to

[3]Other regular members of the Number 12 Committee were Murdo Maclean, the Chief Whip's Private Secretary, John Lacy, Central Office Director of Campaigning, Jonathan Haslam, Gus's deputy, and from the beginning of 1992, Tim Collins, who had been snaffled from Michael Howard's office to go across to Smith Square and look after the lobby correspondents. Richard Ryder's Special Adviser, Robina Finlay, tried to make sense of the discussions in her minutes – a task Shana Hole inherited with the job in September 1991. Eleanor Laing, John MacGregor's Special Adviser, also attended.
[4]The Number 12 Committee survived until the reshuffle of July 1995, when it was superseded by a committee chaired by the Deputy Prime Minister, Michael Heseltine.

make a parliamentary statement, and cannot give up the Commons 'slot' identified by the business managers. Minister C has promised to reply to a Commons Select Committee by such-and-such a date.

Then there are the well-established techniques by which departments bounce an announcement out. The documents have already gone round Whitehall with a date mentioned; if Minister D does not stick to it, there is 'bound to be' something in the Sunday papers. Minister E may utter dire warnings that his Private Office has got wind of a leak. Minister F's Press Office may have pre-warned journalists of a possible press conference: to hold back would smack of confusion, dithering, U-turns. Or so the Number 12 Committee would be told.

But as the election date receded, the Government had to change gear from day-to-day tactics to longer-term strategy. First, if there was to be another parliamentary session, they would have to decide its contents, preferably before the summer break. Second, there would have to be a political campaign to regain momentum. At a Political Cabinet on 23 May, the Prime Minister told his colleagues to gear up for either a party conference, or an autumn election, or possibly both. And third, if the Government ran through the autumn, the Treasury would have to set public spending budgets for 1992-93.

All of which sounded fine. However, bills and budgets – legislation and loot – are the two things departmental Ministers fight for with greatest zest. So what actually happened in the summer of 1991 was that a Government that was supposed to be in pre-election mode settled back into the normal habits of argument and administration.

The legislative programme for the year under way, 1990-91, had been inherited from Margaret Thatcher. The Queen's Speech at the opening of Parliament – at which the final choice of bills is formally announced each year – had taken place on 7 November 1990, just under two weeks before the first ballot of the leadership election.

It was not, to put it mildly, Margaret Thatcher's best. The programme for 1990-91 contained two substantial bills which had to be heavily and embarrassingly revised before the ink was dry on the statute book: both the Child Support Act and the Criminal Justice Act quickly ran into trouble. The former introduced rules for maintenance payments widely criticised as arbitrary and inflexible. The latter suffered from a similar failing, introducing 'unit fines' for criminal offences, heavily dependent on income (a somewhat un-Conservative notion anyway) which left too little to the discretion of the courts.

However, John Major's Government added another bill in the course of the year which was also open to criticism. The measure which became the Dangerous Dogs Act was triggered by a series of horrific injuries inflicted by pit bull terriers. The media raised the alarm; then other dog bite cases which might ordinarily have received a down-the-page paragraph were suddenly the national news headlines. The Home Office had published a consultation paper in the summer of 1990; now it was rushed into action. A bill was hurtled through the House of Commons, all stages from 'Second Reading' through 'Committee' and 'Report' to 'Third Reading' taking place on one day, 10 June 1991, with the aim, as the Home Secretary put it, 'to rid the country of the menace of these fighting dogs'.

The measure had all-party support, though some MPs, even on the Government side, protested at the rush. It was certainly a classic example of 'law-making on the hoof', and various problems emerged soon enough. The regular tragedies of injuries caused by dogs continued – but somehow faded back from national to local papers again. They were replaced by stories of cross-breed dogs languishing on 'death row' while the courts debated the question of whether or not they were proscribed by the Dangerous Dogs Act.

These three bills illustrate a complicated truth about legislation. Long preparation does not necessarily save government from bad law-making: both the Child Support Bill and the Criminal Justice Bill had had a long gestation. But it is almost always a mistake to rush legislation through.

But in the summer of 1991, Ministers' minds were beginning to focus on the next legislative session. The first skirmishes in the annual battle of the bills take place in one of the most important Cabinet committees not chaired by the Prime Minister. Known by its initials, FLG – for future legislation – in 1991 it was chaired by the Leader of the House of Commons, John MacGregor. It meets in the most splendid corner of the Cabinet Office, the old Treasury Board Room; known, in the dead language of modern government, as Committee Room A. FLG also traditionally includes the Chief Whip, the Leader of the Lords, the Lord Chancellor and the Attorney-General. A member of the Policy Unit sits in, to sniff the wind for the Prime Minister.

This membership makes FLG cautious, since it consists largely of the people to whom a bad (or contentious) bill will give most trouble, rather than the political 'big beasts', the feudal lords of the Prime Minister's Cabinet, who are likely to cause trouble if their contentious (or bad) bill is not included. These may come before FLG to argue the case for their bills, but hardly in fear and trembling. The end result of all this is that, whatever the chairman of FLG proposes, the final battle usually takes place in Cabinet.

Once they secure a big bill, departments always empty their lockers, keen to seize this opportunity to get all their pet schemes into law in just a few extra clauses added on to the main bill, as well as tidying up past legislative mistakes. The only limiting factor is that such extras must be within the bill's 'long title' – and here departmental interests conflict sharply with those of the business managers. The wider a bill is drawn, the more scope for MPs to put down amendments, incorporating their pet schemes as well – and the longer and more unpredictable the passage of a bill is likely to be.

Top of the list for the new session running in to 1992 was, of course, the Council Tax legislation. True to form, this became enormous. As first proposed to FLG by the Department of the Environment, it ran to about 150 clauses. Faced with this tanker to pilot through parliamentary channels, the business managers were extremely reluctant to have much else rumbling down the slipway.

But the Prime Minister wanted to use the session for positive policy, not just for undoing past mistakes. In particular, he and Ken Clarke were keen to pass an education bill. Schools that wanted to break free of local authorities and become grant-maintained by the Department for Education were complaining that there were still too many obstacles in their way, which could only be knocked down by legislation. Such a bill was also needed to back up Citizen's Charter plans for independent inspection and published reports. Another Charter announcement which had to be given statutory force through a parliamentary bill was beefed-up regulation of the privatised utilities.

Meanwhile, Michael Heseltine let it be known that he too was bubbling with ideas to cheer up the next session. He just wanted 'a steer' from the Prime Minister – who in turn wanted to know a good deal more before touching such a sensitive tiller.

Jonathan and Sarah went, at Michael Heseltine's request, to have these ideas explained to them. Afterwards, Sarah wrote a slightly despairing note to the Prime Minister saying that they were not a great deal the wiser. Conversing with Michael in enthusiastic mode, her note said, was rather like swimming with a whale:

> A perfectly friendly whale; but one who surges out of the water with grand ideas, leaving you struggling with a feeble breast-stroke of run-of-the-mill questions, and taking in a lot of sea-water.

In September, FLG took a hatchet to the legislative programme, and the Prime Minister handled a difficult Cabinet which resolved the final choice. An extraordinary number of bills did get round the course before the election. Some forty-six bills in all – not all, of course, big Government bills – were to receive the Royal Assent before Parliament was dissolved on 16 March 1992, including legislation on both education and the regulation of utilities. Michael Heseltine did persuade the Prime Minister to announce one of his grand ideas – for an Environmental Protection Agency[5] – but legislation had to wait until well into the new Parliament.

However, as Chris Patten frequently reminded his colleagues, in the Political Cabinets that summer, they had to rediscover the

---

[5]This caused endless trouble with the Ministry of Agriculture. As the Cabinet Minister in charge of that department, John Gummer had the doubtful pleasure of articulating its concerns before the election, only to find himself taking the legislation through Parliament as Environment Secretary some years later.

arts of politics if they wished to go on experiencing the joys of government. The big political exercise of the summer was the 'Labour costings'.

In document after document, Labour politicians had been making expensive promises. In April, the Labour Party published its fourth campaign document, *Opportunity Britain*, which added another cluster. The Conservative Research Department had got hold of a note by Chris Smith, then Labour's moneybag-minder, or Shadow Chief Secretary to the Treasury, with which they then had much fun. This asked rhetorically, not to say despairingly, what the reply would be to one Tory question: how was all this spending to be paid for?

It was clearly time for the Tories to start asking. The first step was to repeat the exercise carried out by John MacGregor as Chief Secretary before the 1987 election: to add up the cost of Labour's pledges. The basic work, done by Norman Lamont's Special Advisers, Bill Robinson and Warwick Lightfoot, was convincingly cautious. Only forty big items were costed. The first was Labour's pledge to raise pensions – at an estimated cost of over £3 billion. Much the same price-tag (a distinct under-estimate) was put on Labour's pledge to equalise state pension age by bringing down the age of retirement for men. The Opposition was committed to spending an extra £3 billion on the health service, the same again on housing, and nearly as much on education. And so on. It was not at all difficult to get to a total of £35 billion.

In the document prepared by Central Office for publication, each pledge appeared in Labour's own words. Some costs were held back, to put into the pot if Labour reneged on any of the pledges listed. Only pledges costing over £50 million – a figure the Treasury did not normally class as 'small' – had been included.

But some of this caution backfired. John Gummer was particularly annoyed. He said he had been urged to attack Labour's expensive pledges on agriculture. Now he looked pretty silly because none were included: although cumulatively large, each was individually under £50 million. For the same reason, the entry for trade and industry was ludicrously low. And because the document was narrowly focused on spending programmes, there was no allowance for other costly Labour promises, such as new tax allowances for industry or an end to privatisation (let alone the costs of re-nationalisation). Chris Patten warned the Prime Minister that the costings had suffered from too little attention from Ministers outside the Treasury; those Ministers, in turn, grumbled that they had not been properly consulted. At Political Cabinet, the discussion was somewhat scratchy.

The £35 billion figure was lower than some already in circulation (including those from independent economists). So when the document was published in June, though David Mellor, the Chief Secretary to the Treasury, put on a good press conference show, it attracted relatively little attention. Saatchi's had not, by then, got back into their stride. The poster slogan 'Labour's going for broke again' did not really hit home. A further weakness was that the costings exercise had been conceived as a one-off, without any plans for a follow-through.

However, the Number 12 Committee picked up and ran with the costings, stopping Ministers sinking into an apolitical summer torpor. Most importantly, Labour never really managed to undermine the figures. And it may have been this early, convincing set of spending challenges that provoked Labour into the consummate campaign error of publishing their tax-raising 'shadow Budget'.

In 1991, however, the press paid more attention to the Government's own spending arguments. These had begun early. The Treasury felt vulnerable because of the poll tax, where damage limitation was proving extremely expensive: to damp the tax down, some £6 billion was given to local government in the 1991 Budget. Early in 1991, the Policy Unit compiled for the Prime Minister a list of other decisions, small in themselves, that had been making the Treasury nervous. A classic, early example was his agreement to allow the Health Secretary, William Waldegrave, to pay compensation to those haemophiliacs (and subsequently other groups, too) infected with the HIV virus through blood transfusions. The decision, the Health Secretary believed, was a clear example of the Prime Minister's decency and pragmatism. But it had been taken outside the annual framework of spending negotiations, and the Treasury smarted.

So the Prime Minister asked the Policy Unit to identify a spending battle which the Treasury could equally publicly 'win'. Unfortunately, however, the biggest spending issue of the early months was one the Treasury were bound to lose.

Very early each year, the Government faces the problem of dealing with the recommendations of the various pay review bodies, established to make key public-sector groups feel that their salaries are not dictated by Treasury whim. In January 1991, although inflation was down to 9 per cent and falling, these bodies recommended increases of between 10 and 12 per cent. Agonised discussions around the Cabinet table followed. With the troops risking their lives in the Gulf, it would be politically impossible to cut back their award. Even paying it in stages, the familiar Whitehall device for delaying the full cost of financing a pay award, was unattractive: it would seem extraordinarily perverse to refuse to give the full increase to those sweating in the Gulf, paying it only when they got home again – assuming they got home at all. Trying to separate Gulf soldiers from the rest of the armed forces was impractical and unfair: some were, after all, also risking their lives in Northern Ireland.

So what about the rest? Departmental Ministers argued for their groups with passion. How could the Government pay the armed forces but not health service groups (some of whom had themselves volunteered for the Gulf)? Supposing doctors and nurses got the full award, what about teachers? How could they be singled out, when the Prime Minister had laid such stress on education? And so on. In the end, it was decided to pay the full armed forces award immediately; the rest would get the full increase at the end of the year. It was plainly a compromise; and it was undeniably expensive. But it was the price of war – and of having allowed inflation to shoot up in the late 1980s.

Through the spring, there was a great deal of press interest in a heated battle between the Employment Secretary, Michael Howard, and the Treasury. The Training and Enterprise Councils (TECs) were complaining that their budgets were being squeezed. Categories of people who found it particularly difficult to find work, such as ex-prisoners and those with learning difficulties, were finding themselves cut off the end of the list. This caused a furore. The grand old men of the Tory party fulminated in the Lords. The Prime Minister's post-bag bulged.

The result was that Michael Howard 'won' a little extra money for the TECs. But – as those lobbying for more never tired of pointing out to him – his new programmes were far more modest than when unemployment was last roaring up, in the mid-1980s. From the Treasury's viewpoint it was at worst a score-draw. The really big spending battles were to start after Easter.

As one seasoned Treasury mandarin puts it, a five-year Parliament tends to be more expensive than a four-year, because two spending rounds take place under the pressure of an election. And if you have two Prime Ministers in this period, you double the pressure, since they will inevitably have different priorities. Margaret Thatcher had agreed to an enormous roads programme; John Major was to give more money to health.

The annual ritual of the public expenditure survey, or PES, was hallowed by tradition. Each spring, the Chief Secretary would invite 'bids' from his Cabinet colleagues, over and above published plans. Briefed by their civil servants on the profound worthiness of every aspect of departmental activity, hounded by single-issue lobbies demanding more for their cause, it was a rare Cabinet minister who underbid.[6] Year after year, come May, two kinds of stories would find their way into the press.

From the departmental end would come horror stories of 'bleeding stumps', vital work amputated by a shortage of funds. The Ministry of Defence was the acknowledged expert at this: planes would be grounded for lack of fuel, tanks would suddenly be short of spare parts. From the Treasury end, via either a real 'leak' or an inspired one, would come a big number for the total of extra bids – designed to demonstrate Treasury success when the final figure came in lower.

In 1991, the Prime Minister, a former Chief Secretary himself

---

[6]The famous example, which discouraged all others, was John (now Lord) Moore, who put in such a 'responsible' bid for the health budget that he ran into trouble almost immediately.

and wise in the ways of both sides, warned firmly against playing this same old game, which would undermine attacks on Labour by demonstrating ministerial appetites for higher spending. This had some effect; though some alarming bids did find their way into the newspapers.

After a Cabinet *tour de table*, Ministers would commit themselves to penny-pinching frugality – with all the conviction of Galileo agreeing that the sun went round the earth. It would then be left to the Chief Secretary to reach deals with individual Cabinet Ministers. If they agreed, no one else was likely to intervene. If they didn't, the phones would get hot, as both would appeal to the Prime Minister. In 1991, David Mellor and William Waldegrave engaged in a classic of the old-style spending trench warfare, expending an enormous amount of ammunition disputing the last few million pounds, sending up distress flares to the Prime Minister almost daily.

This system for managing public spending was ripe for reform. In the 1992 Budget, the Chancellor was to announce an end to the peculiarly British practice of settling the two sides of the Government's balance sheet separately: announcing spending first, and taxes as much as four months later. Later in 1992, he and Michael Portillo – then Chief Secretary to the Treasury – were to evolve a new way of waging the spending battle which would engage the firepower of other senior Ministers on the Treasury's side in a new, all-powerful Cabinet committee.[7]

In all, £5.6 billion was added to spending programmes in the 1991 round – with an additional £3 billion taken from the reserve. By no means all of this, however, was the result of specific decisions. The biggest deliberate act of spending policy

[7]EDX – as it was called – was packed with two kinds of Cabinet beasts; there were the heavyweights – the Prime Minister's A-team; and there were some supposedly disinterested Ministers with small departmental budgets. The former ensured that, when EDX's recommendations came to Cabinet, Treasury ministers could call up some big political guns in support. The point about the latter was that they could be persuaded to help fight the Treasury's battles by early offers of small change from the Chief Secretary's back pocket. So when other Ministers were summoned before the committee, one or other EDX member could be counted on to go for a colleague's jugular.

was to allow William Waldegrave an extra £1.65 billion for health. This was the minimum he considered necessary to avert a collapse of morale amongst those managing the health service reforms at their most sensitive stage. The other big deliberate increase was £800 million for defence, to make up for Gulf losses. But that was not a fiscal problem, since a great deal of money to pay for the war was raised from Britain's Gulf allies, particularly by the Chief Secretary, David Mellor.

Much of the rest of the increase was caused by the underlying momentum of existing programmes, boosted by recession and social changes not fully understood until later: the number of people applying for all sorts of benefits was rising much faster than anyone had forecast. In 1991, the estimate for social security spending had to be raised a staggering £4.2 billion.

There is no disguising the fact that 1991 turned out to be an expensive round: there was a 'real' (that is, after allowing for inflation) increase in spending of 5.8 per cent. But this figure was swollen, ironically enough, by unexpected economic success. Beforehand, the Treasury's plans had suggested spending would rise by 3.5 per cent more than inflation – a substantial increase in real terms, but not a record even for the Tory years. In the event, inflation fell faster than the Treasury had forecast, so the money allocated to departments turned out to be worth more than had been expected.

Finally, a piece of perspective: despite these increases, public spending in the early 1990s still took a much smaller share of Britain's national income than it had in the early 1980s, when the economy had last been in recession.

In August 1991, when the Prime Minister headed off for a brief family holiday in Spain, these figures were still unsettled; yet an autumn election looked a real possibility. The polls suggested that John Major's personal rating had risen again, still further ahead of Neil Kinnock's. In particular, the Prime Minister had won more ground on issues. According to a poll in the *Today* newspaper, conducted after the launch of the Citizen's Charter, people trusted the Prime Minister to handle public services more than they trusted Neil Kinnock.

John Major was pulling the party up above the level of support that might have been expected, given the state of the economy. But he could only pull it so far. During his 'honeymoon', the percentage saying they would vote Conservative had, according to Gallup, risen way ahead of what might have been predicted from the figures for consumer confidence. Since then, the gap between the two measures had narrowed, but seemed to have stabilised at about 4 per cent. That was reckoned to be a measure of the boost John Major had given to his party's chances in the polls.

In mid-August, when the Prime Minister came back from Spain, he asked Sarah to prepare a short balance sheet of pros and cons for an autumn or spring election. He also wanted a note from the Policy Unit on the policies needed to 'open the November window'.

Sarah gave him both on 19 August – a singularly inept piece of timing, since it coincided with the coup in Russia.

The economic arguments seemed finely balanced. The Policy Unit assessment was pretty pessimistic about economic recovery: in the winter, unemployment would rise further, industry was likely to become even gloomier and there would be the usual public-sector pay arguments, all of which argued for going in the autumn. The main argument for spring 1992 was that inflation was falling faster than wages, so people in work should be feeling a bit better off by the spring. That would also be the time when people on mortgage rates fixed annually would get the benefit of lower interest rates.

So far as the Manifesto was concerned, the earlier the better, if the Prime Minister wanted something that looked exciting; the longer the Parliament dragged on, the more buns would have to be thrown out of the sledge to keep the media wolves fed. On the other hand, the Citizen's Charter programme was running well at that time, and a 'second front' could be prepared for 1992.

Opening the November window, the Policy Unit note argued, would require as much progress as possible in reducing interest rates. It would also mean doing some running repairs to the Government's relations with industry, still smarting from what was seen as a bias towards services in the 1980s. And the public spending round would need to be concluded quickly, since the Prime Minister could not go into a campaign with blood still fresh on the carpet, and Ministers still licking their wounds. Finally, what the Prime Minister would need personally to 'open the November window' would be a thumping good party conference, a completed Manifesto, and a personal campaign fully worked out by Central Office.

At the end of September, the Prime Minister was to have his key meeting on all that with the Party Chairman.

It didn't go – quite – according to plan.

8

False Alarm

There is plenty of time to win this game, and to thrash the Spaniards, too.

Sir Francis Drake, 20 July 1588

'During the summer,' the Prime Minister told his party conference, 'I did quite a bit of travelling.' (*Pause*)

'Headingley, Edgbaston, Trent Bridge, Lord's, the Oval . . .' (*Laughter*)

'. . . Also Moscow, Peking, Hong Kong and Kennebunkport.' (*Applause*)

It was a typical Ronnie Millar[1] sequence. The audience loved it. It also told an important story. Chairman of the Group of Seven, head boy of the Commonwealth, Maastricht negotiator – John Major's international role had kept him spinning from China to New England and back again. Old England, long shadows and warm beer had, in fact, hardly got a look in. His stature as a statesman was rising all the time. But in September, as the Prime Minister built up his air miles in the noisy old official VC10, the political classes were rolling back from Tuscany and Provence. The election temperature rose.

On Sunday 29 September, the Prime Minister had called a meeting at Number 10. It took place in the Green Drawing Room, under the gaze of Nelson and Wellington. It was an opportunity for Chris

---

[1]Sir Ronald Millar had arrived on the scene that summer, to speech-write for his third Prime Minister.

Patten and Maurice Saatchi to run through likely campaign themes and show the Prime Minister some possible election posters.

Throughout the summer, Saatchi's had been refining their thinking. Maurice Saatchi's thesis went like this. In retrospect, at least, 1979, 1983 and 1987 appeared very simple elections to win. The choice was clear: 'efficient but cruel' Tories versus 'caring but incompetent' Labour. The difficulty for the Conservatives in 1991 was that the recession had killed the 'efficient' tag – leaving only 'cruel'. While the Tory party had successfully blunted the 'cruel' image by replacing Margaret Thatcher with someone seen as more 'caring', Maurice did not believe that John Major should fight the election on soft 'caring' issues. Instead, it should be fought on the old economic battleground – although the Tories would have to rely on claiming relative rather than absolute 'efficiency'. They would therefore have to demonstrate that under Labour, conditions would be even worse.

However, Saatchi's brief from Conservative Central Office pointed in a rather different direction. The battleground issues were identified by the party as the National Health Service, public services and the environment. So it was perhaps unsurprising that the suggested poster campaign lacked clarity. At this stage, the Saatchi argument had not been taken to its logical conclusion – an all-out attack on Labour, translating the costings of Labour promises into tax bills for the average household. Instead, the posters relied heavily on what Saatchi's saw was the party's chief electoral asset – the Prime Minister. And the attack on Labour was focused on its inexperience, changeability and unpopular leader.

The main poster displayed was hinged on an L-plate, which took the place of the capital 'L' in the slogan 'You can't trust Labour.'[2] Saatchi's had meanwhile prepared a special poster for the Labour Party Conference the coming week. The main wording would simply state that this conference was taking place in Brighton. In

---

[2]This poster, which was used in the campaign, had unfortunately not been subjected to the graffiti test. It was all too easy to amend. All around London, the 't' was removed from the second word, leaving the poster to tell the world that 'You can trust Labour.'

small type, the advert would say, 'Unless they've changed their mind on this as well.'

The Prime Minister was also shown an advert that highlighted the difference between John Major, who listened, and Neil Kinnock, who talked: a blue ear and a red mouth. Much later, just before the election was called, it was shown to a wider group of the Prime Minister's colleagues – the full A-team. They thought it looked very splendid. But why, Ken Clarke asked, had Saatchi's put a picture of Michael Heseltine's mouth next to the Prime Minister's ear?

No one on that Sunday evening mentioned tax – until Jonathan, feeling slightly like the man who coughs in the British Museum reading room, raised the question at the end of the presentation.

After the meeting, the Prime Minister went upstairs to his flat with his closest advisers to decide what to do. Neither he nor Chris Patten wanted to rule November out at this stage. But neither thought the party was ready to go. At the back of everyone's mind was Jim Callaghan's cliff-edge decision in the autumn of 1978. No one wanted to get to the point where the Prime Minister could only jump – or be seen to retreat.

At the Tory Party Conference in Blackpool the following week, there would be constant speculation as to whether the election was on or off, and it would look particularly bad if the party was thought to be backing away. It would suggest that the Prime Minister had been disheartened by Neil Kinnock's performance at the Labour Party Conference, which was due to take place the week before. So John Wakeham, in his role as media link-man, was asked to tone the election stories down before Kinnock spoke, with a little bit of discreet briefing.

To the mortification of the Tory leadership, Monday's television news and Tuesday's headlines screamed with the news that the general election was off. Definitely – off.

In retrospect, John Wakeham thinks his mistake was to brief journalists in the morning. This gave time for the Chinese whispers between them to exaggerate the story through the day. If he had waited until the afternoon, they would have had less chance to blow it up. Delicate steering from London was not made any easier by the fact that the political correspondents were all gathering at the Labour

Party Conference. In truth, the story was probably bound to over-shoot. The slightest hint was certain to be magnified. Although the stories misrepresented the Prime Minister's mood – he continued to toy with the 'November window' for another few weeks – they were instinctively right. The end of September was a watershed.

For the Prime Minister, his first party conference as leader was too all-consuming an event to allow much reflection on election timing. It was fraught with danger. The media were hungrily watching for Margaret Thatcher. How would the Prime Minister's reception compare with hers? Would she speak? Would they speak to each other? How would the Prime Minister speak? He had done six mini-conferences: the annual round of Young Conservatives, Local Government Conference, Central Council, Scottish and Welsh Conservatives, and the Women's Conference. There had been much speculation in the party and the press as to whether John Major could rise to the challenge of a full-bloodied annual party conference.

Tory party conferences are constructed to build up to a prime ministerial star performance on the Friday. In the old days of the grandees, the Prime Minister might not even appear until the Friday. But John Major had to arrive on the Monday, put fire into the bellies of the constituency agents that evening, put himself around the receptions and dinners all week, and finally hit his top notes on the Friday afternoon.

Thank God, it was Blackpool.

Brighton, the other traditional conference venue, has somehow managed to be bad news for the Tories ever since the IRA carnage of 1984. In 1992, it was a bleak backdrop for a party conference sandwiched between Black Wednesday and the coal debacle.[3] None

---

[3]Much of that conference had to be devoted not only to settling his party down again on Europe – but also hammering out a new economic policy. Treasury officials were hauled down from their safe house in Whitehall to the raw political air of Brighton. Norman Lamont's meeting with the Prime Minister was made no more agreeable by the noises off. An enterprising protester had hired a bus, and was driving it up and down the sea-front outside the Grand Hotel, bawling from its loudspeaker. Every time the Chancellor opened his mouth, he would be pre-empted by the booming demand to: 'Cut interest rates now.'

of the Number 10 team were sorry when the next southern conference turn, in 1994, took them to Bournemouth instead.

For all the length of the journey there, and the strength of the wind-chill factor, Blackpool is altogether a better conference bet than Brighton. That is largely because of the hall itself. The Winter Gardens is steeped in the blood of British politics. Age, acoustics, memories – all combine to make for a more electrifying atmosphere than the dead modernity of Brighton's conference hall. In 1963, the Winter Gardens saw the struggle for the Tory party leadership that ended in Sir Alec Douglas-Home's brief premiership. Now, twenty-eight years later, they were to receive another new Tory leader who might have only months to go before election defeat.

The Winter Gardens effect had been forcefully brought home to Sarah at a Blackpool conference in the 1970s, which she and Mark Schreiber[4] attended on behalf of *The Economist*. Mark, who had just joined the paper after working in Ted Heath's office, had a tendency to leap to his feet and applaud each platform speech – something she had to explain was not quite done when wearing a press pass. From then on, Mark stood poker-faced, his arms folded across his chest, unfortunately hiding his press pass. Doubly unfortunately, the next speaker happened to be Michael Heseltine. Hezza was on flying form. The audience loved it. The applause was deafening. Seeing Mark's unmoved countenance, an empurpled constituency chairman seized him by the lapels. 'Clap, damn you! Don't you believe in England? CLAP!' Mark and Sarah crept away to the cinema, to watch *The Towering Inferno*. It seemed safer.

Conference themes, emblazoned behind a platform of politicians, rarely have much impact on voters, but they occupy many anxious hours of discussion in party headquarters. Some words bob up time and again: 'Britain', 'winning', 'forward', 'right', 'strength', 'future'. At a similar stage in the previous Parliament, 1986, there had been a debate between a 'future' theme and a 'developing' theme. The leadership had opted for the latter – 'The Next Move Forward'. Now Central Office preferred the notion of a 'future' theme – hence, in the end, the slogan was 'The Best Future for Britain'.

[4]Now Lord Marlesford.

This was a diplomatic way of putting the conclusion that change was a better electoral bet than continuity. It was to remain the party theme right through the election, appearing on posters featuring the Prime Minister, the Manifesto cover, and the backdrop to countless press conferences.

A perennial difficulty, however, was to persuade Ministers – including the Prime Minister – to stick to whatever theme had been decided. At Margaret Thatcher's ill-starred final conference, the slogan had been 'The Strength to Succeed', but the theme of her speech had been 'Opportunity Britain'.

In 1991, the party was still suffering from a certain amount of cross-sloganitis. While the conference was intended to be forward-looking, Central Office had been expending a good deal of effort on a splendid, well-designed, glossy but essentially backward-looking publication called *Transforming Britain* – a summary of changes for the better since 1979. This did a good deal to fill the dog days of September, when the Government were showing hardly any signs of political activity, but it was not completely in tune with their forward-looking strategy.

Transforming Britain was published in September. In an effort to sharpen its political focus, the Conservative Research Department followed up with a series of publications intended to show how Labour would transform Britain for the worse. In the meantime, they were trying to get Cabinet Ministers to focus their conference speeches on their own version of the 'best future'.

As usual, the Conservative Research Department put together an advance summary of what Ministers thought they were going to say. Equally as usual, these notes varied between the pages of smooth prose supplied by the Foreign Office, to 'no details yet' from Michael Heseltine. One Minister's summary started informatively with two phrases: 'Recognise problems Point to solutions.'

When the Number 10 team left London on the afternoon of Monday 7 October, the Prime Minister's speech was pretty well advanced. Nick True, who as ever bore the main speech-writing burden, had done an extraordinary job, since very little had been prepared before the Prime Minister had embarked on his global travels. Nick had, however, enlisted the help of Ronnie Millar, acting as impresario as well as wordsmith. When the Prime Minister got fed up with the long labour of speech preparation, or worried about his voice, Ronnie was able to tell him it was all part of the game, and that his predecessor had been just the same. And he worked on the Prime Minister's delivery with the same sensitivity and skill that he had applied to Margaret Thatcher's.

The Tory conference audience, Chris Patten recalls, had taken John Major to their hearts in 1990, when he spoke as Chancellor. It took him some time to realise that as Prime Minister he would be judged more harshly – and that more preparation time would be needed. Pleas from his advisers to set aside more diary time received support from an unexpected quarter when he visited the National Theatre and met Sir Ian McKellen, the first actor to be knighted during his premiership.

'Now tell me,' the Prime Minister asked, 'how long does it take to train one's voice?'

'About thirty years,' said Ian McKellen.

John Major's great strength is speaking off the cuff. Some of his best performances have been when he has torn up the notes over which his Number 10 team have laboured, and simply let it flow. These occasions have been all the better for the fact that he has clearly then spoken from the heart. But it is a technique which, when he was tired or under strain, could also flop. All politicians are a bit susceptible to circling-aircraft syndrome – an inability to land a speech successfully after an extended ad lib. Moreover, conference speeches are in a class of their own. They need a good deal of choreography, light and shade, points where the applause can build up, where the audience can feel it is participating. The Prime Minister's speech has to have a broad sweep: the right buttons have to be pressed, the right people mentioned. Whether it is in the speaker's head or on pieces of paper, this requires a text.

With only a few hours' sleep a night during conference week, Nick and Ronnie worked on in the Prime Minister's office in the Imperial Hotel, drafting and redrafting text for him to look at between balls and buffets and stints on the Winter Gardens platform – applauding his Ministers, getting the feel of the hall, and 'Welcoming Margaret Thatcher'. The Party Chairman and she had agreed that she would not speak; but it was clearly an emotional moment for her, receiving – as Chris Patten put it – 'the applause of those she would have led to electoral disaster'. Sarah was reminded of what Nick Budgen, the maverick MP, had once said to her at the memorial service of one of his colleagues: 'The Tory party may be rotten to you while you are alive. But, by God, they bury you well.'

The most sensitive section of the Prime Minister's speech was on the health service. Privatisation scares were still running strongly; Ronnie Millar, in particular, felt that the Prime Minister must use this platform to get across his own personal commitment to the NHS, which would carry far greater conviction than any number of statistics or pledges on spending. As Health Secretary, William Waldegrave's speech came before the Prime Minister's. John Major asked to see it. He was very concerned that it should go well. William recalls with pride that – for once in his life – he got a longer ovation than Michael Heseltine. But then, it has to be said, 1991 was not a good conference year for Hezza: the Tory party had not yet quite forgiven the hand that struck down Margaret Thatcher.

Meanwhile, the Prime Minister's passage on the health service was shuttling between Ronnie, who was turning out some good phrases, and Sarah, who was ruining them in her efforts to make sure the Prime Minister said nothing that could rebound on him. Nick True smoothed the rough edges and injected fluency. The text made progress. The Prime Minister's delivery, however, did not. The conference treadmill was tremendously time-consuming – made more so by the fact that the Prime Minister, who retained his natural love of meeting people to an alarming degree, over-ran his visit to every function. When he reappeared late every evening, he would want to work on his text and set the speech-writers homework for the following day. This left no time to practice. Ronnie was getting frantic.

It had been assumed that John Major would follow Margaret Thatcher in using autocue, and he had agreed. Reading a speech off two reflectors, one on either side of the podium, the speaker is free to shift his gaze and does not need to look down. Reading off paper on a lectern, most people drop their eyes at the end of a sentence, and their voice follows, killing the punch-line.

But autocue is also a trap. The speaker is dependent on the operator winding the text on at the requisite speed – he cannot see far ahead, or feel where he has got to. John Major came to dislike autocue; at the 1992 conference, this dislike was reinforced by the fact that the left-hand reflector faded out half-way through, leaving him to make the rest of his speech to the right-hand side of the hall only. At the 1993 conference, he got rid of the autocue altogether.

In 1991, having decided to use it, the Prime Minister urgently needed to get used to it. He had had one trial run in Downing Street. Now he needed a proper practice in Blackpool. As well as Ronnie Millar, he had another performance adviser in that darling of Tory audiences, Jeffrey Archer. On Thursday, Ronnie, Jeffrey and Sarah finally got the Prime Minister down to the practice room in the basement of the Imperial Hotel.

Barely bigger than a hotel bathroom, this little glory hole was packed to the gunnels with a host of terribly helpful MPs – not all of them, it has to be said, noted conference orators themselves – and eager beavers from Central Office. Each of them could no doubt have done a splendid solo rehearsal job; in combination they provided too much distraction (and too much body-heat). What was worse, Ronnie could not say the things to the Prime Minister he felt he needed to say in front of what seemed like half the Tory party.

The Prime Minister good-naturedly made a start. The temperature rose. He looked hot. Ronnie looked desperate. The Prime Minister ploughed bravely on. Ronnie made a terrible face. Sarah hastily exited and re-entered, inventing an important guest waiting in the Prime Minister's office. The team marched up the back stairs again; Ronnie – not, after all, in the first flush of youth – puffing with exertion and irritation.

The Prime Minister's office was, of course, guest-free. He was mystified, annoyed, and then amused as Sarah tried to talk her way out of this one. She then snaked straight down again to persuade the friendly hordes sweating in the black hole that the rehearsal was best left in Ronnie's hands. When the Prime Minister came down again, only Sidonie Myers (who worked the autocue) and Russ Pipe (Central Office's ITN-trained director) were in evidence. Russ and Sarah saw them get started, then crept out and sank to the floor outside the door, breathing a sigh of relief.

Thursday had been made more hideous by a traditional horror of conference week – rows between Ministers. These disputes usually erupt because Ministers want to brighten up their speeches with little news-breaking nuggets that have not been cleared with colleagues or underwritten by the Treasury. Each year, well before the conference, the Party Chairman of the day sonorously reminds the Cabinet of the need for early clearance; each year, as Ministers scribble last-minute speeches, these strictures are ignored.

The consequent disputes are made more ghastly by the fact that, on such party occasions, Ministers are deprived of their Private Offices, whose staff normally sort things out with others of their kind. Ministers are, inevitably, in a high state of emotional tension, on trial for their political lives before an unforgiving conference audience, some of them for the first time. They all, therefore, tend to appeal instantly to the Prime Minister. Free of the main burden of speech-writing, Jonathan and Sarah had the job of keeping a fire-break around the Prime Minister, running errands between Ministers in an effort to help them resolve their differences without using up his precious speech preparation time.

The longest-running conference battle of 1991 was between Malcolm Rifkind, Secretary of State for Transport, and Norman Lamont, facing his first conference as Chancellor. The issue was a delicate one: what the Transport Secretary could say about the Channel Tunnel Rail Link, a subject on which he was under great political and industrial crossfire. Jonathan had flogged backwards and forwards most of Wednesday, trying to get agreement on the words Malcolm Rifkind could use. Eventually, at 2.00 a.m. on Thursday, he and Sarah clinched a deal between Rifkind and Lamont; the Prime Minister's precious sleep was saved.

But not Jonathan's. He had hardly got to bed when the phone rang. Surely not Malcolm Rifkind – again? Jonathan reached blearily for the receiver. It was even more alarming news. His wife, Alex, expecting their first baby, had gone into labour early. So by 5.00 a.m., Jonathan was heading south. Wrestling with the hospital coffee machine many hours later, he was helped by another father, who looked at his ashen face in deep sympathy. Jonathan didn't feel capable of explaining that in comparison with playing midwife to Messrs Rifkind and Lamont, witnessing a twelve-hour labour was a doddle.

On Friday morning, Nick True and Debbie de Satgé, the Political Office Secretary, who had done a magnificent job of keeping the speech drafts flowing off her machine, also looked as if they'd been through a long labour. Ronnie pored over the precious autocue tape, marking it up for delivery. The Press Office was hungry for the text. Nick True and Sarah briefed Shaun Woodward on the contents. Bits were fed to the *Evening Standard*, whose earliest editions would be printed well ahead of the speech, and to the lunchtime television news programmes. Then Judith Chaplin swept the Prime Minister off to the Winter Gardens, and the rest of his team slumped in front of the television to watch.

The final speech was quintessential Major: a statement of his Conservatism that was to stand the test of time. He paid generous tribute to his predecessor; but he took the debate over continuity and change head on. There would be no change in the 'fundamental beliefs of the Conservative party' but, he insisted, 'we all bring our own beliefs, our own instincts, and our own experiences to politics . . . and I am no exception.'

He summed up his programme in a favourite phrase: 'the power to choose – and the right to own'. The themes of choice and ownership permeated the speech: in particular, lower personal taxes to permit personal choice and encourage ownership of homes, pensions, savings, and businesses. Values are passed on from generation to generation, the Prime Minister argued; he wanted to see wealth 'cascading down the generations', too.

The key passage on health came right at the beginning. He reminded his audience that the National Health Service was not Labour property: for twenty-nine of the forty-three years of its existence, a Conservative Government had been in charge. His anger with Labour for spreading scare stories was very real: he hated such tactics, not just for their political impact, but for the worry they caused people, reflected in anxious letters from elderly, vulnerable people who knew only what they saw on television. He drove his message home:

> So let me say now, once and for all, and without qualification
> – under this Government the National Health Service will
> continue to offer free hospital treatment to everyone . . .
> There will be no charges for hospital treatment, no charges
> for visits to the doctor, no privatisation . . . Not today. Not
> tomorrow. Not after the next election. Not ever while I'm
> Prime Minister.

Why, as the opinion polls demonstrated, was this so much more effective than Margaret Thatcher's assurance that the health service was safe in her hands? Probably because the way John Major led into this passage rang true:

> I know that for millions of people in this country the National
> Health Service means security. I understand that. Because I am
> – and always have been – one of those people.

The Prime Minister also used his speech to make it clear that he wanted to give people more control of public services, through the Citizen's Charter – 'the centrepiece of our policies for the 1990s'. Never mind if Labour tried to steal Tory clothes. ('Did you see how many of them were wearing grey suits last week? Have they no shame?') He rebutted criticisms of his aim for a 'classless society'; he wanted to see:

> . . . a tapestry of talent in which everyone from child to
> adult respects achievement; where every promotion, every cer-
> tificate is respected, and each person's contribution is valued.

He pledged himself to 'fight for my belief in a return to basics in education'. He talked tough on law and order – and on inflation. He was cautious about economic recovery – notably more cautious than the Chancellor, but triumphant about the improvement in our trade in manufactured goods. He reminded his audience – just in passing – that the goal of 'ever closer union' in Europe was set by the Single European Act (signed by Margaret Thatcher's Government). But he unequivocally rejected federalism, and the imposition of a single currency.

He pressed all the international buttons. He celebrated the death of the socialist system in eastern Europe, looked forward to seeing South Africa back in the Commonwealth, picked his way through the debate on defence cuts, with the aid of a few swipes at Labour's disarmers. He relived the war in the Gulf with a very personal passage which he had written, then had cold feet about, and had finally been persuaded to deliver. But the centrepiece of his speech was a credo that was to be echoed in speeches, posters, leaflets, broadcasts right through the general election campaign:

I want to give individuals greater control over their own lives.
- Every mother, every father, a say over their child's education.
- Every schoolchild, a choice of routes to the world of work.
- Every patient, the confidence that their doctors can secure the best treatment for them.
- Every business, every worker, freedom from the destructive dictatorship of union militants.
- Every family, the right to have and to hold their own private corner of life; their own home, their own savings, their own security for their future – and for their children's future.

The newspapers gave a remarkably consistent verdict. 'Major wins Tory hearts' was the *Daily Mail* headline. The paper's leader writer concluded that the Prime Minister had come across as, 'Decent, determined, honest, straightforward.' The verdict of the *Daily Telegraph* was that he had displayed 'a rare talent to make people feel at ease'; his speech, the newspaper reckoned, offered, ' . . . decent Conservatism stripped of the barbed wire girdles worn so enthusiastically by the right'.

After his speech, the Prime Minister traditionally goes to thank his party organisation, then the police, and then heads straight off home. Sarah spoke to him from the car, as Douglas and she drove across the north of England, back to their home in Lincolnshire. He was relaxed, pleased with how the speech had gone; his only worry was that he had not yet been able to thank Nick True or Ronnie Millar, rattling southwards on the London train.

And the election? Well, that would just have to wait. For on Monday, the Prime Minister was airborne again. He left for Harare, to play his part in the meeting of Commonwealth heads of government. It was another international relations success,[5] which Gus O'Donnell turned into a rainbow of television news shots, even enticing his boss on to the cricket pitch. But, at this critical moment in the political calendar, it kept him out of Britain for nine whole days. While he was away, the November election window began to close.

It was just as well that, in his heart of hearts, the Prime Minister had already decided to get through Maastricht first.

[5]There was, however, nearly a diplomatic disaster. Only the heads of government had been asked to the banquet hosted by Her Majesty. Suddenly, to their horror, the British team noticed an uninvited guest: Nelson Mandela, then merely the leader of the African National Congress. Fortunately, one head of government had just cried off sick. Gus and Stephen Wall hastily wrote a name card for Mandela, and the evening proceeded without a ripple.

9

At the Sign of the Golden Tulip

*It has been a damned serious business – Blücher and I have lost
30,000 men. It has been a damned nice thing – the nearest run
thing you ever saw in your life . . . By God! I don't think it
would have been done if I had not been there.*

Wellington, *Creevey Papers*, Chapter X

As midnight approached on Tuesday 10 December in the bleak
Maastricht Provinciehuis, Stephen Wall hastily reached for the
phone. The Prime Minister, his Private Secretary had suddenly
realised, was about to outstay Her Majesty's permission to be outside
the United Kingdom. Would the entire British delegation turn into
white mice, forced to scuttle away with their pumpkins? Number
10 consulted Buckingham Palace. An extension was granted. John
Major could stay at the ball.

It was a vivid reminder of the length of this negotiating marathon.
The Council should have been over by early afternoon. Europe had
been preparing for it long enough.

As the British team left for Maastricht on Sunday 8 December,
the Brussels rhetoric was streaming out against them. That very
afternoon, the President of the Commission was making a passionate
public plea for an 'irreversible commitment to federalism'. The
'F-word' was still up in lights at the top of the draft treaty. The
European People's Party, the grouping of Members of the European
Parliament to which Conservative MEPs were loosely allied, had
just put out a similarly provocative communiqué.

· 138 ·

Whatever now happened at Maastricht, the Prime Minister would have to go to the polls within six months. Disunity in his party would be fatal. If he came back without a treaty, an acrimonious European post-mortem would dominate the early months of 1992. But to come back with a bad deal – a federalist deal – would be worse still.

As the British motorcade wound its way through the suburbs of Maastricht, no one was in very good spirits. Remembering the articles she had drafted for the Prime Minister about this 'small town in Holland', Sarah looked with gloomy astonishment at the miles of north European urban sprawl. The omens were bad. At Heathrow airport that afternoon, the Prime Minister had put his chances of achieving an acceptable agreement at only fifty-fifty.

In July, the European game of musical chairs had thrust the Netherlands into the presidency seat. The Dutch Prime Minister, Ruud Lubbers, would be in the chair at Maastricht. He spoke good English, though in a quick-fire, guttural voice not always easy to understand. John Major found him well-briefed, and at Maastricht itself very ready to negotiate. But the Dutch were not always on the British side.

When they took over the presidency from Luxembourg on 1 July, the political union treaty took a turn for the worse. Hans Van den Broek, the Dutch Foreign Minister, presented a new draft to replace the version produced during the Luxembourg presidency. Britain's design for a new framework for co-operation outside the straitjacket of Brussels institutions had been removed. Centralism ruled, with foreign policy, defence and law and order all in the hands of the European Commission and the European Court. In place of the elegant 'pillared structure' on which Britain had laboured, the Community tower block loomed large over the treaty blueprint.

It was a bad moment. If all other Foreign Ministers supported this when they met in September, Britain would be isolated on too many issues to have a hope of successful negotiation. However, the Dutch had misread the European mood. Luxembourg's Foreign Minister, Jacques Poos, deeply affronted by what he took to be an insult to his chairmanship, began the meeting of Foreign Ministers with a furious attack on the Dutch draft. The Italians had, meanwhile, changed their view. In attacking the Dutch draft, Douglas Hurd was helped by the Italian Foreign Minister, Gianni de Michelis. The Belgians supported the draft, of course, and the Dutch believed Germany would do so too. But Hans-Dietrich Genscher, the arch-coalition politician with sixteen years' survival as German Foreign Minister behind him, played a canny game. He spoke last, briefly and damningly. The earlier, Luxembourg text was perfectly all right, he thought. He might have preferred the Dutch version, but the issue was academic: plainly it would not fly. That settled the matter: the Dutch had lost.

This ill-judged Dutch draft was, in fact, probably a godsend. It sobered up all European governments, giving focus to a feeling that things had been allowed to go too far in the centralist direction. But Britain still had a long list of criticisms of the draft treaties, not least on the by now familiar territory of monetary union.

The first battle, fought doughtily by the Treasury's chief nego-tiator Sir Nigel Wicks, had been for tough preconditions to be met before any European countries tried to form a monetary union – the famous 'convergence criteria'. Secondly, he had struggled to prevent stage two being designed in such a way that the twelve nations would be swallowed up into an effective union even before the decision to proceed to stage three had actually been taken. In particular – and this was made clear by Number 10 – the treaty should not be allowed to make the ERM part of the statute law of the United Kingdom. John Major's approach to the ERM, as both Prime Minister and Chancellor, had always been that it was a system based on co-operation, not law.

Thirdly, Britain was opposed to big 'cohesion' hand-outs to the Mediterranean countries to compensate them for the supposed disadvantage they would suffer on joining the European Union (a big bit of bad economics unfortunately enshrined in the Single European Act). And fourthly, so far as our 'opt-out' was concerned, we had been arguing for the treaty to offer the same right to all member states. The Danes wanted this freedom, too.

A general opt-out did make a brief guest appearance in one 'informal' Dutch draft of the treaty. But others (the French in particular) objected. They did not want the Germans to have an escape clause, since monetary union without the Deutschmark would be a farce. The Danes deserted Britain's stand in November. Their government's defeat in a referendum on Maastricht the following summer proved how ill-judged that defection was. At the time, however, it merely made Britain's struggle harder.

By the time the British team got to Maastricht, they knew that finding a way out would probably depend on securing a special protocol, unique to Britain. Nigel Wicks had a British draft in his briefcase; but no text had been agreed, and no British protocol was attached to the draft treaty.

The Germans, meanwhile, were pressing hard for another change the British Government intended to resist: a big shift of power to the European Parliament. At the June Council meeting in Luxembourg, Britain had agreed to the principle of some form of 'co-decision' – links between the European Parliament, European Commission and national governments, represented in European Councils. What was not agreed before Maastricht, however, was an acceptable mechanism for sharing decision-making between them, or the list of issues to which it should apply.

Even more of a problem was Helmut Kohl's desire to bring immigration under the control of the Commission, as part of his wider ambitions for political union. This issue had a long and difficult history. At the back of everyone's mind was the agreement on frontier controls Margaret Thatcher had accepted in 1985. This was founded on a public political commitment by her European partners in a declaration attached to the Single European Act, not in the act itself. The legal status of this declaration has been in dispute among the lawyers ever since.

Britain was not under immediate threat on frontiers, but the issue was discussed between all the Ministers involved at a Number 10 dinner in November. They decided that entangling the issue with Maastricht would be a mistake. Britain would be the supplicant, asking for change to an existing community text. Other governments would inevitably demand a price in terms of British negotiating objectives, none of which could be sacrificed. If adding a further demand simply led to an impasse, Britain would be worse off than where we started. Better to negotiate Maastricht, then conduct the frontiers battle independently, when the timing was right.

When all the pre-Maastricht skirmishes were over, in late November the Prime Minister took the highly risky step of spelling out his bottom line to the House of Commons. He would accept no commitment to a 'federal' union; no compulsion to join a monetary union; no subjection of foreign or interior policy to Brussels control. He would not consider anything that he thought would undermine either NATO or Britain's economic competitiveness. He also had a long list of Maastricht 'wants'.

He wanted the European Parliament to have more power to investigate fraud against the Community – the misuse of Commission money. He wanted the European Court to have more power to enforce a 'level playing field' for industry, making all countries abide by agreed rules. He wanted a new principle – 'subsidiarity' – written into the treaty: a specific form of words to underpin national sovereignty and clip Brussels back to activities which national governments could not undertake alone. And he wanted the Community to raise its sights above its old boundaries, opening its gates not merely to the rest of western and northern Europe, but to the fledgling democracies further east as well.

He won a very healthy majority of 101 at the end of the debate. Margaret Thatcher and Edward Heath quarrelled openly on the floor of the House. But only six Tory MPs voted against the Government.

Here and elsewhere, John Major tried to give a clear signal to the rest of Europe. He was not out to wreck the Maastricht party. However, he was ready to use the veto if he had to. It was not his style to shout 'no' to everything. But as he told the Commons, where he had said 'no', plainly, loudly and repeatedly, his European partners should not imagine that he would give in at the 'fifty-ninth minute of the eleventh hour'.

Douglas Hurd listed a total of nine unresolved areas at the final Cabinet meeting before Maastricht. The unfinished business included all the big Cs of Maastricht jargon with which commentators had been struggling for weeks: competence, co-decision, cohesion, convergence. He also reported that all other Community members were still determined to have a Social Chapter in the new political union treaty.

Back in the 1980s, Britain had committed itself to a 'social dimension' to the European Community. Other members argued that a Social Chapter was merely the logical expression of this. Most other European countries had much higher social costs – welfare taxes and contributions levied on employers and employees – and more restrictions on working practices than Britain did. The Government knew a Social Chapter – enthusiastically endorsed by the Labour Party – could be a Trojan horse. Other governments in Europe would be only too delighted to blunt Britain's competitive edge by forcing us to burden our industries with the regulations suffered by theirs. They would be able to do so because it was proposed that many decisions under a Social Chapter should be taken by 'qualified majority voting'.[1] Britain, in other words, would not have a veto.

Having put through one piece of domestic legislation after another to free up Britain's labour markets, the Government faced the risk of having all that work undone at the European level. Through the year long negotiations in Brussels, John Kerr had warned his counterparts that this was not a risk John Major would run. Jacques Delors was to reinforce the British Government's argument by expressing the view that our position made Britain a 'paradise for inward investment'. But when the Prime Minister left for Maastricht, no solution was in sight. We were on a collision course. This, above all, looked like a treaty-breaker.

The Prime Minister's Maastricht fighting force was led by three Ministers: the Foreign Secretary, his right-hand man; the Chancellor, there to play Britain's hand in the monetary union negotiations; and the Foreign Office Minister with responsibility for Europe, Tristan Garel-Jones. Tristan was free of the burden of

---

[1] This piece of Brussels jargon describes a compromise between a requirement for unanimity – where no decision can be taken unless all member states agree – and 'Simple Majority Voting' – where a decision can be taken provided more states support than oppose it. The QMV rules are hideously complicated, and became more complicated and contentious after new countries joined. Broadly, they require a proposition to attract something like two-thirds support.

attendance at the main meetings, and so could act as a one-man mobile task force.

Maastricht was dangerously full of disobliging foreigners ready to speak their excellent English on our news channels. Gus O'Donnell would feed the 'Minister for Europe' to the press pack when the interminable meetings made them hungry for news. It was a difficult holding job, when so much was uncertain. Famed for his mastery of the black arts in the Whips' Office, Tristan had learned long ago how to look impressive while giving nothing away.

He had made a visual statement even before leaving London. He and the Foreign Secretary both liked to wear green Austrian Loden coats, dubbed by the frivolous end of the British delegation the 'Single European Coat'. These coats were the bane of Sarah's life on prime ministerial trips. The kindly RAF staff, certain that no real man could wear a coat with a pleat down the back, would always rush up with one at the end of the journey: 'I think this must be yours, Ma'am?' By Maastricht, however, Tristan had been so teased about this politically incorrect garment that he appeared in an incontrovertibly British blue coat, which must have been old when the Empire was young.

It is common to deride the Foreign Office as Euro-quislings and the Treasury as blinkered number-crunchers. Both institutions have their weaknesses: ask the FCO about the Treasury, or vice versa, if you want to hear the worst. But the civil service team at Maastricht was Whitehall's best. The lead officials from the Treasury and the Foreign Office were Nigel Wicks, who had done such a thorough job of the pre-Maastricht work on monetary union, and Michael Jay, a first-class player of the European negotiating game of 'twelve-dimensional chess'.

Lawyers, budgetary experts, drafters from the Cabinet Office, the Treasury and the Foreign Office made up the bulk of the delegation. From Number 10, there were Stephen, Gus and Sarah. She kept in close touch with Jonathan, on standby – or tenterhooks – in London, ready to get the conclusions into the hands of the entire Cabinet as soon as the Council ended.

European Councils are a peculiarly hazardous way of reaching important decisions. Only the heads of government are present, usually flanked by their Foreign Ministers. With agreement, these can be replaced by Finance Ministers; but such an exchange is almost always resisted by the French. As successive Chancellors of the Exchequer have discovered to their annoyance, across much of Europe Finance Ministers are considered mere book-keepers. Only at Maastricht itself did Britain secure European agreement that they should attend the twice-yearly Councils, and even then not as of right.

No officials are allowed to take part in the Councils. There is a small secretariat in the Council chamber, from which one official will emerge to brief – mostly in French the so-called 'Antici group' of officials, one from each country. At Maastricht, the briefer was of course a Dutchman; but by tradition he briefs in French.[2] The Antici group scribble down his words in their own languages. Their scrawls are then passed out to delegation offices, photocopied and circulated amongst waiting teams, who thus receive a blurred, third-hand account of the arguments exchanged among the Council half an hour before. It is hardly the best basis for judging what additional information might be required.

From each national base camp, the holders of a couple of magic inner passes can pop in and out of the Council chamber with 'messages'. John Kerr was the acknowledged master of this diplomatic game. Squatting beside the Prime Minister, avoiding eye contact with those who might object to his presence, determined not to leave while malign German influences were muttering in Kohl's ear, he managed to extend the art of message delivery way beyond any normal interpretation of the rules. The Dutch by and large turned a blind eye. The disadvantage of his floor-level position was that he was not entitled to either of Britain's two sets of earphones, carrying interpretation in English. When the debate was in French (or even German), he could cope; but when Lubbers spoke Dutch, some surreal exchanges ensued between the stowaway ambassador and the Prime Minister.

All, therefore, hung on John Major.

[2]Our Antici official was, of course, British; but just to make things really confusing, he had the thoroughly French name of John de Fonblanque.

The obvious defects of the system – particularly for Britain, with so many points of disagreement to raise – were counterbalanced by just one advantage: John Major's negotiating skills. He had good briefers, and an inexhaustible capacity for detail. But that was not the half of it. Understanding both the issues and the psychology of the players is the key to European Council negotiations: John Major possesses that rare combination of skills to a high degree. One wry ministerial victim of his technique as Chief Secretary to the Treasury described it as 'offering you a toffee-apple while removing your wallet'. It was never more needed than in dealing with his fellow heads of government at Maastricht.

Who were they, this motley crew with the future of Europe in their hands?

All twelve other leaders – including the President of the Commission – were older than the forty-eight-year-old John Major. There were the three old men, with adult memories of a war spent in occupied France, the Cretan hills, the Vatican library: François Mitterrand, Constantine Mitsotakis, Giulio Andreotti. Then there were the men of the middle generation, adults just after the war, now in their sixties: Poul Schlüter from Denmark, the Irish Taoiseach Charles Haughey, Helmut Kohl, Jacques Delors. Finally, there were the younger men: Wilfried Martens from Belgium; Jacques Santer from Luxembourg; Ruud Lubbers of the Netherlands; Felipe Gonzalez from Spain; and Anibal Cavaço Silva from Portugal.

Most had years of leadership under their belts. Constantine Mitsotakis had only been Prime Minister for a few months more than John Major, but he had led his party since 1984. Giulio Andreotti had been only two years in office this time, but had first become Prime Minister of Italy nearly twenty years earlier.[3] Lubbers, Gonzalez, Schlüter, Martens, Mitterrand and Kohl had all been in the job for nine years or more. Jacques Delors himself had been President of the European Commission since 1985.

---

[3]At seventy-one, Giulio Andreotti was still younger than his Finance Minister, former central bank governor Guido Carli; but older in every way than his flamboyant Venetian Foreign Minister, Gianni de Michelis.

What else did they have in common? Sex and politics, for a start. The Maastricht negotiating table was entirely surrounded by men – until François Mitterrand left Elizabeth Guigou, his junior Minister for Europe, in his chair.[4] There were few card-carrying socialists among the leaders, but a number of the others headed coalitions that included socialists, and even those Christian Democrats who governed unconstrained did not see eye to eye on everything with the British Conservative Government. But the two key figures were closer to the British view than most: the Dutch Prime Minister and the German Chancellor. Helmut Kohl – with his stonemason's hands, avuncular beam, dislike of Margaret Thatcher, equal liking for John Major – had been the key to the Prime Minister's construction of alliances. The German leader wanted Maastricht to be a success – continuing disarray would be bad for Europe, and success would improve John Major's election prospects (as well, of course, as his own). Sometimes, however, his efforts to help his friend John were a little naive. There was an awkward moment in the run-up to Maastricht when a beaming German Chancellor offered to come to 'explain Europe' to Tory MPs. John Major had – tactfully – to refuse.

In the back of Helmut Kohl's mind, however, lurked the suspicion that John Major might prevaricate simply to get past the general election. But by November, the British Prime Minister had convinced his ally that he would not. Their final meeting was the culmination of the 'German strategy' which had been the dominant feature of British diplomacy in Europe over the previous year. Its success was – literally – visible at Maastricht. One close observer describes Kohl's body language in the Council. Always restless, shifting his formidable bulk in some inadequate chair, he became really fidgety when Hans-Dietrich Genscher urged him to oppose the British Prime Minister and support Wilfried Martens, the Belgian cheerleader for Europe's federalists. When John Major took a stand, Helmut Kohl's instincts were plainly supportive, whatever his briefs or his advisers might say.

[4]Edith Cresson was still Prime Minister of France at the time, but it was President Mitterrand who came to Maastricht.

All the same, the British contingent knew that they could not count on German support throughout. At any European Council, negotiations can take an unexpected turn. Deals may unravel at the last moment – and frequently do.

Nor – even for two short days – would the rest of the world stand still. When, on 8 December, the British team got to their conference hotel – the Golden Tulip – news was just beginning to filter in from Minsk. The Soviet Union, it seemed, was finally to be dissolved. At an historic meeting, the leaders of the new republics had decided to replace it by a looser 'commonwealth' of independent states.

As so often with news from that part of the world, there was little up-to-date information beyond what was on the wires. But Britain's principal concerns were clear: the security of the former Soviet Union's nuclear arsenal, human rights in the emerging republics, responsibility for Soviet debts. Overnight, Stephen Wall spoke to Brent Scowcroft in Washington. A press line was hammered out, and – equally important – contacts made with the French. A meeting was arranged with François Mitterrand. Here was at least one issue on which Britain and France were likely to take a common view.

On his way to the Council on Monday morning, the Prime Minister was ready with a 'doorstep' comment on the break-up of the Soviet Union. He ran through Britain's concerns. But most of the cluster of journalists, shivering outside the Golden Tulip, wanted to know about the European treaty negotiations. The Prime Minister was notably cautious.

Then it was off to the ball.

Maastricht was by no means the most exotic of locations, but it was very determinedly *en fête*. Its burghers were clearly hoping that the week would bring them a name in history on a par with Vienna or Versailles. On Monday, there was dinner in the town hall for the negotiators, lunch with Queen Beatrix for the heads of government, a watering-hole earmarked for each press pack ('Le Britannique', complete with improbable Beefeater, offered strange combinations of beer and breakfast). There was a kite-flying contest, with an enormous Euro-kite ready to be the star of the show.

In the Provinciehuis, however, Monday saw little progress to celebrate. The meeting began with a full cast: heads of government,

1. 'Starting here and now': John and Norma Major, 28 November 1990.

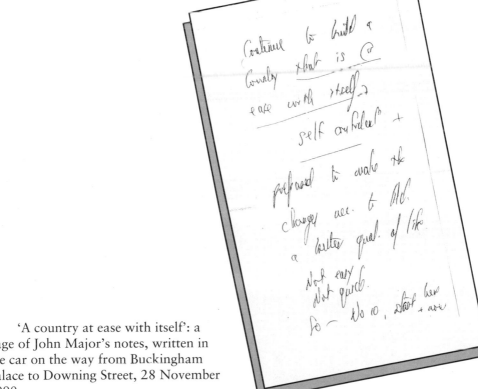

2. 'A country at ease with itself': a page of John Major's notes, written in the car on the way from Buckingham Palace to Downing Street, 28 November 1990.

3.   Cambridge 10, Oxford 7: the new Cabinet. Back row, from left to right: Richard Ryder, Ian Lang, Peter Lilley, Michael Howard, Peter Brooke, Tony Newton, John Wakeham, Chris Patten, John Gummer, David Hunt, William Waldegrave, David Mellor (and Cabinet Secretary, Sir Robin Butler). Front row: John MacGregor, Tom King, Norman Lamont, Lord Waddington, Lord Mackay, John Major, Douglas Hurd, Kenneth Baker, Michael Heseltine, Kenneth Clarke, Malcolm Rifkind.

4.   The 'kitchen cabinet' - according to artist Michael Frith in the *Financial Times*. From left to right: Gus O'Donnell, Sarah Hogg, David Mellor, Chris Patten, John Major, John Wakeham, Richard Ryder.

5. The new boy (second from right, between Luxembourg's Jacques Santer and the Netherlands' Ruud Lubbers). John Major's first European Council, Rome, 14 December 1990.

6. 'Meet John Major': the Prime Minister with troops in the Gulf, January 1991.

7. Roses all the way?: the Prime Minister and the German Chancellor at Chequers, June 1991.

8. Here today, gone tomorrow: Mikhail Gorbachev, Brian Mulroney and George Bush with John Major, London, July 1991.

9. Raising the standard: launching the Citizen's Charter, July 1991.

10.   A special relationship: Kennebunkport, August 1991. From left to right: Marlin Fitzwater, Sarah Hogg, Norma Major, George Bush, Elizabeth Major, John Major, Brent Scowcroft, Barbara Bush, Stephen Wall.

11.   Government meets Party: the No. 12 Committee. Back row, from left to right: Tim Collins, Sir John Cope, Gus O'Donnell, Andrew Lansley, Graham Bright, Alastair Goodlad, Shaun Woodward, Eleanor Laing, Jonathan Haslam, Sir John Lacy, Murdo Maclean, Shana Hole. Front row: Chris Patten, Sarah Hogg, John Wakeham, Richard Ryder, John MacGregor, Lord Waddington, Gillian Shephard, Judith Chaplin.

12.   Not seeing eye to eye: John Major and Margaret Thatcher at the Conservative Party Conference, Blackpool, October 1991. Chris Patten is in the buffer zone.

13.   Taken to the bosom of the party: Blackpool, October 1991.

14.   Team spirit: John and Norma Major with the Cabinet on the last day of the Conference, October 1991. In the background, from left to right: Peter Lilley, John Gummer, Chris Patten, William Waldegrave, Tony Newton and Tom King.

15. Going on and on and on: John Major with Douglas Hurd at Maastricht, December 1991.

16. First things first: John Major with Lincolnshire primary schoolchildren on the opening day of his general election tour, March 1992. Shirley Stotter, Douglas Hogg and Jonathan Hill are in the background; to the left are Norma Major and the Lincoln candidate, Kenneth Carlisle.

17.   'Look, there's a voter!' The Prime Minister with the team on the battlebus. Jonathan Hill is third from right.

18.   Mothering Sunday at Chequers during the campaign: Alex and Jonathan Hill provide the baby.

19.   Campaigning, general election, 1992. Barn owls ...

20.   ... and birthday cake, with staff at Chequers.

21.   Back to basics: getting on his soapbox, Cheltenham, March 1992.

22.   On the night shift: the Prime Minister working on his boxes in the Downing Street flat, April 1992.

23.   'If you don't know what it means by now ...': Chris Patten and Michael Howard at a Campaign Press Conference, April 1992.

The Britain I am fighting for.

A Britain where everyone has the chance to succeed.

A Britain where effort is rewarded, where low taxes leave people free to choose how to spend their own money.

A Britain where money keeps its value.

A Britain where we all have a stake in Britain's future. Where everyone has the opportunity to own their own home, and the chance to build up their own savings.

A Britain where people can pass on the fruits of a lifetime's work to their children — and their grandchildren.

A Britain where our public services set standards for the world.

A Britain where our National Health Service, freely available to all, gets still better every year.

A Britain where every child leaves school well-qualified for life.

A Britain where all our young people have the chance to study or train for a career.

A Britain that offers dignity and security for the old.

A Britain where people feel safe on our streets and secure in their homes.

A Britain that restores our inner cities and cares for our countryside.

A Britain where there's a helping hand for those who need it. Where people can get a hand up — not just a hand out.

A Britain well-defended, admired and respected throughout the world. And a Government that stands up for Britain in Europe.

A Britain that's fair and free from prejudice — a classless society, a country at ease with itself.

That is the Britain I want.

That is the Britain I am fighting for.

John Major

24.   Taking the battle to Fleet Street: newspaper advertisement, April 1992.

25.   Oops ... *Daily Mirror*, first edition, 10 April 1992. Stephen Sherbourne in the Policy Unit; Nick True is in the foreground.

26.   The home team in Number 10, April 1992. From left to right: Tim Collins, Shirley Stotter, Nick True, Edward Llewellyn, Jonathan Hill, Claire Jones, John Major, Norma Major, Sarah Hogg, Sir Norman Fowler, Stephen Sherbourne, Sir Ronald Millar, Debbie de Satgé.

27. Cowley Street celebrates, July 1995.

28. Done it again: the Prime Minister after the leadership election, July 1995.

Foreign and Finance Ministers. They circled round monetary union. Basic positions were agreed. Then the Finance Ministers were sent off to argue out the detail amongst themselves. Norman Lamont gave a 'doorstep' interview explaining why Britain wanted 'an opt-in/opt-out clause' on monetary union. This was, he said:

> . . . a very serious matter and we ought to decide it on its merits at the time. When we see whether it is going to work, Britain would have the complete freedom to decide to do what it wanted to do on the merits of the case and we don't think we should make up our minds today.

The opt-out was not, he admitted, 'in the bag'; but 'we are very happy and quite relaxed about the way this is going'.

At the Finance Ministers' lunch, however, the French and Italians launched their missile. It was, said one seasoned observer, a classic Council attack: late, precision targeted, hard to duck. Finance Ministers had been working over the famous convergence conditions. They had more or less concluded that a monetary union should only begin in 1997 if a majority of countries met these conditions, and – a second requirement – if a still larger majority formally agreed that it was right to go ahead. Now the French made a further proposal. If we are serious, they said, there must be a fall-back date. In 1999, those who met the economic conditions should join a single currency automatically, with no further ado. The Italians supported the French with enthusiasm; they presumably had not realised how slim Italy's chance was of meeting the conditions on that time-scale.

Since Britain was now determined on an opt-out, they could hardly fight the others' battle for them on this. The Germans were uneasy. But they had been put on the spot, obliged to demonstrate their commitment. They agreed. The deadline of 1999 was written in. (The final act of that particular play will open on 1 January 1998, when the countdown to the 1999 deadline begins. The supreme irony is that on that date, Britain will hold the presidency.)

In the main Council, John Major had carefully held back the

list of issues on which he was ready to agree co-decision until the discussions on political union began in the afternoon. He now started by treating the Council to a list of points unacceptable to the British, on everything from competence and Council voting to the Social Chapter. Then he began to play a lot of small cards, out of a pack prepared by John Kerr: he listed areas where he thought change would be useful, like the creation of a Community ombudsman and increased status for the Court of Audit (Ruud Lubbers's pet idea). He was happy for the European Parliament to have a greater supervisory role, over financial control and the appointment of the Commission, as well as a greater legislative role (carefully-defined); and he wanted to see national parliaments more involved. He also supported proposals for co-operation on interior and justice matters.

This last point was distinctly two-edged, since it said equally clearly that he was only going to agree to co-operation – not Community 'competence', or authority. But his little list was skilfully timed. It was a surprise. There was applause from Helmut Kohl. Ruud Lubbers said, 'Now I know we shall succeed.' From then on he was ready to pay a price for the success he thought was in sight. Britain's leverage had been increased. What's more, the Prime Minister had still held back about a third of his co-decision ammunition, ready to fight with on the second day.

As the Council broke up that first evening at Maastricht, the Prime Minister took stock. On the monetary side, mixed news. The notion of 'cohesion' subsidies to the poorer countries had survived, but Nigel Wicks had managed to ensure that the language was tougher than in the Single European Act. No sums were agreed; these were put back for settlement, along with other financial questions, at the Edinburgh summit a year later. There had been modest progress on the political side.

The biggest problem was that Britain was still being pressed to accept a Social Chapter. On this, the Prime Minister found the draft completely unacceptable. As he had said on the doorstep that first morning:

. . . it would impose huge costs on British industry and

commerce; it is very strongly opposed by British industry and commerce; it would cost jobs; it would cost competitiveness.

The Foreign Secretary was fully engaged in protecting NATO from confusion or duplication in the defence proposals, and in retaining the veto on key foreign policy decisions. The Chancellor was focused on monetary union. So there was no Minister at the Maastricht table to fight the battle over the Social Chapter. It was all down to the Prime Minister.

Gus O'Donnell and Sarah were concerned that the Social Chapter should not get through by default. Before leaving London, Sarah had gone to see Michael Howard, then Employment Secretary, who had brought his rigorous lawyer's mind to bear on the draft. The Prime Minister insisted Michael Howard was kept informed about the detail of the negotiations at Maastricht, and John Kerr did so throughout. Sarah also kept in close touch with John Banham of the Confederation of British Industry.

Meanwhile, officials worked on alternative drafts, trying to see if it was possible to reduce the Social Chapter to a meaningless shell. But it was dangerous territory, and the Prime Minister did not like it.

Late that Monday night in Maastricht, the news got worse. Michael Jay and Co. received from the Dutch the all-important draft conclusions of the Council, reflecting the first day's work. They were appalled. Belgian-inspired federalism had forced its way back in. This would turn Britain's precious pillared structure into mere temporary accommodation, a staging-post on the journey to full Community competence. Much else in the draft conclusions was also unacceptable.

And the Social Chapter was still there. The Dutch, like most other member states, thought that John Major was bluffing. They remembered a previous Prime Minister who had said no until the eleventh hour, then done a deal.

The team slaved through the night on a new 'back-to-back' version of the conclusions. A back-to-back document has the draft of whatever text is under negotiation on one side, with officials' comments on the other. Each contested phrase should be marked with a warning note, a suggested alternative, a fall-back position, a final trench.

The Prime Minister's basic working tool at Maastricht was a back-to-back of the entire draft treaties, prepared by Michael Jay and others, who had worked round the clock on it before they left London. John Major had then ground through this at long preparatory meetings with Ministers and officials until he was completely at home with the substance of all sensitive articles. The new back-to-back was merely a supplement which showed how far negotiations had got. The answer, from Britain's point of view, was: not far enough.

An enormous amount of judgement is involved in the construction of a back-to-back. Inevitably, officials will tend towards overkill, rather than risk missing any points. Even when they think the proposed language is good, they feel obliged to worry round it. So the Prime Minister, with the help of the Foreign Secretary, has to go through these products of official art, and decide which points to take.

Douglas Hurd's brisk, slightly schoolmasterly style was a huge asset on such occasions. At some Councils, the Prime Minister would leave the Foreign Secretary to chair the session with officials on the back-to-back. Presenting their overnight homework, the Upper Remove of officialdom would not be encouraged to waste the headmaster's time. On Tuesday 10 December 1991, however, the long list of points required the attention of both John Major and Douglas Hurd. And it would be the Prime Minister who would have to argue them in Council.

His team had a breakfast meeting with the Prime Minister at 7.45 a.m. His mood, not surprisingly, was bleak. John Kerr reported the overnight news. The Prime Minister's mood became even blacker. Those who worked closely with him knew that this was a necessary part of the process of working himself up for the immense strain of a negotiation. But John Kerr thought he had better ring Michael Jay, already at the Provinciehuis, to warn him that the session on the back-to-back was going to be a difficult one.

That meeting started grimly, too. There seemed to be just too many obstacles in the way of agreement. On the Social Chapter,

John Kerr believed we just had to go on seeing if they were bluffing, keeping the issue to the end, when the table would be piled high with other agreements. Michael Jay said that he believed the Prime Minister could get a treaty without a Social Chapter – if he dug in and sweated it out beyond the last minute. But no one was certain.

Important tactical decisions had to be taken. The text for the special protocol enshrining Britain's opt-out from monetary union had still not been agreed. Other finance ministries kept demanding to see the British draft. Nigel Wicks was coming under heavy pressure. But the Prime Minister was adamant: Nigel Wicks was not to show them anything until lunchtime. Scarred by the experience of the famous declaration on frontiers, British officials had constructed a long, legalistic set of defences. The Prime Minister did not want other Finance Ministers to have time to unpick language carefully lawyer-proofed at home.

At lunchtime, the Treasury duly circulated our proposed monetary union protocol. When Finance Ministers met, the British Chancellor, however, ran into difficulties. Some of the others raised points of detail, they felt they had a right to do so since this protocol – unlike a declaration – would be attached to the treaty. Tempers rose. Norman Lamont found he was getting nowhere; he decided to walk out of the meeting.

In the main Council, the Prime Minister was grinding on – under a handicap. For, earlier that day, there had been a disaster. His treaty back-to-back had disappeared. Not only did the official notes in the document reveal our negotiating positions, but this particular copy was covered with the Prime Minister's own personal amendments. Stephen Wall searched everywhere, white-faced. It was a Private Secretary's nightmare, likely to lead to a loaded revolver in the Foreign Office library. Everybody searched. Nobody could find it.

The Prime Minister could have been excused for disembowelling his entire Number 10 team. He remained extraordinarily cool, even amused by the sight of an upturned ant-heap of officials hunting frantically around the building.

Tristan Garel-Jones had an inspiration. He turned to Sarah. 'Did he leave it in the Gents?'

The only woman in the room, she struggled not to say what she thought of that question. Meanwhile, the room emptied, as every able-bodied male official rushed off to check. But it wasn't there.[5]

The Prime Minister had to go back to the conference table with a substitute. The pressure was rising. As at all European Councils, there came a point when Chancellor Kohl began to get bored with sitting still and President Mitterrand began to think longingly of dinner in Paris. Their officials began to mutter portentously about Cabinet meetings back home. The trick, John Major knew, was to engage these emotions for him rather than against him.

At about a quarter to seven, the Council took a break – but not for refreshment. The Dutch, wisely, had decided to starve the delegations into agreement. Hospitality in the Provinciehuis, lavish until the afternoon, was down to the last dried-up cheese roll. At seven o'clock, Ruud Lubbers sent a message asking if he could see the Prime Minister, who went down shortly afterwards to the presidency office, accompanied by the Foreign Secretary, Stephen Wall, Michael Jay and John Kerr.

Beer, wine and sandwiches were now brought in to fuel this all-important meeting. The first thing the Prime Minister had to do was secure Britain's opt-out from monetary union, still not agreed between Finance Ministers. The Chancellor was called in, along with his Dutch equivalent. The Prime Minister nailed the protocol into place. The mood lightened. Finance Ministers left. Then Ruud Lubbers and John Major moved on to the big outstanding issue: the Social Chapter.

At a Europe-wide meeting of employers and trade unions, a Confederation of British Industry delegate had given rash agreement to consultation between the 'social partners' – industry and unions – and the European Commission, which had rather undermined the British position. The Dutch had taken this as a signal that Britain was ready to give in. Ruud Lubbers pressed the point. John Banham had, however, told Sarah that the CBI had repudiated this agreement.

[5]Eventually, officials told the Prime Minister that they had found it in the Council Chamber itself. In the confusion, it had somehow found its way under a pile of Normal Lamont's papers.

John Major now made this clear. Britain could not accept that Community rules should be dictated by the 'social partners'. Ruud Lubbers backed off a little.

The Dutch Prime Minister then offered Britain another opt-out. There would be a Social Chapter in the treaty, but a protocol indicating British reservations would be tacked on at the end.

It sounded tempting. But the experience of negotiating one protocol on monetary union did not encourage the Prime Minister to think it would be easy to construct a watertight equivalent on social policy in a few short minutes. He wanted to keep the Social Chapter out of the treaty. So he took the high-risk strategy. It was time to see who was really bluffing. He rejected this offer. Stalemate.

Next, Ruud Lubbers tried to persuade the Prime Minister to accept Community control over immigration. Again John Major dug in. Britain had already gone as far as he thought reasonable. A common format for visas had been agreed and, more significantly, common lists of countries whose citizens would be required to apply for them. If, by the beginning of 1996, member states could not agree unanimously which these countries should be, then – he accepted – this decision should be taken by qualified majority voting (QMV).[6] But the Prime Minister would not agree to Community control over who should be allowed to immigrate to Britain. When Helmut Kohl joined the meeting, the German Chancellor did not press the point.

Now officials left the room. John Major, Ruud Lubbers and Helmut Kohl were down to the end-game. John Kerr had been working on a cosmetic Social Chapter, in close consultation with Michael Howard. The Prime Minister began the game by proffering this, knowing that it would be unacceptable to other governments. Helmut Kohl went off to find a German interpreter so he could read it properly, but both he and Ruud Lubbers knew it was only an empty gesture. Then the Dutch Prime Minister moved to his fall-back position. He hinted at a solution now credited to Jacques Delors' adviser, Pascal Lamy – a separate deal amongst the other

[6]In fact, the list was agreed, unanimously, in July 1995.

eleven, outside the treaty. This meant that they, not the British, would have to rely on a protocol.

Helmut Kohl left to put Giulio Andreotti in the picture. John Kerr, Michael Jay and Stephen Wall went back in, to be told that – if Lubbers and Kohl could get their agreement – the other eleven would sign their own declaration. Officials then worked through some details. There were still loose ends – including responsibility for the administrative costs of any Social Chapter measures. But in effect, they all knew, the Prime Minister had won. The Social Chapter was dead.

Shortly before 9.00 p.m., the Council reassembled. By now, President Mitterrand looked very tired. Helmut Kohl was cheered up by the light at the end of the tunnel. The rest had plainly had enough. We were into what Tristan Garel-Jones called 'zimmer-frame time'. But the Prime Minister had not given up. At the last minute, well past 10.00 p.m., the one outstanding issue was how to handle the treaty provisions for research and development – one of the largest elements of European Community spending.

Ruud Lubbers asked for views. Around the table, other leaders complained of the difficulty of reaching agreement in the Research Council on R & D 'framework programmes' under the present rules, which required unanimity. It was clearly a case for QMV. The Chairman looked to the Prime Minister.

With exquisite politeness, John Major insisted on his right to disagree. Britain, which had fought so often to hold down European spending, could not abandon its veto on the size of the research budget by accepting QMV. Decisions on the research budget must continue to depend on the Council reaching unanimity. He had noted others' views, but his had not changed. Nor would they change, however long the debate continued. There was a tense pause. Then Helmut Kohl flung up his hands, and slapped the table, roaring with laughter. 'Unanimity,' said Ruud Lubbers quickly and quietly, and closed the meeting before anyone else had a chance to speak.

Then they got out the champagne. And John Major was the first to propose a toast – to Ruud Lubbers's chairmanship. It had indeed been skilful; but everyone knew whose bluff had been called.

Up in the delegation office, Sarah phoned Jonathan to tell him Britain had a deal, and began writing furiously. Over in the press briefing room in the bowels of the Golden Tulip, Gus O'Donnell was the most exposed. He was working steadily through his evening briefing, discounting nonsensical accounts of the day's negotiations which were being fed to English journalists by the French: tales of a single European army, an end to NATO . . . On the issue of the Social Chapter, Gus had been sitting firmly on the fence. The Prime Minister's briefing line had been 'Hard pounding – and we are still pounding on; let us see who pounds the longest.' Gus filled the gap by talking vaguely of 'treaty language' – the well-known briefer's code for 'God knows'.

Suddenly there were rumours that the Council had broken up. Was it a fudge? Journalists wailed about their deadlines. They threatened to write about 'British concessions again' unless Gus gave them chapter and verse. He continued doggedly to the end of the briefing. Only when he could get back to the British base could he discover what had really happened. Then he learnt that the Social Chapter had been removed from the treaty. His next briefing was short and to the point: victory.[7]

The first formal press conference was held, following tradition, by the Presidents of the Community and the Commission. Ruud Lubbers and Jacques Delors took questions; the latter made no secret of his discontent about Britain's obduracy on the Social Chapter. The Prime Minister could not have asked for a better advertisement for the success of the negotiations. National leaders then began to meet their own press. Helmut Kohl was asked point-blank whether it was not the case that Britain was the only victor. He confessed to some disappointment, particularly about his failure to win more powers for the European Parliament, but without rancour. Even François Mitterrand was generous in his disagreement.

The Prime Minister, weary but content, worked his way through the points Britain had secured. Subsidiarity was in; federalism was out. The pillared structure was cemented into the treaty, keeping

---

[7]But not 'Game, Set and Match', which crept into the briefing later – and which the Prime Minister always disliked.

law and order, foreign affairs and defence away from the Brussels institutions. The protocol on Britain's monetary union opt-out was signed and sealed. There was no Social Chapter. The Council had agreed to allow the European Parliament more of a check on Community action; and he had enthusiastically endorsed more of a watchdog role for the Parliament on fraud. He had also secured agreement on a declaration that the Community was ready to open negotiations with any democratic European country applying for membership.

The Prime Minister expressed his satisfaction in characteristically moderate terms. He was 'very happy' with the outcome. It was 'a success both for Britain and for the whole of the Community'. Would staying outside the Social Protocol which had replaced the Social Chapter give Britain a 'leg up' on its competitors? 'It will certainly do us no harm.'

He was still answering questions at three in the morning. Only one asked about parliamentary ratification of the treaty, and it is interesting to note the slant that was put on the question. A senior British journalist inquired what would happen if the other eleven, and the European Parliament, were so annoyed with Britain's excision of the Social Chapter that they – not the United Kingdom – refused to ratify. It was not a question that gave the Prime Minister much difficulty.

Even though Brussels was an hour ahead of London, this was too late for the newspapers to do a very thorough job in Wednesday's editions. The headlines, however, were clear enough. 'Major wins all he asked for at Maastricht', announced *The Times*.

Thursday's newspapers were full of admiration for the Prime Minister. *The Times* leader described Maastricht as an 'emphatic success'. John Major had returned to what that paper's reporters called a 'hero's welcome' among MPs.

The positive verdict in the press outlasted the euphoria of the moment. On 16 February 1992, the *Sunday Telegraph* leader opined that:

So far from being the Conservatives' Achilles heel – as many assumed before Maastricht – the issue of Europe makes the party look increasingly purposeful.

Meanwhile, around 4.00 a.m. on Wednesday 11 December, Stephen Wall had asked the Prime Minister whether he wanted to fly straight back to London. To the great relief of his team, he said he would rather have a few hours' sleep first.

At the hotel, Sarah rang Jonathan again, and they activated the machinery they had put in place days before, and were to replicate for all important European Councils thereafter. Their aim had been to ensure that by breakfast, every Cabinet Minister would have a summary of the 'bull points' of the Maastricht agreement. Other key figures – the members of the Number 12 Committee, for example – would get the same service, transmitted by Shana Hole, the Chief Whip's Special Adviser. At Number 10, the Press Office had been watching a direct television 'feed' of the Prime Minister's press conference, and would prepare a transcript – but that took time, and would be lengthy to read. A clear summary of a confused story was the first essential.

Sarah worked on it through the night, checking points of fact with Michael Jay, John Kerr, Nigel Wicks – everyone in command of different pieces of the jigsaw. Jonathan worked on it again in London, completing the transformation from Euro-speak to plain English. Eventually both were satisfied. The distribution began. It worked according to plan.

The following day, one of the broadsheets concluded magisterially that this exercise was, 'a hallmark of the politically acute and tactically alert style that is fast becoming the defining quality of John Major's premiership'. Before Sarah or Jonathan could get big-headed, they spotted the accompanying photograph. The whole exercise had mysteriously been credited to someone else.

Before the British team set off for home the following morning, Tristan Garel-Jones had been in touch with several of the Cabinet, too. Warmest in his praise was the Home Secretary, Ken Baker, who sent messages of congratulation to the Prime Minister. The day after Maastricht was, indeed, one on which it seemed the Prime Minister could do no wrong. Success overcame tiredness, carrying him through another demanding forty-eight hours.

When he finally left Maastricht, the Prime Minister's sitting room at the Golden Tulip was a tip, littered with coffee cups, papers and, worst of all, the debris of two chain-smokers, Tristan Garel-Jones and John Kerr. Glancing round, the Prime Minister was suddenly horrified. 'We can't leave it like this.' Tristan's face was a study. He bustled the Prime Minister out of the door while, meekly, Sarah, Stephen and Gus began to clear up the mess.

The team got back to Number 10 mid-morning. On the plane, John Major suggested a proper Number 10 breakfast – a health fascist's nightmare of eggs, bacon, sausages, beans and fried bread. Stephen Wall, who had carried the heaviest official burden, had been too busy for food for the past twenty-four hours: his plate emptied faster than the average dog-bowl. Then he went down to work on the next stage of the Maastricht marathon: that afternoon's parliamentary statement.

John Major sailed through it. The Tory benches were in high spirits. Even Margaret Thatcher was reported as 'smiling and nodding' through the statement. She was still warmer when the Prime Minister made a last-minute decision the following night to go to the party for her fortieth wedding anniversary. 'I'm absolutely thrilled – I do congratulate him' were the quotes that appeared in the newspapers – even though some of her friends were later heard to mutter that she had been 'thrilled' about the Prime Minister's arrival at her party rather than his treaty.

By then, the Prime Minister had finished Maastricht week off with a party political broadcast. There had been much debate beforehand as to whether he was wise to commit himself to making one. Supposing he had nothing to report? Supposing Maastricht had broken up unresolved, and the political air was thick with recriminations? But the party had a television 'slot' that night, and the Prime Minister thought it would be both wasteful and cowardly to give it up. He had committed himself in advance and the gamble paid off. The bull points came into their own again as Sarah drafted the broadcast on the plane home.

Even the following week, when the excitement had died

down, the details had been picked over and the headlines had switched to the Chancellor's package of measures to boost the ailing housing market, the Maastricht afterglow carried the Prime Minister smoothly through the Commons debate. There were only seven Tory rebels, led by Norman Tebbit. There were some abstentions, too – among them Margaret Thatcher. But the majority of eighty-three was a firm platform for an election.

As the *Daily Telegraph* put it at the end of February 1992:

> By his handling of the negotiations in which he held out on principle but conceded just enough to keep Britain in the game and head off an electorally damaging split among Conservatives, Mr Major has a strong claim not just to the gratitude of his party, but to that of his European partners.

For a moment it looked as if a quick dissolution of Parliament would be the right decision. But Christmas was looming, in less than a week. Wiser counsels prevailed.

In the sorry aftermath of 1993, when the Maastricht Bill had passed only under threat of another, premature election, one question nagged at all the Prime Minister's team. Should he have put the bill enacting the Maastricht treaties through Parliament before the election, on the crest of his party's applause?

With hindsight, John Major certainly saw this as a lost opportunity. At the time, however, it looked like an unnecessary complication. He would have had to wait for the full and final, legal versions of the treaty documents, and these would not be available until well into the New Year. He would then be very short of parliamentary time before an election. There was no hurry: other European governments, particularly those which were subjecting the treaties to a referendum, would take months to turn them into law. The Prime Minister, meanwhile, surely had his European mandate.

Nor were the business managers keen on a quick bill. They were already overloaded. In the short, final parliamentary session of 1991-92, they had to resort to the 'guillotine' – securing a decision to curtail parliamentary debate – no fewer than six times.

Most important of all, they had the Council Tax legislation to see safely on to the statute book. The final, damaging ripple from the disaster of the poll tax was the parliamentary time required to put it right.

As this chapter began with Her Majesty, perhaps it should end there, too. The full, final, English versions of the European Treaties on Political and Monetary Union were signed by Douglas Hurd and Francis Maude – on behalf of the Chancellor – on 7 February 1992. The intervening weeks had been spent proof-reading, polishing, passing the documents between experts, getting every tiny last detail tied down and into the proper constitutional form.

At Maastricht on 7 February, Nigel Wicks opened his copy of the final document, about to be signed with due pomp and circumstance by the statesmen of Europe. His eagle eye detected an error. He immediately called over a colleague from the Foreign and Commonwealth Office. It was quite appalling. There was a dreadful mistake in the text. Why was the Treasury paying for all these diplomats, if they couldn't be relied on to avoid this kind of thing in an international treaty?

'What mistake?' our man in the FCO asked nervously.

'Well,' said Nigel, pointing to the text, 'don't you know she isn't the Queen? She's "The Queen".'

The FCO was not amused.

10

'If This Is Tuesday,
It Must Be Transport'

*What you have to understand is that the Prime Minister is just
wallpaper. All he's got to do is provide the pictures. OK?*
Central Office 'strategist', general election campaign 1992

Political campaigners, like generals, tend to fight the last war.
Central Office's last war had been the general election of 1987.
They still bore the scars. Despite having won a 101-seat majority,
they were judged by the pundits to have 'lost' the campaign.

It was Labour, with their new-found slickness, who had won the
plaudits in 1987. Donkey-jackets were out, suits in. Red roses had
sprouted in button-holes and blossomed on conference platforms.
All the tricks of modern communications – the sound-bite, the
photo opportunity, the use of staging and lighting, the campaign
theme-tune – had been deployed. Neil Kinnock had been made to
look almost electable in a party political broadcast filmed by Hugh
Hudson, the director of *Chariots of Fire*. Meanwhile, as Labour
marched purposefully on from themed day to themed day, over
at Conservative headquarters, the Tory campaign seemed to be
lurching from crisis to crisis, deteriorating into the farcical excesses
of 'Wobbly Thursday', when ministerial lapels were grabbed and
expletives exchanged. The conclusion drawn in Smith Square, as
they worked up their plans for a general election in 1991 or 1992,
was therefore that their next campaign should be like Labour's last
campaign – only more so.

The view amongst key Central Office staff that at the next election 'news management' would be more important than ever was reinforced by a trip they made to America in the late summer of 1991 to study Republican campaigning techniques. Dazzled by the sophistication of the town mice from George Bush's campaign team, the Conservative country mice concluded that they would have to redouble their efforts to control the media agenda.

Labour had drawn similar conclusions from the 1987 campaign. Since they believed their own propaganda, it would obviously be perverse of them to change the basic format with which they had 'won' the campaign. But it could no doubt be improved, made more efficient, modernised – which in practice meant that everything should be even more ruthlessly choreographed and regimented.

So the cross-party consensus was clear: the coming general election campaign would be the most carefully orchestrated ever. In the probing light of the television camera, in the shadow of the instant headline, one slip of the tongue could lose the election. Therefore the aim should be to reduce risk, to eliminate spontaneity, to curtail the cut and thrust of political debate. Words should be written down on autocue, photographs plotted in advance, sound-bites pre-cooked and wrapped in clingfilm: for Britain was bound to follow the Americans further and further down the path of candy-floss politics.

One other factor was much in Central Office minds as they prepared for the election: they knew that Labour would play the card called 'Time for a Change'. And as the Conservatives ground on through their thirteenth year in power, it looked like an ace. To trump it, the Tories would have to show that they had neither run out of steam nor lost their appetite for politics. They would also, as Maurice Saatchi kept telling them, have to hammer home to voters the dangers of switching to something worse.

Once November 1991 had passed, it was unlikely that the general election would be called before the spring. But that did not mean the Conservatives could afford to relax over their roast turkey and stuffing. The parties were neck and neck in the polls. Whoever got their nose in front first in the New Year might be hard to catch. There was, therefore, much to be said for coming out with all guns blazing after the Christmas holiday.

This was the thinking that lay behind the so-called 'Near Term' campaign. The basic idea was simple. First, identify key campaign themes, then, draw up a detailed plan of action, running week by week, covering one theme after another. So, for example, week one might be 'tax'; week two, 'prices'; week three, 'transport'; week four, 'agriculture'; week five, 'health', and so on.

Taking the initiative in this way — instead of merely reacting to events as they cropped up — would have two benefits. It would help wake Secretaries of State up to the fact that a general election was just around the corner and that they were, after all, politicians and not mere administrators. And it would keep Labour on the defensive, forcing them to react to a Conservative agenda, rather than devising one of their own which might help them open up a lead in the opinion polls.

A Central Office paper on the Near Term campaign was endorsed at a meeting of the Political Cabinet on 21 November 1991. The next steps were for Maurice Saatchi and Andrew Lansley, the head of the Conservative Research Department, to flog round department after department, badgering and encouraging Ministers into activity, and to draw up a detailed campaign plan. It was agreed that this would kick into action in the first full week of the New Year — a period when politicians normally have their feet up. The first campaign target would be: tax.

The launch of the first tax bombshell poster on 6 January caught Labour on the hop. Based on a simple calculation — Labour's total additional spending commitments, divided by the number of households in the country — it brought home vividly the cost of Labour's economic policies. As Maurice Saatchi had hoped, it established tax as a key election issue. By the end of January, the Conservatives had opened up a lead of 2 per cent in the opinion polls and there had been a huge increase in people's expectations that taxes would go up under Labour.[1] The Near Term campaign had so far proved its worth and justified the faith of those who had argued that with effort and planning it was possible to impose one's will on the tide of day to day events.

But after a flying start, the Near Term campaign did not live up to its early promise. Michael Heseltine and others had put their finger on its weak spot at the Political Cabinet on 21 November, when they reminded colleagues of the old campaigning truth: elections are decided by at most two or three themes repeated *ad nauseam*. The first salvo of the Near Term campaign had worked because the debate over tax was such a key election issue. When, however, the campaign rolled on to 'agriculture week' or 'transport week', so the shells fell wide or dropped short. The Conservatives' opinion poll lead at the end of January was turned into a Labour lead by the end of February.

Summing up at the end of the November Political Cabinet, the Prime Minister had endorsed the need for planning, but warned of the need for flexibility. In elections, like war, if a gap opens up in the enemy's defences, you have to be ready to press your advantage home. Political campaigns, like real life, do not always go according to plan. The other side is trying to do to you what you are trying to do to it. Just as you are poised, watches synchronised, to launch a frontal assault, so the enemy bursts through from behind and captures your baggage train. If John Major were ambushed by Neil Kinnock on the health service at Prime Minister's Questions, it was no good trying to stick to a plan to talk about transport. The news that evening would be about the NHS. Equally, the Prime Minister might see an opportunity at Questions to press home his attack on tax – even if the plan said it was supposed to be 'housing week'. The problem with the Near Term campaign was that in order to give every Minister fifteen minutes of fame, too many secondary themes were rigidly pursued for too long.

---

[1] That the poster would be so effective was not immediately apparent to everyone. When Norman Lamont first looked at the picture of a bombshell labelled with the cost of Labour's plans, he said: 'Yes, but why have they done a drawing of a fish?'

The Near Term campaign suffered from a further handicap: it gradually became part of the Whitehall landscape. And in Whitehall, anything that seems to have become a fixture tends to get colonised by the official machine. Government departments had quickly twigged that in being offered a week all to themselves, they were being handed a golden opportunity to slip out some new regulation long awaiting a suitable window. For a while, it was like watching *The Sorcerer's Apprentice*: statements, press releases and White Papers poured out from Whitehall in an apparently unstoppable flow. A political exercise was in danger of being hi-jacked by a bureaucratic one. By February, the process had become something of a joke in the press. The Prime Minister had to turn off the tap before everyone drowned in the deluge of departmental announcements.

Media interest in the nuts and bolts of the Near Term campaign had also been fed by too much chatter. For a while, it was difficult to open a newspaper without finding a moody black and white photograph of a 'strategist' with a copy of the Near Term campaign document placed tantalisingly on the desk; a 'spin doctor' – the phrase coined to describe the press briefers – draped over a piano; a diary column full of gossip about the Central Office 'brat pack'; or yet another feature on the Near Term campaign itself.

Some of this was, of course, inevitable. But there were instances of the classic communications mistake of confusing the mechanism for the message. No one, as Jonathan said, should even have been aware at the time that there was such a thing as a Near Term campaign. Its success should be judged by its results, not by the number of column inches it generated. Apart from giving advance notice of the Government's plans to the Labour Party, the chatter had a further harmful side-effect. All the talk of 'spin doctors' made the media morbidly afraid that they were being manipulated. Inevitably, perhaps, they over-compensated, studiously ignoring announcements to which they would otherwise have given some decent coverage.

Equally inevitably, the publicity the spin doctors attracted ended up by rebounding on them. Having built them up, the media were poised to knock them down again. So when the campaign seemed to be faltering, the press had its ready-made scapegoats. The youth and inexperience of the Central Office 'brat pack' was derided, and every failing, real or imaginary, was laid at their door.

Looking back at the election much later, Chris Patten summed up the problem. Central Office, bruised by the criticism after the 1987 general election, had wanted to prove that they could win the 'war of the campaigns' as well as the real thing. Chris blamed himself for allowing some of his team to spend too much time fighting a kind of 'shadow campaign', trying to get one over their opposite numbers at Labour Party headquarters, rather than concentrating on the main task in hand: persuading people to vote Conservative.

There was also, perhaps, another reason why Central Office felt it had to try so hard to impress Fleet Street. Chris Patten had indicated early on that he did not intend to spend large sums of money on newspaper advertising. He was sceptical about what had happened in the wake of Wobbly Thursday in 1987, when nearly £3 million was splurged in the last week of the campaign on saturating the newspapers with full-page adverts. But it wasn't just that Chris questioned the effectiveness of the newspaper advertising. There was a good practical reason why he was resistant to it: he had inherited big debts at Central Office, so the money was not there to chuck around.[2]

One lesson from across the Atlantic the campaign strategists were, however, slower to learn. In the modern media age, differences over policy have increasingly been reduced to a conflict between personalities. It sounds more sensational. It fits more easily into headlines. It sells more copies. So, no matter how often the Prime Minister or Neil Kinnock might say – and mean it – that the election should be about policies, not personalities, the press would present it as a straightforward bare-knuckle fight between John Major in the blue corner and Neil Kinnock in the red.

Central Office thinking, however, was developing along different lines. Believing that campaign themes were more important than individuals, the Prime Minister's main job during the campaign was seen as providing 'illustration' for the themes which the planners

---

[2]An expensive 1987 campaign, the Euro-elections and the refitting of Central Office left a £12 million accumulated deficit by 1991.

had selected. John Major was, as one of the Central Office team told Jonathan, 'just wallpaper'.

This approach infected the preparation of the prime ministerial programme from the earliest planning meetings onwards. A first detailed session with the Prime Minister was held at Chequers on 10 June 1991. There was a lot to be decided. A team had to be organised, and a safe and secure means found of getting the Prime Minister around as much of the country as possible. Decisions had to be taken about media handling and how to try to set the political agenda for the day; about how many speeches the Prime Minister should make, and to what kind of audience he should make them. It was also an opportunity for the Prime Minister to get to know some of the Central Office team – and for them to meet him.[3] Most of them had not been through a general election before, and nor had John Major as party leader. In 1987, as a fairly lowly Social Security Minister, he had only had a walk-on part in the national campaign. So everyone was on a steep learning curve.

Two issues in particular were trawled over at length at the Chequers meeting in June 1991. The first was what the Prime Minister would do on a 'typical' day on the campaign. From the beginning, John Major stressed that he wanted to get out and about among people as much as possible. And there had to be a real purpose to any visits he undertook: he did not want stunts or contrived photo opportunities. He did, however, agree that his programme should be tied in with the theme of the day.

In theory, this looked a good plan. Everyone in the party would be singing the same tune on the same day of the campaign. In practice, however, it revealed another problem with the themed approach. Hooking the Prime Minister's programme for each day on to a particular theme weeks, sometimes months, in advance meant that his freedom to manoeuvre at short notice would be seriously restricted. Because of the pressures of the moment, the

---

[3]The earliest draft of the Prime Minister's campaign programme contained a small, but significant, slip. At one point it referred to the Prime Minister as 'she': he had been served up with a plan originally prepared for Margaret Thatcher, and now churned off the word processor almost unamended.

day's campaign theme might have to change; but the constraints of security and planning meant that the Prime Minister's visit would have to go ahead as originally planned. As a result, there occurred situations like the one Jonathan experienced at Melton Mowbray in the second week of the campaign.

Struggling to find a decent fit between the theme of the day originally planned and the part of the country the Prime Minister was scheduled to visit, his tour manager, Shirley Stotter, had arranged for him to 'illustrate transport day' by visiting a pet-food manufacturer called Pedigree Petfoods. Why Pedigree Petfoods? Because it transported its product by rail. However, the previous night it had been decided to switch the morning press conference from transport to an attack on Labour's policies on the economy and home ownership. It was obviously too late to change the Prime Minister's programme. The visit had to go ahead. So later that morning, the Prime Minister, watched by a bemused travelling press pack, tried hard to look as if the tins of dog food being loaded on to a Charter Rail freight train were a clear symbol of economic recovery and a pungent comment on Labour's housing policy. The press, not surprisingly, started to play up:

'Hey, Tim. Why are we at Charter Rail? Today was supposed to be transport, wasn't it? You've had to change your plans, haven't you? Is the campaign collapsing?'

Tim Collins, whose job it was to handle the press corps, struggled to maintain order – and a straight face. He solemnly insisted that there had been no change whatsoever, that it had always been intended to attack Labour's economic policy on that day, and it was precisely for that reason that Pedigree Petfoods in Melton Mowbray had been hand-picked as a perfect example of the kind of business that would be hardest-hit by the economic policies of a Labour government. The fact that they were all standing in a marshalling yard had absolutely nothing to do with transport.

Themed visits have further drawbacks. Because it is only possible to cover a fairly small geographical area on one day, you will probably be pushed to find enough good illustrations of the day's chosen theme. The Prime Minister may therefore end up being sent to places because they provide a suitable photo opportunity

– rather than because they are important politically.[4] During the campaign, this had the bizarre effect of obliging John Major to spend a disproportionate amount of time in safe Labour seats, and not enough in key marginals.

Organising any prime ministerial visit – even outside an election period – is difficult enough. Members of Parliament always think there is an extremely good reason why the Prime Minister should come to their particular constituency. They expect to be consulted on the details of his programme, are mortally offended if they are not – and then profess surprise when advance notice of the visit finds its way into the local paper. During a general election, when nerves are jangling, the sensitivities are all the greater.

The second key issue debated at the June 1991 Chequers meeting was what form the Prime Minister's speeches should take. In the earliest discussions, some had argued that the traditional party rally should be dropped altogether. Instead, the Prime Minister should chat informally to smaller audiences, maybe taking some questions as well. By the time of the Chequers session, it had been accepted that it would not be possible to go into an election campaign with no rallies at all. As in previous elections, large-scale events would be needed to raise the spirits of party workers, to provide drama, and to set out campaign themes at greater length than the thirty-second sound-bite would allow. Little time was, however, spent talking about the rallies. Instead, the discussion concentrated on a meeting format first called 'In the Round', which quickly came to be known as 'Meet John Major'.

Modelled on the Prime Minister's successful meetings with the troops in the Gulf, 'Meet John Majors' were for audiences of two to three hundred, seated in a circle around the Prime Minister. They were to be deliberately folksy in feel: John Major was to be perched on a bar stool, plonked on a little circular blue and white rug. Although it was planned that the Prime Minister would make

---

[4]Everyone agreed afterwards that this was an experiment that would not be repeated. Once Jonathan got his hands on the Prime Minister's programme for the 1994 European elections, he stripped it right down. He limited it to one, or at most two photo opportunities a day, and only took the Prime Minister to places that were interesting in their own right.

some opening remarks – preferably providing sound-bites for the evening news – the main focus would be on questions and answers. The aim was to show a relaxed and confident John Major dealing in a calm and convincing way with everyday concerns – rather than the traditional political rhetoric delivered at full belt from a towering stage set.

The 'Meet John Majors' were another idea that had been brought back from the Republicans in the United States. But in transporting them across the Atlantic, two important differences were overlooked. First, George Bush's campaign could buy air-time on television to broadcast the meeting uncut, so that people had the chance to watch it develop – and need not form a judgement based on an unrepresentative half-minute excerpt. And second, Bush employed the format during the primaries, when he was seeking the support of those who were already committed members of his party, in order to win the Republican nomination. During a British general election, neither condition applied.

So how should the Prime Minister play the in-the-round game? His instinct had always been to throw them open and run them as genuinely public meetings. But there were two arguments against:

'I'm sorry, sir,' said the detective in charge of security, 'it's too risky. You could be shot.'

'It could be even worse than that,' the man from Central Office chipped in, 'you might make a mistake and be filmed on television.'

With hindsight, considering the risks to which the Prime Minister ended up exposing himself by using the soapbox, neither argument looks compelling. But at the time, they carried the day. The threat from the IRA *was* real – after all, the first discussions with the Prime Minister about the 'Meet John Majors' took place only weeks after the Downing Street mortar attack.[5] Furthermore, the wisdom at the time was that the campaign should show John Major being

[5]The terrorist threat hung over the whole campaign. On one occasion, Central Office had to be evacuated and the Prime Minister stowed away in Alastair Goodlad's house nearby in Westminster. And the terrible bomb at the Baltic Exchange the evening after polling day was a stark reminder that the IRA were still very active.

prime ministerial and authoritative, not being heckled or tripped up at a public meeting. The provisional decision was taken to go for Conservative-only audiences.

The first dress rehearsal was at Bristol in September 1991; the second, at York in January 1992. Having watched them, Jonathan felt uneasy. It was a good way of holding an internal party meeting. But was the format right for the election? If a 'Meet John Major' went well, the Prime Minister would be criticised for dodging tough questions by only speaking to Conservatives. If it went badly, the verdict would be: 'facing hostile questions even from his own supporters, John Major was left reeling today'. Jonathan therefore argued that the meetings should either be thrown totally open – or even more rigorously controlled, with the questions pre-arranged. The Prime Minister was once more tempted to go for an open meeting, but in the end the format was unchanged. Jonathan had probably left it too late in the day – and too much capital, financial[6] and political, had been invested – for the debate to be re-opened. But there was soon another reason why it was pointless to expend more energy worrying about the 'Meet John Majors'. Party rallies – the staple of so many election campaigns – were back on the agenda again in a big way.

At Chequers in June, and for the following six months, there had been no suggestion that the rallies should follow anything other than a conventional format. There was some talk about having a brass band playing 'classical hits' and asking Jeffrey Archer to act as a warm-up speaker – but that was the extent of 'new' thinking. Then, in early 1992, Andrew Lloyd Webber, who had offered to help the Conservative Party, came up with a totally fresh approach that would make a decisive impact on election plans. Drawing on the 'Meet John Majors', he came up with a set-design that put the Prime Minister on a small-ish circular stage, surrounded on all sides by banked rows of chairs. But there the similarity ended. Instead of rugs and barstools, the rally set was high-tech, state-of-the-art glitz, using videos, music, lighting, and every imaginable piece of communications wizardry. The Prime Minister saw his first

[6]The dress rehearsal at York had cost in the region of £30,000.

mock-up of the set at the New London Theatre, where Andrew Lloyd Webber's *Cats* was showing. The first draft design did not come across to Downing Street until early February, yet hardly more than a month later, the Prime Minister was using the new set for the first time at Manchester.

Adding seven rallies – one more than in 1987 – increased the pressures on the Prime Minister's day. He had said early on that he wanted to visit as many different parts of the country as possible. That raised another logistical question: how to move him and his team from A to B.

The old battlebus had been put into honourable retirement after 1987. But although some argued that it was too closely identified with Margaret Thatcher, there was in practice no better way to transport so many people and so much equipment speedily – and securely – around Britain. So the battlebus was taken out, dusted down, re-painted, fitted with a new engine and driven down to London. There, it was transformed into a mobile office. In addition to the obligatory phones and faxes, there were word-processors, printers, a disc-fax, a photocopier, an autocue printer, a television, and a scrambler for the telephone – installed in case any top secret Government business couldn't wait until the Prime Minister got back to Number 10 in the evening.

In February 1992, Jonathan and his team took it out for a trial run. All went smoothly – except for the driver's clutch control. He hadn't driven an armour-plated coach before, and it was many thousands of stomach-churning miles before he fully mastered it. The travelling team were, however, cheered by the news that, as well as the armour plating, the windows were bullet-proof. Given the constant terrorist threat, this seemed extremely reassuring, until one of the detectives told them: 'Should a bullet by any chance get into the bus while the door is open, the bullet proofing will unfortunately mean that it won't be able to exit. It will simply carry on ricocheting around inside the bus – that is, until it lodges in something, er, soft.'

The next job was to choose the bus-people – the team who would support the Prime Minister and Norma on the campaign trail. Norma was a powerful vote-winner in her own right. Day in, day out, she campaigned tirelessly with the Prime Minister as well as carrying out her own programme. By her enthusiasm as much as by hidden acts of thoughtfulness, she helped to keep the bus-party motivated and cheerful.

It was agreed that Jonathan, as Political Secretary, would be in overall charge. The second key role would be the Prime Minister's minder: traditionally a senior MP with a safe seat. John Major plumped for Sir Norman Fowler. Although Norman had supported Michael Heseltine for the leadership, Chris Patten thought he was the best man for the job and he was signed up as early as mid 1991.[7] Shirley Stotter, a tough and resourceful ex-constituency agent with an extremely sharp pair of elbows, was a natural choice for tour manager. The Prime Minister's tour briefing was to be provided by Edward Llewellyn, a member of the Conservative Research Department – who subsequently went to Hong Kong as Chris Patten's Special Adviser. As the campaign got under way, Edward performed another vital role – he used to interpose his (admittedly not very large) body between the Prime Minister and incoming eggs, so much so that he was rapidly re-named Eggward.

Tim Collins, who had been looking after the press lobby since Christmas 1994, brought his sharp political instincts to his job of handling the travelling press.[8] Also on the battlebus would be the Downing Street detectives, the man who looked after the electrics, and a succession of Garden Room Girls, one of whom has to accompany the Prime Minister at all times. Propping everyone up would be one or other of the two Political Office secretaries, Deborah de Satgé and Claire Jones, who kept everyone sane, fed and watered.

There was one other central piece of the pre-election planning jigsaw that had to be put in place: the Manifesto.

It is always supposed by journalists that the Manifesto is 'written'

[7]Sir Norman Fowler had been Secretary of State at the Department of Health and Social Security in the 1980s, when John Major was his junior Minister. He was to become Party Chairman after the general election.
[8]After the election, Tim Collins became Central Office's Director of Communications.

by one, or at most two hands – the Party Chairman and head of the Policy Unit. The truth is much more complicated. A Manifesto is a kind of treaty between the various different forces in a political party. In government, that means a treaty between Ministers. The Manifesto has to 'go to Cabinet': like official policy documents, therefore, it goes through a tortuous process of consultation and drafting, to and fro between departmental barons before finally being hammered down into a platform on which all of them can stand.

As before the 1987 election, the first step was for the Prime Minister to ask the Cabinet Minister in charge of each department to set up a policy group. Since this had to be done well in advance of the earliest likely election date, Margaret Thatcher had already asked Brian Griffiths,[9] Sarah's predecessor as head of the Policy Unit, to start the ball rolling.

The membership of these groups is always a sensitive issue. Secretaries of State are torn between wanting to bring in original ideas from outsiders and a desire to keep the whole system under tight control. The Party Chairman wants to make sure the party workers get a look in. The various Conservative backbench committees expect to have their say. Junior Ministers want to feel that they can play their part. And so on.

Jonathan's experience of policy groups, having been a member of two before the 1987 election, did not lead him to have high expectations of the contribution they could be relied upon to make. That judgement was confirmed by a warning Sarah got from Brian Griffiths. Although, by December 1990, the pre-election policy groups had already been at work for some months, he confessed that they had, in truth, produced hardly anything. The Number 10 policy cupboard was bare.

Since at that stage it was possible that the Prime Minister might need a Manifesto very quickly, he asked his Ministers (some, of course, new to their departments) to start work again straight away. Chris Patten set a deadline for the contributions from the policy

[9]He was created Lord Griffiths of Fforestfach in Margaret Thatcher's resignation honours list.

groups: the end of February 1991. In March, the Policy Unit summarised these for the Prime Minister. They were . . . patchy. In the Conservative Research Department, Andrew Lansley did his best to weave these into a document for use in an emergency. But, to be honest, he was trying to make bricks without straw.

It was clear that there was a big job of work to be done. The Prime Minister and the Party Chairman had a first canter round the Manifesto course at Chequers in March 1991, with a series of meetings with Ministers: Norman Lamont, Tony Newton, John Wakeham, Michael Heseltine, Michael Howard, Ken Clarke, and Malcolm Rifkind. They touched on tax and social security – where it was decided not to waste time on grand schemes for integrating the two, but to confine themselves to looking again at the situation of older and poorer pensioners. They reviewed energy and industry – and agreed to motor ahead with the privatisation of British Coal and British Rail, but not the Post Office. Instead, Peter Lilley would work up plans for increasing competition from other postal carriers.

Ministers had a first look at housing, but decided much more work was needed before any decisions could be taken. Home Office policies were not reviewed until rather later, and yielded less than the Prime Minister would have liked. Nor did Ministers tangle with inner city policy at this early stage in the Manifesto game. Michael Heseltine was already working on 'City Challenge' – a radical scheme under which authorities had to bid for funds on the basis of the quality of their projects.

As the June 1991 window for an election closed, so interest in the Manifesto faded and energies were channelled into the Chairman's political 'summer offensive' against Labour. All Ministers were asked to update their draft sections of the Manifesto (or write them from scratch) before the party conference at the beginning of October. The Prime Minister had been spelling out the themes of choice, opportunity, responsibility and ownership, against which Ministers' proposals were tested. The results varied. Some Ministers produced good copy. Others seemed bent on demonstrating that they could not function without the aid of their civil servants (who could not, of course, get involved).

Even the best contributions could not simply slide into a Manifesto unedited – the Prime Minister needed an editorial team. John Wakeham, John MacGregor, David Waddington and Richard Ryder were all closely involved in his early election preparations; but they were also immersed in the day-to-day management of issues, through the Number 12 Committee. So in December 1991, as the Manifesto preparations reached the final lap, the Prime Minister decided to convene another committee of 'big beasts'. Soon christened the 'A-team', its members were Douglas Hurd, Norman Lamont, Kenneth Clarke, Michael Heseltine and of course Chris Patten – who, as Party Chairman, had overall responsibility for delivering the Manifesto.

Chris had originally intended that each senior Minister would make a presentation on their Manifesto proposals to the Political Cabinet, with which almost every regular Thursday Cabinet meeting now concluded. Ken Clarke batted first at the final Cabinet before Christmas, describing his ideas for getting 'back to basics' in education. But time ran out before everybody could do their party piece. Instead, Ministers were paraded before the A-team, as their Manifesto contributions came under review.

The A-team – plus, on this occasion, the Chief Whip – met for the first time on 9 January 1992. There was just one small problem, on which warning bells sounded at that very first meeting. The group gathered at lunchtime. Sandwiches were brought to the Cabinet Room. Ministers munched their way politely through them. The following day, there was another meeting, this time to resolve policies on the countryside and housing. More sandwiches. The same sandwiches? Michael Heseltine peered at them unenthusiastically. As the weeks rolled by and the load of meetings increased, he and the Foreign Secretary – both meat and two veg men – went on strike for hot food. The final clearance of the Manifesto by the A-team, on the evening of 5 March, had to be fuelled by a three-course supper in the Small Dining Room.

Sandwiches aside, Michael Heseltine seemed particularly glad to be taking part. But then: 'I like any team, so long as I'm a member,' was his retrospective verdict. He took it as a sign that he was back on board, not just on sufferance after his challenge to

Margaret Thatcher. He was, as Chris Patten records, an enthusiastic team player – right through the election. But when it came to the Manifesto, his proposals – new development agencies, grand designs for London – tended to arouse instant suspicion in the Treasury. Finally, in early March – only a day before the A-team was to clear the final Manifesto – the Prime Minister agreed to let the Environment Secretary make a presentation in the Cabinet Room of his vision of the regeneration of London and points east. There was a ripple of unease when Canary Wharf, then very definitely in trouble, suddenly featured in the slide-show. Michael, never one to lose his nerve, stormed boldly on. But on learning that the whole of east London and part of Kent would become part of a 'hot banana' curving through Europe to Milan, some Ministers evinced signs of alarm.

Through this series of meetings, Policy Unit members – Nick True, Alan Rosling, Jonathan and Sarah – would take the minutes, and re-draft again and again according to instructions. The Policy Unit's first idea was that the Manifesto should be a relatively short document, with just a chapter on each of the four themes of choice, opportunity, responsibility and ownership. Ministers, however, were not keen, and instead the challenge became to try to stop the final version growing to Biblical lengths, as Minister after Minister insisted on just one more paragraph. Even at the final Manifesto Cabinet – on 12 March, the day after the election had been declared – some small but much-cherished initiatives were squeezed back in.

In 1987, the Manifesto had been split into two parts: one describing the past, one the future. They were published together in a natty little plastic folder. It looked good, but nobody really looked at the retrospective volume.[10] In 1992, therefore, the Chairman decided on only one volume. But for a time Central Office continued to believe there would be two versions of the Manifesto – one long, one short.

---

[10]Ammunition from the past is provided by the Conservative Research Department's *Campaign Guide*, edited by Alistair Cooke – in its careful detail, a propaganda compendium without parallel in the publications of any of the political parties.

This idea was eventually dropped. It would be hard enough to get ministerial agreement to what should and should not be in one text: to have to fight a parallel battle over the contents of another would be impossible in the time allowed. Even if it could be done, the existence of two versions would set the party up for endless arguments with the press as to what was and was not 'in the Manifesto'.

Inside Whitehall, most excitement was aroused by an issue that in the rest of the country wouldn't even blip on the radar screen of public interest. Having decided to absorb the Energy Department in the Department of Trade and Industry (with a little bit going to Environment), but keep a Department of Employment (with a little bit going to Trade and Industry), the Prime Minister could create an entirely new Whitehall empire. He decided to bring arts and libraries, sport, the media and tourism together, and give this amalgam a seat in the Cabinet. But what on earth could such a ministry be called? The A-team scratched its collective head, struggling to find a way of stringing all these different beads on a single titular string. The Ministry for Recreation? Awfully fifties. The Department for Leisure? Terribly seventies.

The Party Chairman became frivolous with impatience. 'How about: the Ministry for Things I Want to Do on my Weekends?' He sent Alan Rosling from the Policy Unit upstairs for a thesaurus. Eventually, the team settled on National Heritage, after a spirited argument as to whether sport fell under this heading.

But the A-team proved better at the christening game than Whitehall, left to its own devices. In the Manifesto, the Prime Minister announced he would give a Cabinet Minister responsibility for the Citizen's Charter. He had agreed with Robin Butler that this would be based in the Cabinet Office, which would enable him to use one of the non-departmental Ministers loosely attached to that administrative hinterland. Not until after the election did this department acquire a label: OPSS – the dreary acronym for the Office of Public Service and Science.[11]

---

[11]At least William Waldegrave, the Minister put in charge, resisted a final 'T' for Technology. 'Oh – pissed' did not quite sound the right note for the title of a government department.

Potentially the most controversial element in the Manifesto were undoubtedly the plans for privatising British Rail. These had been long and hotly debated between Ministers. At one stage, Malcolm Rifkind had wanted to publish a Green Paper on rail privatisation before the election was called, but as the wrangles continued, it became clear that this would not be possible. The Manifesto would therefore provide the first detailed statement of the Government's conclusions.

Jonathan had trudged back and forth between his old friend, Francis Maude – handling privatisation in the Treasury – and his by-now-even-older friend, Malcolm Rifkind. It was even harder to get agreement than it had been over the Channel Tunnel Rail Link. Each one of the 450 or so words that summed up the final conclusion of this classic Whitehall battle was bitterly contested by the Treasury and the Department of Transport.

The day after it was cleared by Cabinet, Sarah sent the proofs of the finished text up to the printers. She, Nick and Jonathan went home that night exhausted by the tension of the last-minute wrangles, but satisfied that they had hit their deadline. However, when the final page proofs came back, Jonathan went storming into Sarah's office.

'What the hell have you done to British Rail? Rifkind will go berserk!'

Sarah looked at him in astonishment. Then she looked at the text. Someone had changed just a word here, a phrase there, a tense, a bit of punctuation. Compromises battered out through weeks of hard pounding had been swept away at a stroke of a blue pencil. Cabinet Ministers' cherished prose, lovingly written in their own hands, had been unravelled. It soon became clear what had happened: the person from Central Office sent up to oversee the printing had taken it upon himself to do a bit of freelance editing.

Though the changes to the passage on British Rail were undoubtedly the most likely to cause ministerial explosions, there were lots of other little tweaks to a text that had been formally signed off by Cabinet. With any document, a few chances usually have to be taken, trimming this and that sentence and hoping no one will object; but this has to be done by someone who knows where the sore bits are. These changes would certainly cause a backlash. Ministers had not agreed them. The Party Chairman had not agreed them. The Prime Minister had not agreed them.

Sarah and Jonathan considered the options. Another trawl round Cabinet? Delay the Manifesto? Resignation? Suicide? Murder? All night, they crawled through the text, tweaking it back to ministerial purity. Then Alan Rosling went up to the printers with it, standing guard to prevent any further flights of fancy. The Manifesto was published on time – and problem-free. But only just.[12]

It may be that all Manifestos are dogged by such problems. When, just before the 1987 election, Jonathan was Special Adviser at the Department of Employment, he discovered that the section dealing with the Conservatives' plans for trade union reforms somehow seemed to contain Labour Party proposals. Horrified, he rang Robin Harris, the then Director of the Research Department.

'Robin, bad news, I'm afraid. You're going to have to change the Manifesto. I don't know how it has happened, but the bit on trade unions has got Labour's proposals in it.'

Robin Harris exploded.

'Of course we can't change it. Don't be ridiculous. Don't you realise it has been approved by Cabinet?'

Whether it had been or not, the changes were made. And for his pains, Jonathan was given the task of proof-reading the entire Manifesto. Now it was his turn to foul-up. When he got home that night to start work, he realised to his horror that he must have left the text in his local off-licence. Dry-mouthed, he raced back to the shop. There, in a plastic bag, propped up against the counter, was the Manifesto – the scoop that never was.

But in 1992 there was one complication the editors of the 1987 Manifesto were spared. An April election meant that the Manifesto and the Budget had to be produced in tandem. And the Budget was every bit as important as the Manifesto in a battle that would be fought on the traditional Tory ground of taxes and the economy.

---

[12]This episode was reported to have cost Central Office an extra £50,000.

11

'The Economy, Stupid'

No real English gentleman, in his secret soul, was ever sorry for the death of a political economist.
Walter Bagehot, *The First Edinburgh Reviewers*

Just after Christmas 1991, the Party Chairman took his family away for a brief holiday. Politics must have been far from Chris Patten's mind when he chose Bruges – a name which, ever since Margaret Thatcher's famous speech there in 1988, had been associated with Euro-scepticism: not his scene at all. But politics would not leave him alone. For Bruges had another disadvantage – a full supply, via satellite, of British television news. Switching on each evening, the Chairman of the Conservative Party had his darkest hours of the whole pre-election period. Bad news on the economy was followed by worse. Never before, nor afterwards, not even during the campaign itself, did he feel so doubtful that the general election could be won.

In his March Budget in 1991, the Chancellor had forecast that the economy would begin to recover during the course of the year. In the autumn of 1991, the Treasury stuck doggedly to the view that 'we are probably now past the trough', and that the economy would grow by over 2 per cent in 1992. In October, Norman Lamont told the Tory party conference that he already detected the 'green shoots of economic spring'. At the beginning of 1992, however, they still seemed to be deep in the permafrost. The economic cliché of the time was that we were 'bumping along the bottom' of an 'L-shaped recession'.

There was no gleam of that pearly-fingered economic dawn depicted, a year earlier, in the Chairman's note on the 'full term strategy'. Yet public and private opinion polls continued to show the Government comfortably ahead of Labour on the gut issue of economic management. Of the four issues that voters said they considered the most important, the economy was the only one on which the Tories were thought to have better policies than Labour. One of the great ironies of the 1990s is that the Government should have maintained a reputation for economic competence through recession, only to lose it with recovery.[1]

The polls showed that the Government's broad economic strategy attracted widespread support, not least in the City. Policies on Europe and the economy seemed consistent, mutually reinforcing, and were strongly supported by British industry and most of the media. Furthermore the Government was, by early 1992, clearly winning the fight against inflation. In double figures by the summer of 1990, it was back down below 5 per cent a year later; producer prices were down below 3 per cent by January 1992. Memories were still fresh enough for the fight to seem worthwhile. Though Norman Lamont was never forgiven for saying that unemployment was 'a price worth paying' (and the Prime Minister had some trouble with his own edict that 'If it isn't hurting, it isn't working') they were not out of tune with the mood music of the times.

The Government did also seem to have got across the message that the recovery had been delayed by the plunge into recession of Britain's major export markets. In January 1992, Gallup found that 50 per cent of voters blamed 'worldwide recession' most for the state of the economy. Moreover, it seemed that the Prime Minister had

---

[1] A brief contrast with 1995 highlights the irony. By then, Britain could look back on an *annus mirabilis*. At nearly 4 per cent, growth was well above the trend in 1994, and unemployment had been falling sharply; yet inflation was below 2.5 per cent, and mortgage rates lower than they had ever been in the 1980s. Britain's external deficit, which had topped £22 billion in 1989, was virtually in balance. Yet in 1995, the polls humiliatingly recorded that voters believed Labour would manage even the economy better than the Tories.

escaped the incumbency effect: almost all the rest put the blame on the 'Thatcher Government' rather than the 'Major Government'.

The roots of recession ran back deep into the 1980s. While Margaret Thatcher, Geoffrey Howe and Nigel Lawson argued about Europe, the economy had been left on auto-pilot. The old monetary targets were broken and discredited, the ERM forbidden, efforts to stabilise the dollar or shadow the German mark offering only a draughty, half-way house.

Anxious about the effect of the 1987 stock-market crash, over-confident of the economy's capacity to expand, the Government had given an extra boost to the economy with tax cuts. Growth had accelerated to a heady 5 per cent by 1988. Meanwhile, the housing market had become a breeding-ground for inflation. The monetarist Tim Congdon, one of the earliest to sound the alarm at the time, summed it up in 1995:

> The Lawson boom was due, above all, to an overheated housing market, which stimulated excessive mortgage credit and so led to extraordinarily rapid rates of monetary growth.

House prices more than doubled between 1983 and 1989, rising by 23 per cent in 1988 alone. By the autumn of 1989, bank base rates had had to be raised to 15 per cent. The squeeze was painful. The housing market was suffering an agonising cure. House prices went into reverse – at a time when general inflation was as high as 10 per cent – making the 'real' fall in property values even greater. Those of 'Thatcher's children' who had bought in the boom years were struggling to come to terms with the burden of a debt which now sometimes exceeded the total value of the property they had bought, and would go on doing so. The bleak phrase 'negative equity' made its appearance in the jargon of political analysis.

There were not many signs of voter joy elsewhere in the economy. Overall, retail sales fell only 1 per cent in 1991. But superstores and out-of-town shopping centres were taking a bigger share of the cake, and the high streets of south-east England displayed rows of boarded-up shops and bankrupt businesses. The car market was dead. Registrations had dropped 20 per cent that year. The forces of recession had also begun to work their way through to unemployment, always their final and grimmest port of call along the economic cycle. The dole queue began to lengthen in 1990; by early 1992, unemployment had risen by a million, and in the one month alone of January 1992, it jumped by nearly 56,000.

So the impression was of an even worse recession than in the early 1980s. In fact, what was happening was that the economy was adjusting to the squeeze much more quickly – and this meant, in the end, a shallower recession. Britain's output fell just over 2.75 per cent between 1990 and 1992, compared with a 4 per cent drop from 1979 to 1981. And unemployment began to fall again much earlier in the subsequent recovery than it had in the 1980s.

But the voter could hardly be expected to be grateful for suffering less pain than the last time boom turned into bust. And indeed, many Tory voters were suffering more – if the recession was less painful in manufacturing, it was more painful in the services sector. Manufacturing production fell only half as much in the early 1990s recession as in the early 1980s – and in the long run, a stronger manufacturing sector was very good news for the economy. But the services sector, concentrated in the south-east of England, was hit hard. It was also suffering from the introduction of the Uniform Business Rate, which was based on a revaluation of commercial property and led to steep rises in tax for small retail businesses in the south-east. In London, the unemployment rate doubled, to 10 per cent, between early 1990 and early 1992.

This was, so the story goes, the 'middle class recession'. In fact, unemployment was still far more severe among the unskilled and semi-skilled than in the professions and managerial classes. But the shake-out in services, combined with the collapse in house prices, undoubtedly hurt the Conservative heartlands of southern England.

Even in early 1992, therefore, the Government did not lack critics. The Chancellor was attracting a lot of flak, even from Conservatives, according to Central Office. Half the party complained he sounded too gloomy; the other half that he angered people by sounding too optimistic. At the same time, a number of monetarist economists, who believed that the Government should focus on the growth of the money supply, not the exchange rate, kept the ERM under constant fire. They argued that the Government should be cutting interest rates faster, and that only the effort to defend the pound's ERM position was preventing them from doing so.

Bank base rates had been reduced to 10.5 per cent in early September 1991, but that looked like being the last cut before the election (as, indeed, it proved to be). The Prime Minister was not happy about this. If interest rates had to be kept high to kill off inflation, well and good. If Britain was killing off recovery by keeping interest rates high simply to prop up the pound, that was another matter.

The two 'ifs' were not, of course, easy to separate. Membership of the ERM had clearly helped the Government bring both inflation and interest rates down, because it had restored the credibility of British policy. To let the pound slide now would be to throw that gain away, at a dangerous point in the cycle, and before inflation had been brought as low as the Government wished.

However, there might be a way forward – though not one that could ever be discussed openly for fear of precipitating an exchange rate crisis. The ERM did allow for realignments – changes in the exchange rate within the overall system. So in the autumn of 1991, the Prime Minister asked Sarah – very privately – to do him a paper on ways in which the pound might be allowed to settle at a lower rate without leaving the ERM. This just might give the Government a chance to cut interest rates without causing a crisis.

With a central rate against the mark fixed at DM2.95 and 6 per cent margins either side, sterling's 'floor' in the ERM was just under DM2.78 and its ceiling just under DM3.13. Sarah's note worked through four options for realignment, based on principles Nigel Lawson had set out at the International Monetary Fund in 1987.[2] The lowest of the options in her note suggested a new

[2]The key point, Nigel Lawson argued, was that the new range must overlap with the old, to such an extent that the new mid-point is still at or above the old floor. That way, you avoid giving speculators a one-way bet. If they sell sterling right at the floor, they take a risk that after a realignment they may have to buy it back at a higher price.

central rate at DM2.78, with the range stretching down below that to DM2.61. This would have lowered the central rate by 6 per cent, and created a new floor 11.5 per cent lower than the existing central rate.

On reflection, the Prime Minister decided not to raise these options with the Chancellor. There were a number of reasons for this. First, the Treasury was still relatively optimistic that economic recovery would begin soon, without any change in policy. Second, the Bank of England was still concerned about inflation, making it reluctant to cut interest rates anyway. Third, the pound was still trading fairly comfortably within its existing range, averaging DM2.89 in the final three months of 1991. So the Prime Minister put the idea aside, and robustly supported existing policy by ruling out realignment whenever he was questioned about it. There was no debate in Cabinet on the value of membership of the ERM – and as late as January 1992, a Gallup poll indicated that membership had the support of 80 per cent of Tory MPs.

The moment passed. By the end of 1991, the election was too close for any Government to contemplate a realignment. Though the pound was a little weaker in early 1992, it was difficult to disentangle underlying pressure from pre-election jitters. Readings on the 'real economy' were also confused by the election effect. And indeed, both the pound and consumer confidence did rebound after a Tory victory.

There were worries that the pound might come under more severe pressure during the actual election campaign. Pessimists had argued that if speculators sold sterling on the threat of a Labour victory, this would force the Government to dig its own grave. To protect its ERM position, it might have to raise interest rates at positively the worst political moment. In practice, however, the bluff worked the other way. John Smith was desperate to demonstrate financial responsibility, so he had to commit himself publicly to maintaining the pound's position in the ERM. The City, by and large, believed him. So, though the pound occasionally weakened a little on polls showing a strong Labour lead, the alarm bells never sounded.

The Chancellor, meanwhile, had decided to tackle the troubles in the housing market not by cutting interest rates but by trying to cut repossessions directly. Although fewer than 1 per cent of mortgage-holders had their homes repossessed in 1991, 1 per cent of 10 million households amounted to a lot of trouble. Mark Boleat of the Council of Mortgage Lenders (CML) was thought of as a sensible fellow, not prone to panic, so when he sent up alarm signals, the Government listened. And on 19 December, Norman Lamont announced a package of measures to help those whose homes had been repossessed and to try to perk up the housing market.

The most important measure cost nothing. The CML had complained that some claimants were diverting the money given specifically for mortgage payments to meet other bills. In future, the Chancellor announced, income support for mortgage payments would be paid direct to the lenders. He also tried to give the housing market a boost by announcing a 'holiday' from stamp duty on houses costing less than £250,000, bought before August 1992. In return, mortgage lenders committed themselves to providing up to £1 billion of their own money to help keep people having difficulty with their mortgages in their own homes as tenants.

This package did not win many plaudits. The Government was accused of sharp practice in claiming a '£1.5 billion package', when two-thirds of this was coming – at least Ministers hoped it was coming – from mortgage lenders themselves. Looked at from the Chancellor's viewpoint, however, this amounted to an effective bit of leverage: a big bang for a modest Treasury buck. But the real problem with this package was that it increased the Government's deficit again, only six weeks after the Autumn Statement, the Chancellor's annual announcement of the Government's spending plans. This had not passed altogether quietly. Although the markets took the figures pretty well, there had been some raised eyebrows in the City at the size of the increase in public spending.

So the Government ended 1991 with very little room for manoeuvre. The political and economic cycles were clearly out of kilter. The Party Chairman was not alone in worrying that economic opinion polls might also turn sour.

In political folklore, three economic indicators were considered crucial to voting intentions. First, the mortgage rate. Second, the various opinion poll indicators of 'consumer confidence' – the 'feel-good factor'. Third, 'real personal disposable income', which means the amount of money in people's pockets, after inflation and the taxman have both taken their toll. A number of City firms had dedicated highly-paid manpower to modelling the effects of one or more of these factors. When the London Business School[3] published a noted analysis of the links between economic and political fortunes, it concentrated almost exclusively on mortgages.

Although interest rates had got stuck at 10.5 per cent, they had by then fallen 4.5 points from their peak in 1990, before Britain joined the ERM. So mortgage payments had come down by over £70 a month for an average mortgage. For the increasing number of home-owners on annual payment systems, part of this change would not come through until January to April of 1992 – nicely timed for a spring election.

All the same, this was a pretty frail basis for an election intended to be fought on the issue of economic competence. For mortgage rates were still in double figures. And consumer confidence, the second of the three conventional economic indicators of electoral performance, was still dismally low. That left only the third of those three – disposable income, or take-home pay – on which to rest electoral hopes.

There was a chink of light here. Prices had been slowing down more than wages, which made people's pay-packets worth more. This effect, however, was blunted by recession, which was still putting people out of work.

The election strategy therefore had to depend on persuading voters to look forward: to convince them that the Tories offered a better chance of future income, a better prospect of higher living standards than Labour. In doing that, two arguments were

[3]The London Business School Centre for Economic Forecasting had a high public profile – not least because it had produced both the present Chief Economic Adviser (Alan Budd) and his predecessor (Terry Burns, who by 1992 had become Permanent Secretary to the Treasury).

important: one, that economic recovery would be stronger with a Tory government; and two, that taxes would be higher with a Labour one.

Up to and right through the campaign, the Government hammered home its message: 'Vote for recovery – not for the start of a new recession.' Independent surveys of business opinion supported this view of Tory and Labour policies. On 18 March, for example, a MORI survey of businessmen indicated that 90 per cent of them thought a Conservative win would be very or fairly good for the economy, while only 6 per cent thought a Labour victory would be.

However, the tax message was – as ever – going to be far more powerful than views on general economic prospects. The obvious, traditional way to deliver this message was to cut personal taxes. But the Government had very little in the kitty. It could not afford a big pre-election tax-cutting Budget.

So why wait? If the Budget was going to be a damp squib, why not go for an early election? Back in early December, Sarah had done the Prime Minister a note on the various complications of election timing. The first practical date in 1992 was 23 January. But to make that, the Prime Minister would either have to blight Christmas with a long campaign – or recall Parliament on 27 December in order to fire the starting gun, which would look a bit panicky.

So effectively, the first date was 30 January. 6 February was also possible; 13 February would look a bit odd as a choice, because it was only three days before a new electoral register was due to come into force. The following three Thursdays would involve starting the campaign on one register and finishing on another, which constituency associations would not like.

After 5 March, however, the Prime Minister would run into Council Tax problems. The parliamentary experts had told Number 10 that with an election on or before 5 March, there would be sufficient time after it to get the Council Tax Bill through Parliament by the end of May. This was the deadline by which local authorities had to have legal authority to start setting up new systems, if they were to be ready to raise the new tax in 1993.

However, if the Prime Minister waited until after 5 March, he would have to get the Bill passed before the election – or kiss goodbye to a new tax system in 1993. The earliest date possible on this scenario was 2 April. But if he waited that long, the Prime Minister could hardly avoid having a Budget. If he did not, he would be accused of 'hiding the figures'. If, on the other hand, he allowed the Treasury to follow its normal Budget timetable, with a Budget in the second half of March, the earliest practical date for a general election would be local election day, 7 May. There were plenty of possible dates after that; the election need not take place for a further two months.

Norman Lamont continued to argue that the Prime Minister should wait for recovery – all the way to June, or even July – before calling a last-minute election. In strict logic, he had a point. The longer the Government waited, the closer the campaign would be to that turning point in the economy, which did indeed come in midsummer. But there were two difficulties with the Chancellor's argument. First, on current poll showings, the Conservatives could expect to do badly in the local government elections in May. A poor performance then would rattle MPs and party workers and get the general election campaign off to the worst possible start. Second, the recovery would not come in sufficient time or strength to affect how people felt about the economy even if the latest possible date were chosen – and in the meantime, confidence might continue to drain away, weakening the Government's position.

Ironically, however, the Chancellor's view may actually have helped the Prime Minister. It found its way into the newspapers, widening the range of dates the Government was thought to be considering. When the Prime Minister announced that there would be an election on 9 April, there was a useful element of surprise. The decision was described by *The Times*, for example, as 'curiously bold'.[4]

It certainly involved some fairly hideous internal complications.

---

[4]As well as all the good political reasons for choosing 9 April, John Major has his own personal fondness for the date. It was the anniversary of the day he had met his wife.

The Prime Minister had had to persuade the Chancellor to bring the Budget forward from 17 March – the natural date, because by then all the background economic data would be available – to 10 March. The Budget would then have to be co-ordinated with the Manifesto.

The Cabinet would not see the Budget until the morning of 10 March; no trace of its content could appear in Manifesto copy circulated around Whitehall or sent to the printers before that date. But if the Manifesto was going to be launched the following week, the final proofs would have to be cleared by Cabinet on 12 March.

The Budget is a piece of domestic policy whose security is still taken very seriously. A 'Budget list' is compiled, of people who may see the figures and tax proposals. Papers circulate in special orange folders containing numbered copies overprinted with warnings. This fuss has some real sense to it, in that foreknowledge of tax changes is a highly valuable commodity. It is, however, often over-done. Every year there is some last-minute trouble when it is discovered that a Minister whose policy area is affected, or the one official who really understands the practical issues, has not been consulted.

One other traditional security practice has, however, now fallen out of fashion – Budget 'purdah'. Those on the Budget list are supposed to steer well clear of any journalistic contamination in the weeks before it is published. By the early 1990s, purdah had developed its own traditions – notably a mid-day snooker school amongst senior Treasury officials, who would normally have been lunching their way around the financial pages of the national newspapers.

These features of purdah had little effect on anything (except perhaps a few bureaucratic waistlines). But the parallel ministerial habit of steering clear of interviews in the pre-Budget period caused an immense amount of angst in 1992. How, the Party Chairman would demand, could the Tories fight an economic war with Labour if the Chancellor was going to stay off the field? Eventually he persuaded Norman Lamont to break with convention, and there-after the Chancellor attacked tenaciously on tax. David Mellor got on the airwaves too. The 'purdah' habit was to depart with Norman Lamont, since no fuddy-duddy tradition was ever going to keep Ken Clarke quiet.

The other essential exercise in co-ordination was to get the Manifesto costed alongside the Budget. Norman Lamont was reluctant to talk about the Manifesto until his Budget was concluded – from his point of view, that was understandable, since the main Manifesto meetings, at the beginning of January, were due to take place before his meetings with officials on the Budget position. But from the Party Chairman's point of view, it was frustrating. The situation was complicated by the fact that Treasury officials could work on the Budget, but not the Manifesto. Only the Chancellor could give the Prime Minister an overview of the two.

The Prime Minister took the view that the Chancellor should announce whatever he wanted to in the Budget; John Major would not deliberately keep back 'goodies' to announce himself in the Manifesto. For several weeks, policies hopped back and forth between the Manifesto and the Budget, as the Chancellor kept his options open. The two most important moveables were the package of help for pensioners, which it had been decided to give to those on income support, rather than spread amongst all older pensioners – and the lottery.

The Treasury had never been keen on a lottery. Officials disliked the idea that a big new revenue-raiser would yield funds for special causes, rather than mainstream public programmes; and they were anxious about the effect on revenue from football pools, which went straight into public coffers. The Chancellor did not, however, share this institutional view. Would he be the one to launch the national lottery?

In the end, not wanting to distract attention from his tax changes, he decided against announcing it in the Budget. Instead, it was launched by Kenneth Baker, the Home Secretary, in an officially-drafted White Paper published before the election was called, with the idea of establishing a Millennium Commission held back for the Manifesto. The Chancellor did, however, decide to announce a package of measures to help poorer pensioners, originally proposed for the Manifesto.

The costings provided by the Treasury advisers suggested that all the new Manifesto commitments put together added up to under £600 million – and over half of this was accounted for by the poorer pensioners package. Of the rest, the biggest cost – estimated at the time at £100m – was for inner cities; and that was only for later years of the Parliament. Debates between Ministers about childcare and nursery education ended with a commitment to spend a mere £30 million supporting after-school care – and that was to be spread over three years. The Government therefore had no difficulty in saying that a net £250 million or so of new commitments could be met out of existing spending plans.

By contrast, the full-year cost of Budget measures, over and above the poorer pensioners package, was £2.1 billion in 1992-93, and £2.6 billion the following year. But then that included something central to the Government's strategy – an announcement that was far more important than anything left for the Manifesto and played a key part in the Tories' economic battle. Norman Lamont utterly wrong-footed Labour by introducing an income tax rate of 20 pence in the pound.

The goal of a 20 pence basic rate of income tax had been Tory policy since the mid-1980s. But 1992 was not a year in which the Government could do anything expensive. To bring the basic rate down by only 1p, to 24p, would hardly strike a ringing note, but would surely raise questions about when the next reduction would come. The alternative was to bring as large a slice of earnings as possible into a new, lower band. The Chancellor took some time to make up his mind which way to jump. Finally, to the Prime Minister's satisfaction, he suggested cutting the tax on the first £2,000 of people's taxable income to 20 pence, at a stroke.

This had a number of advantages. First, it concentrated help at the bottom of the income scale. Every taxpayer would benefit, but the better-off would gain no more than poorer taxpayers. Second, it reduced the 'poverty trap', in which a number of poorer families found themselves simultaneously losing means-tested benefits and paying a 25 pence basic rate of tax as their income rose, so that they gained little from earning more. Third, it established a much more flexible way of making progress towards the goal of a 20 pence basic tax rate. While the Government could only take something off the basic rate at a minimum cost of over £2 billion, it could widen the 20p band as much or as little as it liked, at a cost of only about £80m for each £100 of people's income exempted from the higher 25 pence rate. So, in answer to questions about when the Government would make further progress towards 20 pence, the Prime Minister could say that it would come 'a bit at a time'.

Apart from the poorer pensioners package, which passed almost unnoticed, there were only two other big ticket items in the Budget. First, the painful effect on business rates of the revaluation of commercial properties was alleviated, at a cost of nearly half a billion pounds. Second, the Chancellor halved the tax on new cars, from 10 per cent to 5 per cent of their price. This cost over £600 million, which he recouped through higher tobacco, petrol and vehicle excise duties. But neither of these measures attracted a great deal of attention. It was the 20 pence tax band that hit the headlines.

The press gave the Budget a generous send-off. 'A Mint If You're Skint', said the *Sun* perkily. *The Times* congratulated Norman Lamont on his 'ingenious' Budget, displaying 'remarkable dexterity' – and contrasted the Government's 20 pence tax objective with the implications of Labour policies, which they considered to be a basic rate of 30 pence in the pound.

The Tories, meanwhile, were claiming that the Labour Party would cost voters a lot more than that. At this point the Opposition made their strategic error: attempting to close down the tax story by publishing their own 'Shadow Budget'.

Every effort was taken to make the Shadow Budget look responsible and governmental. The Shadow Chancellor had himself filmed outside the Treasury. The document was printed between red covers, and titled in the same typeface as the genuine Budget. This caused the press to suffer from a bout of schizophrenia. Hungry for show, they applauded the Shadow Budget as a brilliant campaign initiative. Alarmed by the tax proposals, they booed Labour's policies as an assault on hard work and skills. Commentators seemed to find it difficult to draw these threads together, and realise that the only effect of all this show of statesmanship was to make the tax increases proposed in the Shadow Budget seem more real – and hence more threatening. They lost sight of the fact that the Shadow Budget offended against the most basic principle of campaigning: raising the 'salience' of one of Labour's weakest issues. It could hardly have done more damage if Neil Kinnock had had himself filmed leading a CND march.

The Economist, for example, praised the Shadow Budget as a *'coup de théâtre'*, showing John Smith as the 'unflappable Chancellor in waiting'. Three pages later, it condemned the Shadow Budget for promising to make Britain's tax regime 'one of the most severe in the world', adding that its underlying economic philosophy was 'not just flawed, it is dangerous'.

In *The Times*, Anatole Kaletsky – not one to flinch from criticising the Tory Government – said that after a Labour victory 'the pips will squeak much louder . . . than they ever did in the days of Arthur Scargill and Tony Benn'. The *Independent* said that 'the housing crisis would be given a savage new twist' and 'the recession will be intensified'.

The net effect of the Shadow Budget was said to be increased expenditure of £1.9 billion in 1992–93, to pay for Labour's recovery package. But the tax increase needed to pay for the proposed hike in pensions and a cut at the bottom of the national insurance system was rather larger. It included some sharp bites at the better off – not just a top tax rate of 50 pence, but the abolition of the ceiling on national insurance. This would hit skilled workers and the professions hard.

This Shadow Budget had another ill-effect for Labour. To make the sums add up, John Smith had committed his party to voting against the new 20 pence income tax band. From the very beginning of the election campaign, therefore, the party was branded as opposing tax cuts as well as threatening tax increases – with the further political embarrassment that the cuts they were opposing were targeted at the lower-paid. As Michael Heseltine put it, this was 'the electoral equivalent of the Charge of the Light Brigade'.

But it did make some complications for the Tory campaign. For a while it was uncertain what the target was: Labour's Shadow Budget, in which the party admitted to planning tax increases for the higher-paid; or Labour's spending pledges, which had been added up in the Tory costings exercise, and translated into a threat of much larger and more general tax increases. In the 'bombshell' campaign, the two Labour tax threats were finally brought together.

In revising their calculations, the Tories had raised their estimate of the cost of Labour's promises from £35 billion to £38 billion. Under questioning on the Shadow Budget, Labour had effectively ruled out all substantial sources of revenue except basic income tax. To raise this money, Norman Lamont's advisers calculated that – over and above the Shadow Budget increases – Labour would have to put income taxes up by 12.5 pence in the pound. The total cost to the average taxpayer was put at £1,250 a year.

Labour politicians did not make much of an attempt to dispute the individual cost estimates. But they did complain about the aggregation, arguing that their spending programmes had not been given a fixed time-scale. However, even here they ran into difficulties. Their own literature lacked the vital get-out clause: 'when resources allow'. And in the BBC's *Election Call* programme on 24 March, Robin Cook stated unequivocally that, 'All our commitments in our Manifesto are intended to take place over the lifetime of a Parliament.'

The Tory campaign took some time to find its range, but gradually the artillery began to score hits. Press conferences were brightened up by graphics and videos. John Maples, a junior Treasury Minister who was good at presenting, was drafted in to help. Step by step, he worked through the bills for all sorts of different people: a nurse on inner London rates (£2,010 extra), a middle manager (£3,361), a crane driver (£960). Neatest of all, perhaps, were the calculations for the average reader of each newspaper, from the *Daily Mirror* (£678) to the *Financial Times* (£3,153).

Tax 'bombshell' posters appeared around the country, bearing the figures. And the message seemed to be getting through. Francis Maude's experience was typical. An irate voter in his constituency, answering the doorbell, treated the candidate to a torrent of abuse.

The Tory campaign was 'useless'. Labour was 'running away with it'. He could tell Francis how to fight the campaign. Why, said this voter, don't you just tell people it'll cost them over £1,000 to vote Labour? That, said Francis Maude, was the moment at which he believed the Tories should win – at least in less marginal constituencies than his own.

Saatchi's steamed on. The tax 'whammy' became the 'double whammy' of the impact of Labour policies on both taxes and prices; then the implications for mortgage rates of all this extra pressure on public finances were milked as well. The rhetoric mounted. 'Dogs bark, cats miaow, Labour puts up taxes,' intoned Chris. 'Hezza' leapt into the farmyard too:

> A vote for Labour, a vote for the Liberals, is a vote for tax increases. It's turkeys voting for Christmas, it's lambs voting for the big slaughter, it's lemmings voting for the big drop.

The Prime Minister, meanwhile, was bearing the brunt of the questioning about the Government's own tax plans. He was much more cautious than is generally supposed. More than once, he was reported as having made a 'gaffe' in refusing to rule out an increase in taxation. This sprang from what can now be seen to have been one of the greatest ironies of the morning press conferences during the campaign. Day after day, under the television lights in the bowels of Central Office, Tony Bevins, perhaps the most persistent of all lobby correspondents, would bombard the Prime Minister with different versions of the same question. How could he claim to be the leader of a tax-cutting party, when the Treasury's forecasts said that taxes would be taking a bigger share of our national income in the next Parliament?

Tony Bevins had a point. The Budget Red Book did, after all, show the tax take going up from just under 36 per cent in 1992-93 to 38 per cent in 1996-97. Day after day, the Prime Minister would seek to explain. Economic growth automatically puts up the tax take: as more people become taxpayers – and more of them higher-rate taxpayers – and more companies make profits on which they have to pay tax, so taxation rises faster than national income. So what Tony considered a mark of failure would actually be a mark of success.

The irony is that both the Prime Minister and Tony Bevins turned out to be wrong. Instead of rising, the tax share of national income actually fell. By 1994-95, it was down to 34 per cent, depleted by recession and the scaling down of Inland Revenue estimates of the yield from various corners of the tax system. On Tony Bevins's score, that made the Tories a successful tax-cutting party: people were keeping a bigger share of their incomes – a substantially bigger share than the Government had forecast. Success? Well, not exactly. Less tax had meant a bigger deficit – so the Government had had to change the tax structure to claw the money back again.

On VAT, most questioning was focused on the rate. This was natural, since the Government had only just raised it to 17.5 per cent in the 1991 Budget. (Norman Lamont appeared as 'Vatman' on Labour election posters.) The Prime Minister was not subjected to detailed forensic cross-examination on the exemptions (such as the zero rate on domestic fuel), though at a press conference on 27 March he did say that the Government 'had no plans and no need' to extend the scope of VAT; and the Conservative Research Department's *Campaign Guide* gave the same reassurance.

So far as other taxes were concerned, John Major was most forthcoming on the 20 pence income tax band:

> This is the way we mean to go on – taking more and more taxpayers out of twenty-five pence tax by widening the band. This way we can make progress, year by year, towards a twenty pence basic rate for all.

Even here, however, he added that, 'I cannot give a categorical promise that we would be able to do it each and every year.' In fact, even through the darkest tax-raising days of 1993-94, the Government did manage to widen the 20 pence band.

The Manifesto pledged the Government to making progress on the 20 pence band, on Inheritance Tax and business taxes, and in general 'to continue to reduce taxes as fast as we prudently can'. It gave no pledges on timing; nor, indeed, on the scope of VAT. It did contain a pledge to reduce public spending as a share of national income. And, indeed, public spending's share did peak in 1992.

But the question that has to be answered is: could Ministers – should Ministers – have known and said more?

The estimates of the Government's deficit published before the election had been increased sharply since 1990. The year 1993-94 was expected to be the peak – as indeed, it turned out to be. In 1990, it was supposed that the Government would not need to borrow any money in that year. But by the spring of 1991, this forecast for 1993-94 had been raised to £8 billion; by the autumn, to £22 billion; then, in the 1992 Budget, to over £32 billion. However, the final outcome was higher still – £46 billion, even after tax increases. So what happened?

The Treasury's figures suggest that only about a fifth of the increase since 1990 could be accounted for by specific decisions to increase public spending – most of which were taken and announced, by both Margaret Thatcher's Government and John Major's, before the election. Tax decisions announced in the two Budgets of 1991 and 1992 roughly cancelled each other out, in that the first increased VAT revenue by just over £2 billion a year, while the second cut the yield from income tax by not quite as much.

Three other factors really did the damage. First, and most obviously, the recession lasted longer than expected. Second, spending simply kept on rising faster than forecast, as more and more people applied for benefits. John Major inherited an endemic failure to get to grips with the fearful momentum of so-called 'demand-led' programmes: those where the Government offers money to all who fulfil certain criteria, whether for higher education, legal aid or social security benefits. One of the tougher post '92 tasks was to bring all three of these budgets under some kind of cash control.

Third, and least obviously, the yield from taxes fell well short of officials' estimates – not just because of the recession, but because of a more fundamental problem. Following the changes begun in the mid-1980s, in corporate taxation in particular, forecasting proved unexpectedly difficult. The extent of this shortfall, which accounted for up to a tenth of the total £46 billion deficit, only became apparent in early 1993.[5]

No one can pretend that either what the Manifesto stated, or what the Prime Minister and the Chancellor said in the campaign, prepared people for the two tax-raising Budgets of 1993. But in the light of persistent Labour complaints that the Government 'knew' there would have to be tax increases after the election, two points are perhaps worth making.

First, the extent of the tax shortfall, the momentum of demand-led spending, and the greater weakness of the economy were all features that better forecasting would no doubt have identified. But these were not known facts; they came as nasty surprises to John Major and Norman Lamont more than anyone. Indeed, the estimates of the size of the deficit that were published before the election were very much in line with independent forecasts.

Second, these are not features on which the Labour Party can rest their claim to have been 'more honest' about taxes in the 1992 election. For the tax increases stipulated in John Smith's Shadow Budget were all earmarked for specific extra increases in public spending – for pensions or health – over and above what was being spent anyway. Given that Labour were relying on the same forecasts, they would have had the same deficit increases to deal with. Of course, the 1993 Budgets damaged the Government's reputation for tax-cutting, and left voters feeling bitter about its election campaign. But had Labour won the election, they would either have had to renege on their spending promises – or put taxes up even more than the Tories.

---

[5]When, in early 1993, the Prime Minister received the latest Treasury forecast on which Norman Lamont's 1993 Budget would be based, he was astonished. He found that the borrowing forecast for 1993-94 had leapt by over £7 billion in only two months – despite the fact that the economic forecasts had barely changed – simply because of 're-estimates' by the taxmen.

12

They're Off

*My centre is giving way, my right is in retreat; situation excellent.
I shall attack.*

Marshal Foch, message sent during the
second Battle of the Marne, 1918

Wednesday 11 March did not start well. Labour were three points ahead in the opinion polls published that morning. Nevertheless, a few hours later the Prime Minister walked out of Number 10 into Downing Street to speak to the assembled press. He told them that he had just got back from the Palace, where the Queen had agreed that Parliament should be dissolved. Polling day, he announced, would be Thursday 9 April. The starting gun for the 1992 general election had been fired.

As its impact ricocheted around Whitehall, so the official machine started to melt away. The whole civil service life support system which had sustained the Prime Minister was, at a flick, turned off – very clinically, very professionally, but very firmly. The great government press machine, which only the day before had been churning out its usual mammoth briefing on the Budget, fell silent. Now it would become clear which Ministers had remained politicians, and which had become robots programmed by their departments.

The leap from Whitehall baron to political animal is a big one, which gets harder to cross the longer Ministers are in office. Between elections, the system militates against active party politics.

All the Rolls-Royce services of a department – speech-making, press releasing, briefing – are at the disposal of Ministers, provided they are not used for overt attack on the Opposition, which the politicians and their political advisers must add for themselves. As elections approach, Whitehall rightly becomes even more sensitive to this convention. So, ironically, it becomes more difficult for Ministers to rediscover the ancient arts of party politics at the very time they need them most.

Then – suddenly – party politics are all there is. No speech drafts. No Cabinet papers. No Private Office. Only the most necessary Red Boxes for the most necessary Ministers. Though they continue in office, and on the state payroll, the business of government shrivels to a core of unavoidable decisions or meetings.

At Number 10, the best civil servants behaved with great personal decency, but for most of them the Prime Minister was now someone else's problem. If, against the odds, he should win, they would be warm in their congratulations. But if, as seemed more likely, he should lose, well, it would be an interesting intellectual challenge to work for a Labour administration again. To those who had been appointed from outside the system, and whose allegiance to the Prime Minister was personal or political, such apparent indifference was sometimes difficult to understand – but it is a necessary part of maintaining a civil service built on the principle of impartiality.

From that moment, Sarah, Jonathan – who was officially appointed as Political Secretary the same morning – and his tiny team in the political back offices of Number 10 had to fill the hole. In theory, they could simply replace the Whitehall support system with well-oiled Central Office machinery. But when they tried to change gear, it coughed and spluttered, the victim of too many years of neglect. Central Office always has a difficult task when the party is in power: it is ignored for four years, and then is expected to perform miracles in the last six months before polling day.

By 1992, it was thirteen long years since the party machine had last known the hunger and discipline of Opposition. Chris Patten, out of the old Research Department stable himself, was appalled to find the place split into little empires, sometimes more concerned with internal turf battles than with the Labour Party. There were still many unsung heroes and heroines with a great deal of experience. But Central Office did also have its fair share of time-servers and political novices. And it certainly suffered from the handicap of having a new Prime Minister with whom very few of them had worked. That, of course, was about to change.

Over at Number 10, the heart of the operation was the small Political Office team. Before every election, someone suggests that everybody concerned with the campaign should be brought under one roof – namely Central Office – to streamline communications and lines of command. In Opposition this works, but not in government. The Prime Minister's base remains at Number 10. It is where he returns at the end of a long campaigning day. And it is where he needs to find his team, at his beck and call when he gets back. Moreover, for John Major, the Special Advisers on his staff remained his link with the official machine, and could not simply transfer to Central Office.

Nick True had the daunting task of producing seven major rally speeches in four weeks, some of them only forty-eight hours apart. Ronnie Millar put on the greasepaint and came in to help out and phrase-monger. With Ronnie sitting opposite him across the desk, Nick would sit at his laptop computer, tapping out line after line, racking his brains to come up with fresh ways of saying the same old things. When a draft was ready, it would be disc-faxed through to the battlebus, where Jonathan would be waiting to scoop pages off the floor as they spilled from the printer. As the bus swayed sickeningly along winding country lanes, he would then have to carry out the delicate task of arbitrating between the various authors. Back in the bunker, Nick True would be trying to prevent his cherished phrases from being mangled and the rhythm of the speech destroyed. Norman Fowler would be making helpful suggestions of his own: 'I think you'll find that if you change that semi-colon to a colon, it will make all the difference.' And the Prime Minister himself would stamp on some of Nick or Ronnie's prize blooms of oratory: 'No, I couldn't possibly say that. I do not want to attack Mr Kinnock.'

The other key person who joined John Major's team was Stephen

Sherbourne, Margaret Thatcher's Political Secretary from 1983 to 1987. Stephen had also run Ted Heath's Private Office when he was Leader of the Opposition, so had long – and varied – experience on which to draw. He quickly got to grips with the Prime Minister's media schedule, which had fallen into a Central Office black hole. Bids for interviews had gone unanswered. There were no records of agreements that television companies were certain had been made. Dates, times and venues had never been confirmed. One evening, Stephen turned on his television to see that the Prime Minister was being billed to appear on a particular programme on a certain date, when he had no idea that a bid had been submitted, let alone accepted. As Stephen searched desperately through the Central Office files, he realised that he would have to construct the whole media programme from scratch.

He turned for help to Shana Hole, the Chief Whip's Special Adviser who, along with Lord Fraser,[1] had been asked to set up an office for the Prime Minister in Smith Square. She quickly got stuck in and sorted out the logistics.

But she experienced a different sort of communication problem on her first evening at Smith Square on the Sunday after the campaign was launched. She was unpacking office equipment when Shirley Oxenbury, who ran the Chairman's office (and has done so for successive Chairmen since 1970), came in.

'I've had a message from security on the front desk to say that there is a large freezer for you down in reception,' she announced.

'What on earth would I want with a large freezer?' asked Shana, nonplussed.

Then the penny dropped. It wasn't a fridge down in reception, but Lord Fraser, whose name had been deliciously mangled by the security guard. The name, which suited him, stuck; for the rest of the campaign he was known as the 'Large Freezer', or sometimes the 'Big Fridge'.

The final member of the Downing Street team was Dermot

[1] As Peter Fraser, he had been a Member of Parliament until 1987. He was another member of the Blue Chips.

Gleeson, another veteran from the old Conservative Research Department stable. Dermot had initially come in to give Nick True moral support, but he was soon helping out on a wider front, in particular with newspaper articles. Election campaigns generate a huge demand for articles by party leaders (or, more accurately, for articles that go out in their name – the party leaders themselves obviously do not have the time to sit down each evening and dash off a dozen pieces) from national and regional papers, and other special interest publications. So a team of ghostwriters has to be assembled. Everything has to be very carefully cleared; any slip, even in an obscure publication, would certainly be picked up and could reverberate through the whole campaign. This problem is much more acute for a Prime Minister, whose words will be scrutinised for the slightest deviation from departmental policies, than for a Leader of the Opposition, who can enjoy the luxury of attack.

During the 1992 campaign, the draft articles from Central Office ended up on Sarah's desk for clearance. Most of the drafts needed a bit of work – some, perhaps inevitably, a lot. Articles for regional papers had been put together with a blithe disregard for geography. Everyone pitched in, but as the flood increased, Sarah's laptop overheated. So did she.

The Conservatives' campaign had to hit the ground running, partly to demonstrate that they were still full of beans, but also because of continuing fears that if Labour were able to hold on to their early lead, it would prove almost impossible to claw back. The Conservative campaign in 1987 had come in for a lot of stick for having got off to a slow start. That was a mistake that Chris Patten did not intend to repeat. He wanted to come out with all guns firing, and then blast away every day for four weeks until polling day.

After the endless speculation about tactics and timing, the Prime Minister's own relief that the campaign was finally underway was apparent. It was the moment when all the complexities and calculations of the last sixteen months were stripped away, and the whole paraphernalia of political life reduced to a simple gladiatorial contest between Labour and Conservative, Kinnock and Major.

Although so much was at stake, those around him sensed that the Prime Minister felt freer than at any time since taking over from Margaret Thatcher, and that the feeling of liberation grew stronger as each day of the campaign passed.

The first salvo of the campaign came early in a speech to the Conservative Central Council on Saturday 14 March. John Major ran through the record:

> After sixteen months as Prime Minister, the immediate tasks I set myself and my colleagues have been completed – winning the Gulf War, bringing inflation down, putting the Council Tax safely in place, giving a new face to public service with the Citizen's Charter, safeguarding the interests of Britain at Maastricht, and setting out in Tuesday's Budget our strategy for recovery and growth.
>
> That is now done ... Now is the time to seek a new mandate from the British people.

He then set out the themes to which he would return time after time during the campaign:

> Wherever freedom can be extended, there we will be. Wherever choices can be widened, there we will be. Wherever wealth can be created, there we will be. Wherever care must be given, there we will be. That is the Conservative philosophy: wealth and welfare, hand in hand.

Of all the issues that would be debated over the coming weeks, he singled out three that he said he wanted to share with the audience at the start of the campaign:

> The place of Britain in the world; the cohesion of our country; and the future of the battle against inflation.

That the Prime Minister should have chosen to highlight the importance of the fight against inflation came as no surprise. It has been a constant refrain in his political life. His is not the economist's or the businessman's dislike of what inflation does to the economy. It is a deeply personal, gut loathing – born of his own experience – of what it does to the weekly budgeting of people on small fixed incomes.

Talking about Britain's place in the world was also to be expected. It is an area where no Leader of the Opposition can ever compete with the incumbent; John Major had an impressive record in overseas affairs since becoming Prime Minister; and all the evidence showed that the combination of Neil Kinnock and his Shadow Foreign Secretary Gerald Kaufman did not fill the electorate with confidence.

What was more striking, perhaps, was the emphasis the Prime Minister placed in this, his first campaign speech, on constitutional issues. Later on, there was quite a lot of press comment that John Major had suddenly 'discovered' the constitution. In fact, his defence of the Union, the constitutional arrangement dating back to 1707 that binds England and Scotland together, was woven like a steel thread throughout the campaign. It was a theme to which he returned time after time, dealing with it at length in six of his seven rally speeches.

In order to keep the initial momentum up, it had been decided to hold the first 'Meet John Major' of the campaign in Huntingdon the next day – Sunday. Unfortunately, there had been a good deal of pre-briefing by Central Office, and expectations had been raised sky-high. The meeting had been billed as a bold new departure, John Major's secret weapon, carefully crafted to reflect his personality and style. It was going to be like nothing ever seen in a British general election before.

In fact, when the press turned up at tea-time at Sawtry Village College, what they found were two or three hundred solid burghers of Huntingdon, a bit drowsy after Sunday lunch. Even the typically ringing tones of Jeffrey Archer, who introduced the Prime Minister at all the 'Meet John Majors', could not compete with the effects of the roast beef and Yorkshire pudding. The audience listened politely as the Prime Minister chatted to them, perched in their midst on his bar stool. Dubbed a 'talkabout' by *The Times*, the press concluded that the whole thing was a set-up, the questions all carefully planted, the audience hand-picked for their docility. Once they had formed that judgement, the 'Meet John Major' format was doomed for election purposes.

The next day's papers had some good pictures, but the comment was disappointing. The 'Meet John Major' setting was seen as confirming the Prime Minister's reputation for being a nice but grey man. They seemed to fit with the judgement that the campaign was 'lacklustre'. They were clearly not going to win the election for him. But there was no time to sit and reflect. Parliament was dissolved that day, and in the afternoon the Prime Minister came to Central Office to take delivery of the battlebus – and pose for the inevitable photo-call.

The bus had its first outing on a war-footing the following morning, a Tuesday. With Ken Clarke, the Prime Minister had launched a special mini-Manifesto on education entitled *The Thirty-Nine Steps*. This publication was the last twitch of a debate that had been going on for months between those who wanted to trail the Manifesto proposals in a series of pre-launches, and those who wanted to keep them back for a bigger bang when the whole Manifesto was launched. The argument in favour of trailing policy pledges in the Manifesto? It would demonstrate that the Government had not run out of steam in the pre-election period. The argument against? That when the Manifesto proper came to be published, journalists – having seen most of the policy ideas before – would rubbish it for having nothing new. Opposition parties can get away with re-hashing old proposals. Governments, particularly after thirteen years in office, cannot.

After unveiling the proposals on education at a Central Office press conference, the Prime Minister headed to the East Midlands to visit a primary school and the new City Technology College in Nottingham (the only example of a themed day working properly). In the afternoon, he did the second 'Meet John Major'.

As the campaign got under way, a regular daily routine took shape. The Prime Minister would get up at about half-past six. At around seven, while he shaved and had a cup of tea, Andrew Turnbull, Stephen Wall or Gus O'Donnell might pop up to the flat to deal with any pressing government business. Jonathan would have gone up to start the process of winkling the Prime Minister out to make sure he left on time. Sarah would be scribbling down the Prime Minister's amendments to that morning's press release. Just before twenty-five past seven, Norman Fowler would arrive, and he and the Prime Minister would drive across to Central Office together. Jonathan and Sarah would scramble into the second car, loaded up with their travelling library of Budget Red Books, statistics and fact sheets – an inadequate substitute for the huge governmental infrastructure on which the Prime Minister had come to rely.

At seven-thirty, in a large meeting room specially adapted for the election, just along from the Chairman's office on the first floor of 32 Smith Square, the briefing before the morning press conference would start. With Ministers, their Special Advisers and Central Office staff, the cast list was up to twenty before Chris Patten had time to blink, and the room was normally filled to overcrowding.

The Prime Minister would begin by signing off that morning's press release – provided there were no more last-minute attempts to re-write it. Responsibility for producing the press release had travelled the well-trodden path from Smith Square across to Number 10. The original plan had been for yet another large meeting when the Prime Minister arrived back in the evening, so that the following day's release could be drafted in good time. That lasted two days – until exhaustion set in. After that, Sarah produced the drafts on the policy themes, which she, the Prime Minister and Jonathan would go through together last thing at night. Once the Prime Minister had given his instructions and turned in for the night, Sarah and Jonathan would re-draft into the small hours.

More and more frequently as the campaign gathered pace, they would find themselves drafting from scratch. Of the nineteen morning press conferences held after the Manifesto launch on 17 March, only four followed the pre-election plan. Flexibility was essential, but it did add to the strain on Chris Patten. When he staggered back to Central Office from Bath, often after midnight, it would be Sarah's sometimes uncomfortable task to let him know what theme the Prime Minister had decided to run with at the following morning's press conference.

It was to break the glad tidings of such a change that Sarah went across to Central Office in the early hours of 30 March. Chris, understandably, was less than overjoyed. Weary and a bit on edge, they eyed each other silently. Then Chris picked up the phone.

'Get me Michael Heseltine, please.'

By now it was nearly two o'clock in the morning. Michael had just got home from making what he later described as his best campaigning speech ever. He came straight round, still fired up by the speech he had given. As he replayed the best lines for Chris and Sarah's benefit, Michael's eyes gleamed, his hair started to bounce, and his voice took on its trademark lilt. Firing on all cylinders, he began to scribble notes for the morning, not just for himself, but for Chris and the Prime Minister too. Dazed, they sat there meekly drinking it all in.

Once the press notice had been finally approved at the morning briefing, Tim Collins would run through a summary of the day's papers. Then the Prime Minister would look at the questions-and-answers briefing, which the Conservative Research Department had been working on since dawn, and which dealt with the various issues that had arisen in the previous twenty-four hours. Other members of the brat-pack would join the meeting to report on the Liberal Democrat and Labour press conferences which they had just attended.[2]

By this stage, time would be running short and the press would be gathering downstairs for the press conference, due to kick off at eight-thirty. Ministers would be getting fidgety, keen to get the show on the road. This was the moment when they were supposed to agree a key message for the day which everyone could then bang home for the next 24 hours. By the time that Jonathan or Sarah would enquire plaintively – and no doubt tediously – what it was supposed to be, the meeting would be breaking up in a flurry of powder puffs and combs as Ministers started to prepare for the

[2]The three main parties always send observers along to each other's press conferences.

television lights. Failing to sort out an agreed daily message was a basic communications mistake.

At half-past eight, Chris Patten, the Prime Minister and the relevant Secretary of State would troop downstairs for the press conference, sent on their way by a few bars of the Purcell theme tune yowled atrociously off-key by Sarah in an attempt to get them smiling – or at least grimacing – for the cameras.[3] Then came the best part of the day. Jonathan had discovered that it was possible to watch the proceedings on a screen in the meeting room. More importantly, he had also found out that it was possible to have breakfast brought up from the Central Office canteen. So there he and Sarah would sit, keeping half an eye on the television, eating their eggs and bacon – and, as the campaign went on and sugar levels plummeted, beans, fried bread and sausages. (And chocolate, Crunchie bars, crisps and fizzy drinks – a diet familiar to anyone working in the engine room during a general election.)

After the press conference, the Prime Minister and Chris would come back up to the meeting room to discuss how things had gone – but really to have an excuse for coffee and toast, and to put off the evil moment when they would have to pile into stuffy cars and noisy helicopters and rattle off round the country. As the clock ticked on, first Shirley Stotter, then Jonathan, and finally Norman Fowler would try to prize the Prime Minister away from his coffee cup.

Eventually, they would get under way, roaring off from Central Office with their motorcycle outriders, speeding through the heavy morning traffic to catch their plane or helicopter. Skilled police outriders dazzle with their speed, deftness and sheer economy of movement. In London in particular, they have perfected the choreography to the point where four motorcyclists are enough to cope with the heaviest rush-hour traffic. The further one gets from London, however, the greater the number of motorbikes and the more clumsy their movements. It is like the difference between a thoroughbred and a carthorse.

Back in Central Office, John Wakeham would be starting his

---

[3] Andrew Lloyd Webber had re-scored Purcell's hornpipe from *Abdelazer* specially for the campaign.

stint as caretaker Chairman until Chris Patten returned from his daily visit to his Bath constituency. John Wakeham was also acting as caretaker Minister, on standby in case the civil service needed someone to put their thumb-print on some official document or other. As the campaign hotted up, a daily meeting was introduced – at which Maurice Saatchi took the lead – to tackle the problem of forward planning.

On his flight to whatever region he was scheduled to visit that day, the Prime Minister might work on a speech, give an interview to one of the travelling press pack, or – just possibly – look at his briefing for the day. When the plane touched down, the battlebus would be waiting on the tarmac, ready to lurch off to the first destination.

At the beginning of the campaign, the day was packed full. A typical day would have up to four visits, a speaking opportunity – a 'Meet John Major' or a rally – a series of press interviews, and perhaps a walkabout. It certainly demonstrated activity, but this sort of over-crowding caused problems. It meant the Prime Minister ran late. It meant he did not have enough time for thinking, speech-writing or simply putting his feet up for five minutes every now and again. And having so many visits meant that each photo opportunity competed with the next for coverage, so that good shots were crowded out by bad.

More generally, not enough thought and preparation had gone into working out what the day's picture should be. Decisions tended to be taken on the hoof. Too often the Prime Minister had to push his way through a scrum of photographers and television crews, sometimes so dense that it was difficult for him actually to meet any voters. The result: shots of him posing uncomfortably in front of yet another dreary piece of unphotogenic machinery, miles from any other human beings. The Labour Party, by contrast, had meticulously planned every shot and plotted every camera angle. Some of the writing press might have commented that it all looked rather too staged, but on television, where it mattered, Neil Kinnock looked good.

The programme had been stuffed so full with the best of intentions: to keep the travelling press pack busy. Journalists and photographers were being charged large sums of money for the privilege of accompanying the Prime Minister. To keep their news desks happy, they wanted as many stories and photographs as possible. But what the Prime Minister needed was a single message and a single image. The mistake his team had made was to allow journalistic needs to come first.

Overload on the Prime Minister's programme was also caused in part by trying to please too many people. All the Conservative Party's Area Agents[4] were understandably keen to get their money's worth from the Prime Minister, wanting to take him to as many places and to meet as many people as possible in order to repay debts and win brownie points with the local party. 'Quick' photo-calls or 'short' visits would be slotted into the diary – even though the quick photo-call or short visit involving the Prime Minister has yet to be invented.

As they clocked up the miles in their bomb- and bullet-proof world, carrying everything they needed with them like a snail with its house on its back, it was surprisingly easy to get cut off from what was happening back at base. Just as the Prime Minister's tour team were focused on their own world of visits, rallies and walkabouts, so the London end was busy fighting a different campaign of opinion polls, advertising campaigns and media gossip. Sometimes, it seemed as though the two parts of the campaign were operating in separate dimensions, with little communication between them.

Although scant information filtered back to the bus from Central Office, Jonathan kept in regular touch with Sarah at Number 10. However, worried about reports that one of the Sunday newspapers had followed the battlebus in 1987 trying to eavesdrop on phone calls, they developed a simple name code. Frankly, it wouldn't have fooled a child, but it might, they hoped, protect the bus against casual listening in. Above all, it acted as a reminder to everyone to be careful about what they said. Sarah became Piglet – for obvious reasons; Jonathan was Pooh; Tim Collins,

[4]For organisational purposes, at the time of the election, England was divided into ten areas, with an Area Agent in charge of each. Scotland and Wales had their own Area Agents.

Eeyore; Nick True, Wol; Edward Llewellyn, Tigger, or sometimes Very Small Beetle. Central Office became collectively known as Rabbit's Friends and Relations. The Prime Minister, of course, was Christopher Robin.

Halfway through the campaign, Ronnie Millar announced to Sarah that he would be Alice. Alice? Help! A change of author? Ronnie looked pained.

'My dear,' he said reprovingly, 'they're changing guard at Buckingham Palace, Christopher Robin went down with *Alice*.'

The days when the Prime Minister was speaking at a big rally were inevitably the most fraught for the travelling team. Out on stage, television or sports personalities would give warm-up speeches to get the audience in the mood. Stirring music and powerful images on huge video screens helped create a sense of drama. Meanwhile, there would be pandemonium going on in the Prime Minister's room in a nearby hotel. In one corner, Debbie de Satgé would be running off the 'final' version of the speech for the autocue. In another, the Prime Minister would already have started fiddling with his text again, leaving Jonathan in a desperate scrabble to incorporate those changes by hand on to the autocue script. Then the Prime Minister would decide he needed a new beginning. Next, it would be a new shirt or tie. Then the whole speech would be wrong – as would his suit.

Finally, he would agree to go across to the venue where the rally was taking place. Into the Green Room, where the whole process would start again. The final warm-up speech, the final video, and then, to the crash of 'his' theme music, the Prime Minister and Norma would walk in through the audience as the applause rose to a crescendo.

To Jonathan, the whole process was like preparing a prize boxer for the big fight. Surrounded by his trainers and camp followers, the champ would walk towards the ring. There would be a constant stream of chatter: 'Listen to them in there. They're a good audience. They're on your side. They really want you to win. Now, go in and sock it to them. Give it everything you've got.'

The rallies were a success. The Prime Minister liked the feeling of having the audience all around him. The atmosphere was highly charged. As the campaign went on, so he relaxed, and the speeches got better and better. But even after the first one, in Manchester, George Jones wrote in the *Daily Telegraph* the next day:

> It looked good on television and the audience loved it. The verdict afterwards was that it had worked well. The Major campaign had at last come alight.

George Jones – clearly shocked went on to say: 'Some of the phrases in Mr Major's speech . . . were his own.' The view that the Prime Minister was slightly less articulate than a speak-your-weight machine was, indeed is, widely held among the press. They clearly believed that he merely read out, without amendment, a text prepared for him by others. It never seemed like that to the speech-writers.

When the Prime Minister finished his speech at Manchester, the applause went on and on. However, as he and Norma Major left the set, shaking hands as they went, Norma spotted one person who was not clapping and who wouldn't look her in the eye. 'Not one of us,' she thought, and hurried past. In fact it was one of the local Special Branch officers who, needing to be ready for a quick draw, are never allowed to applaud.

But although the rallies went well, they did not have the impact they deserved. His team knew that the Prime Minister was an incorrigible re-drafter, and should have written more time into the diary before a big rally for him to work on his speech. As the speech got more and more delayed, so the press, worrying about their deadlines, got rattier, and Tim Collins's job of briefing them became more difficult.

Then, as the Prime Minister himself started to fall behind schedule, so the timing of the rallies had to be pushed back – meaning not just restive audiences but, more crucially in a general election, missed television headlines. On one occasion, everything had been arranged for the rally to make the top slot on the BBC *Nine O'Clock News*. But that day the Prime Minister was running even later than usual. In the event, he didn't start his speech until just before the news went on air. That night, it wasn't just the top slot at the beginning of the news that was missed – but the whole programme.

As the campaign went on, Jonathan overcame some of the problem by releasing key extracts from the speech earlier in the day, a technique which was used subsequently for party conference speeches. But delays in producing the text, problems with over-running – sometimes the warm-up speakers went on for so long that everyone cooled down – and failure to identify key themes early enough for Tim Collins to pre-brief all blunted the impact of the rallies.

The launch of the 1992 Manifesto was set for Wednesday 18 March,[5] a week after the election had been called. Copies of the finished document, complete with John Major's smiling face on the front cover, were available in abundance. The Prime Minister was predictably uncomfortable about the picture, worrying that it smacked of a personality cult – a point duly made by the *Guardian* the next day. But the campaign needed all the help it could get, and the Prime Minister was more popular than the Conservative Party. Labour, implicitly revealing two of their electoral weak spots, sought to reassure voters by plastering the front of their Manifesto with the Union flag, and consigning Neil Kinnock's picture to page six.

The Prime Minister's photograph was at least cheerful – which was more than could be said for the staging of the launch press conference. A throw-back to the monumentalist design favoured in the 1980s, it looked like a huge grey battle-ship. Arranged in two rows as though appearing on *University Challenge*, sat the Cabinet, little pin-heads peeping over the top of the set, looking for all the world like cut-outs at a fairground shooting range.

Watching them line up in the Green Room before they trooped on made Jonathan sympathise with the seedy-looking photographers who used to take school photos with the old cameras that panned steadily from right to left. Just as they thought they had got one side

[5] A letter from the Prime Minister to over a million voters had already been sent out in sixty-seven marginal seats a fortnight before the election was called – astonishingly, the first direct mail letter from the Prime Minister of the day in British political history.

settled and all looking at the camera, so there would be a disturbance over on the far side, and the whole process would have to start all over again. Meanwhile, there was always the little girl or boy who, as the camera panned, ran quickly along the back row so as to appear in the picture in two places. Eventually, the Cabinet were arranged in some semblance of order and they shuffled on to the sound of the Lloyd-Webber theme tune.

Journalists commented on the difference between the Conservative and Labour launches. Mr Kinnock, enjoying being well ahead in two opinion polls published that morning, was described as having 'a smile on his lips', and a 'pronounced swagger' to his gait. The Conservatives, by contrast, were said by the *Daily Telegraph* to be 'glum-looking'.

The Prime Minister's opening remarks drew out the Manifesto's core themes:

> It's about a world in which people are free to rise as far and as fast as they can; in which enterprise creates the prosperity that enables us to take care of others . . .
>
> During the 1980s, we beat a path to that door through the tangle of regulation, state control and taxation that choked our economy . . . A new generation is coming along now – which wants to open the door wider. A generation that takes what's been done for granted, and now wants more choice. More ownership. More responsibility. And more opportunity.

He then singled out some of the key policy pledges: on the economy, progress towards stable prices; on taxation, a widening of the 20 pence tax band, plus a commitment to cut the burden of inheritance tax; on public services, a focus on quality – and openness – through the Citizen's Charter; further privatisation, including an end to BR's monopoly; a package of law and order measures, including tougher sentences for a variety of offences and an extension of community policing; housing measures to encourage both home ownership and private renting; the Millennium Fund, to be financed by a national lottery.

Press reactions were mixed. Hugo Young of the *Guardian*,

no friend of the Conservatives, commented: 'This party is not intellectually dead. It has ideas about the future.' According to Peter Riddell of *The Times*: 'The Tories succeeded yesterday in conveying an impression of freshness and liveliness; along with the gimmicky ideas about a Millennium Fund, there is even some radicalism.' Norman Tebbit, writing in the *Standard* was enthusiastic:

> It is neither narrow nor dull. It does not depart from Thatcherite fundamentals but finds new ways of adapting them into everyday life. It is . . . full of prudent ambition, short on slogans, full of practical ideas. Some commentators may call it dull, but if you are waiting for the council repair team or the hip operation which never seems to be on time, Major's Manifesto is the most exciting for years.

Other commentators did indeed call it dull, claiming not to be able to detect a Big Idea. 'The whole is less than the sum of the parts,' said the *Telegraph* leader. 'The document, like the press conference that launched it . . . lacks an electric charge.' Andrew Rawnsley of the *Guardian* was also in search of the Big Idea: 'The Conservatives' Big Idea was harder to locate,' he wrote. 'But it finally turned up on page 43', in the form of a commitment to introduce a Hedgerow Incentive Scheme for farmers – a mini-item much prized by Environment and Agriculture Ministers (and stoutly defended by the Prime Minister), but deemed by the – largely urban – press to be too trivial for inclusion in a Manifesto.

The Manifesto should undoubtedly have been hacked down further – journalists were right to say there was too much detail in the final version. That said, there are two good reasons for having the detail there. For Ministers, the purpose of a Manifesto is to cover all the points on which they feel vulnerable to lobby groups – which are only too ready to complain that party A cares about such-and-such, while party B obviously does not because there is 'nothing at all about it in their Manifesto'. As single-issue politics increases, so will these pressures.

Secondly, for the Prime Minister its purpose is to ensure there is an agreed language on anything that may come up during the campaign. That way he does not have to spend time fighting fires of disagreement between what colleagues have said, or make policy in the heat of the campaign.

Journalists were struck by the extent to which so much was being pinned on the Prime Minister. Hugo Young reckoned that 'Never has so much been expected of a single leader, to efface the past and personify his party's renewal.' The Prime Minister may have contributed to this impression by the answer he gave when asked who was responsible for the Manifesto.

'It's all me,' he said, 'every last word of it is me.'

(Which came as something of a surprise to the rest of the Cabinet.)

The Prime Minister, who as usual fielded nearly all the questions himself, was in good form, the *Daily Telegraph* noting how relaxed he seemed. He struck only one false note, and that out of old world courtesy. Asked whether it was tokenism that Gillian Shephard was on the platform when she wasn't in the Cabinet (which at that time was still all-male), the Prime Minister explained that she was there because she was Deputy Chairman of the Conservative Party. He had been warned not to rise if the question were asked, but he had clearly forgotten his politically correct briefing. 'And isn't she looking nice?' he added.

The press conference was followed by television interviews with Sky, ITN and the BBC, before an afternoon spent with *The Times* and the regional and foreign press. The day was rounded off by a party political broadcast: the culmination of over six months' work.

All through 1991, Chris Patten and Maurice Saatchi had been pressing the Prime Minister to record some personal recollections, to be made into an election broadcast called – simply – *The Journey*. John Schlesinger, the director of *Midnight Cowboy*, was to make the film. In the spring, he had been in to meet the Prime Minister, who felt comfortable with him. Nevertheless, John Major was deeply reluctant to exploit his past. He recalled with distaste the 1987 election film of the Kinnocks wandering the cliff-tops. It took another six months for Chris Patten to grind him down and get his agreement to have a film made.

When Sarah was sent the film schedule to see if she could sell it to the Prime Minister, her heart sank. It was no doubt perfect for a professional actor, but completely impractical for a Prime Minister. It would demand an enormous amount of his time, and indicated filming locations which were bound to draw a crowd. The detectives weren't happy, either.

Eventually a compromise was reached. John Schlesinger and the Prime Minister toured Brixton together, jammed with the cameraman and essential detective into the back of the Daimler. John Major was persuaded to talk about his life, his feelings when he got into Parliament, his hopes and plans. The result was moving and carefully understated. But the Prime Minister was never happy with it. He demanded more and more editing – particularly to take out references to Norma and his children, whom he tried hard to protect from political exposure. And when it was eventually finished? The Prime Minister could never bring himself to watch it.[6]

That night, as Jonathan and Sarah watched *The Journey* for the *n*th (and final) time, they looked back over the first full week of campaigning. The Prime Minister had come sprinting out of the traps. He had made his first rally speech, held two 'Meet John Major' sessions, chaired his first morning press conference, done his first full day's campaigning, attacked Labour's Shadow Budget, been interviewed by the national and regional media, launched a Manifesto, and starred in the first election broadcast.

And the result?

After week one, the Conservatives had gone from being three points behind Labour in the opinion polls to being five points behind.

---

[6]There has been much debate about the impact of this broadcast, made at a cost of some £250,000. The most frequently made comment by those who rang Central Office was to complain that the Prime Minister had not been wearing his seat belt in the back of the car.

13

Barn Owls and Birthday Cake

It's dogged as does it. It ain't thinking about it.
Anthony Trollope, *The Last Chronicle of Barset*, 1867

A week before polling day, the Prime Minister appeared on the *Jimmy Young Show*. He summed up what he felt about campaigning:

> What are elections about? Elections are actually about people. They are not about hiding away in photo opportunities and striking an image. They are about meeting people, finding out what they think, taking their questions, dealing with them, getting the feel of what the country really wants and what the country really feels.
>
> Now I do not believe that I can do that sitting . . . behind a desk in Whitehall with reports from other people. Everyone operates their own way. I need to be close to people, to feel what they are thinking and to be with them and that is the way that I get an instinct for what I believe is right for us to do. I do not have a shred of doubt that this sort of campaign is right for me. It is how I started politics, that is how I like politics, and everywhere I go between now and April the ninth, I shall take my soapbox with me.

The soapbox, by then, had become the Prime Minister's talisman.

Since the election it has been seen as the symbol of his whole campaign. Yet until the end of the second full week of campaigning, no one – not even the Prime Minister – had even mentioned it.

There had, however, been a sniff of it at Bolton the previous week. Thanks to the local Labour Party, a walkabout in the town centre had degenerated into some ill-tempered shoving. It had been raining and the cobbled streets were slippery underfoot. The police managed to keep the situation under control, but there were moments, as tempers frayed, when it hovered in the balance between order and disorder. When the Prime Minister finally made it through the crowds back to the battlebus, there was such a press of people that he was shot up the stairs like a cork out of a bottle. Jonathan was there ready to shake his head about the behaviour of the crowd and make sympathetic noises about being jostled. But he had read the runes wrong. The Prime Minister wasn't bothered: 'Nothing wrong with that. It was good fun. That's more like it. Do you think I should go back and do some more? What do you think, Norma?'

There was colour in the prime ministerial cheek, a gleam in his eye. It suddenly dawned on a horrified Jonathan: the Prime Minister was actually *enjoying* himself. He liked the rough and tumble of street politics. And it was no good looking to Norma for moral support: she was every bit as bad. Fortunately for Jonathan, the detectives had also had enough. They ruthlessly played their trump card: 'Sorry, Prime Minister: security.' As eggs started to land on the battlebus, it pulled slowly out of the town square, still surrounded by chanting students.

The next day's headlines seemed to take some pleasure in what was described as 'a near riot'. 'Crowd forces Major to abandon visit', said the *Guardian*. 'Walkabout in Bolton ends in jeering student ambush', chortled the *Independent*. But however much the newspapers might have enjoyed what they saw as the Prime Minister's discomfiture, they recognised that the events in Bolton had brought him and the campaign to life.

When the Prime Minister spoke at a rally in Manchester later that day, journalists claimed to detect a new toughness in his delivery. 'Being pushed and shoved by a crowd of students and Labour supporters,' wrote George Jones in the *Daily Telegraph*, 'provided the shot of adrenalin he needed . . . After a week of shadow-boxing, Mr Major landed a few direct hits.'

The crunch point did not, however, come until the following week. On Friday 27 March, the Prime Minister was on his way back from Wales. It had been a dull and uninspiring day, ragged at the edges. The high point was refuelling with fish and chips on the runway at Cardiff Airport. The third 'Meet John Major' had come and gone that afternoon – perfectly successfully, but by now the press had hardened their hearts against them. Criticism of the campaign was steadily increasing in volume.

On the way back to London in the aeroplane, the Prime Minister worked himself into a grump. Stung by criticism of the 'Meet John Major' format, he allowed his frustration at the press coverage to show through. Why wasn't he meeting any real voters? Why wasn't he being allowed to speak to them direct? He was becoming cut off. His message wasn't getting across. Well, he'd had enough of it. He wasn't going to sit there while the campaign collapsed around him. Why shouldn't he do what he had done all those years ago when he first started out in politics: find a street corner, get on a soapbox – and talk? Damn it, he was going to do it, no matter what anyone said.

When Prime Ministers are in that kind of mood, people hop to it.

'How about tomorrow?' hopped Jonathan. Tomorrow was Luton.

The Prime Minister spent the Saturday morning at a sports ground in Welwyn Garden City supporting David Evans – who, never slow to criticise others, had been one of a number of MPs who had publicly attacked the campaign. A walkabout in Luton was planned for the afternoon. The Prime Minister was going there to support the local Tory candidates, Graham Bright and John Carlisle. That, it was agreed, was where the soapbox would get its first outing.

Luton was, in fact, about the worst place that could have been chosen from a security point of view. First, news of the Prime Minister's visit had leaked well in advance. Second, Luton is a tough town. It has more than its fair share of political roughs

– and they were out in force by the time the Prime Minister arrived.

To add to the problems, the Prime Minister had had to delay his arrival to give the travelling press enough time to get to Luton ahead of him. Reports started to come back from the local police that a large and hostile crowd was building up. As the delay lengthened, the numbers swelled still further. The message was sent back that it might be sensible if the visit were cancelled. The Prime Minister, chafing at his enforced idleness, was snappy: 'We are not cancelling. We are going ahead. And I've just about had enough of all this hanging around.'

The visit went ahead.

That day, there was no battlebus, so organisation was more difficult than usual. As the team got out of their cars, they swiftly became separated, strung out in a long line, trying to work their way through the crowd. Edward Llewellyn, lumbered with the loud-hailer, pushed and jostled to keep up. Someone else struggled along with an old packing case which had been discovered in the hold of the battlebus. The Prime Minister, surrounded by his detectives, the local police, TV crews and the Socialist Workers' Party, surged ahead at the front.

They were in a modern pedestrian precinct, punctuated with benches, litter bins, bollards and flower beds, and lined with glass-fronted shops – a dangerous combination with a big and hostile crowd. Labour supporters were howling. The SWP were spitting and swearing. Some were screaming, 'Stab him, stab him.'

An old lady was knocked back against a glass shop window. A small child, frightened by the uproar, started to cry. There was a whiff of panic in the air. The police looked nervous. Shirley, who was used to this sort of thing, looked nervous. Jonathan, who was not, looked very nervous.

But the Prime Minister kept plunging deeper and deeper into the crowd. Then, in the midst of the scrum, he became aware that a huge man was bearing down on him. Tattoos. Cropped hair. Thick neck. Grubby T-shirt. Hairy arms. A vast hand reached out towards John Major, who later admitted that he thought his final hour had come. The hand grabbed hold of the Prime Minister's: 'Good on yer, John. Best of luck.'

Eventually, the Prime Minister, the loud-hailer and the packing case were reunited. The Prime Minister clambered up and started to speak. He had to rely on a small, tinny, hand-held loud-hailer, since the one that had been laid on for him by the local Conservative Party association had failed to work. As he began to address the crowd, the SWP's much bigger and better loudspeaker burst into life, drowning him out. Only occasionally could a prime ministerial peep make itself heard over the booming bass of the SWP.

He soldiered on, but it was pointless to continue. The crowd was growing restive. To the relief of the police, the Prime Minister decided to call it a day. The team retreated to the waiting cars – pursued by howls of derision and showers of spit. Someone tried to force their way into the car in which one of the Political Office secretaries, Claire Jones, was sitting. The convoy pulled away, amidst jeers and much banging on car roofs.

And that was how an old packing case became the Prime Minister's secret weapon.

It did not look that way at the time. Back in Number 10, Sarah received call after call from his 'friends' saying he must have gone mad. Old-style campaigning had no part to play in the modern age of sound-bites and stage management. The Prime Minister's team were behaving like total amateurs. Kinnock had been getting it right with clever photo-calls. He looked *really* prime ministerial. What the hell did John Major think he was playing at?

That had been Jonathan's immediate reaction as well. Back in the car, he sat with his head in his hands, appalled at the shambles and dreading the television pictures of the Prime Minister's rout.

The next day, the press were split. Some praised the Prime Minister for taking the gloves off and coming out fighting. Others, however, were hostile. Peter Hillmore, writing in the *Observer*, was typical: 'The organisation of Mr Major's campaign last week was nothing short of disastrous.' Edwina Currie was equally critical: 'John in a Barbour jacket and on a soapbox looks more like the Leader of the Opposition than Labour's Mr Kinnock smoothing round in a

Daimler.'[1] Many of the commentators and pundits were clear: the gamble had failed. The Prime Minister had got it wrong – again.

The commentators reported that the campaign was 'wobbling'. There had apparently been an outbreak of jitters at Central Office. 'Friends' of Margaret Thatcher were making it known that she thought the campaign lacked 'oomph'. Brendan Bruce, the former Director of Communications at Central Office, couldn't resist chipping in: 'The Tory Party is currently losing this election . . . because the Tory Party has neither clarity nor conviction in its arguments.' Faxes arrived at Number 10 from former Thatcher advisers announcing that the election was lost unless the old guard were called back in.

But what the battlebus team rapidly realised was the effect the experience had had on the Prime Minister himself. He had come out of the crowd positively crackling with electricity. He was a different person. No more Treasury-speak and whirring sub-clauses. Instead, a tough street-fighter who drew his strength from direct contact with a crowd and knew how to speak their language – simple, uncomplicated English spoken straight from the heart. They had found the key that unlocked the real John Major. And, typically, he had had it in his pocket the whole time.

Why did the soapbox work? Certainly not because it offered good sound-bites or was presentationally slick. Rather, because it showed the Prime Minister as he was: a bit homespun maybe, but transparently honest, physically courageous, and prepared to fight for what he believed in. At a time when all the clever talk was that electioneering in Britain was destined to draw on techniques copied

[1]The Prime Minister was typically forgiving of Edwina Currie, offering her the job of Minister of State at the Home Office after the election. She declined, saying that her future lay in the European Parliament and that she would find it difficult to work with the Home Secretary, Ken Clarke. It was Ken who, when he was Health Secretary, had been obliged by the Whips' Office to give her the black spot after her remarks about salmonella in eggs. She had obviously never forgiven him. In fact, he had fought to keep Edwina Currie as a Minister.

In the European elections of June 1994, Edwina Currie suffered from the swing against the Conservatives and failed to secure election as an MEP.

from across the Atlantic, the Prime Minister instinctively went back to an older, truer British political tradition. In doing so, he turned conventional wisdom on its head and destroyed the whole premise on which his own campaign had been constructed.

There his team had been, spending hours debating to and fro whether the 'Meet John Major' sessions might run the risk of exposing the Prime Minister to hostile questions. There he now was, in a situation where a few hostile questions would have come as light relief – if, that is, they could be heard over the noise of the crowd and the splat of rotten eggs.

Eggs now became the Prime Minister's closest companions. Wherever he went, they followed. At Southampton, in the full glare of the television cameras, he was hit smack in the face by one hurled at him from point blank range. It struck him on his right cheekbone with such force that, as the evening news showed, he was momentarily stunned. It had also drawn blood – and for a split second, the detectives had thought that something far worse than an egg had hit him.[2]

Much later, after he had left Number 10, Jonathan asked the Prime Minister how aware he had been of the dangers he faced during the election, or of the ever-present threat from the IRA. He shrugged: 'I've never liked the security. I've always been a fatalist. If they're going to get me, they're going to get me.'

It wasn't only critical press comment that the Prime Minister woke up to on the Sunday morning. It was his forty-ninth birthday. He and Norma were spending it at Chequers. As it was Mothering Sunday, they had decided to go to the nearby church for the family service. Jonathan, his wife Alex, and their six-month-old daughter, Georgia, joined them in their pew. Norma, like all the mothers present, was given a pansy. Georgia, who was sitting next to her, promptly bit off the flower and started chomping – much to the amusement of the congregation. The Prime Minister, unlike most politicians, is genuinely fond of

---

[2]This was the only time that the change of clothes always carried on the battlebus – in case of emergencies – was needed. The man responsible for the attack was arrested by the police, charged and fined.

small children. He started clucking like a mother-hen, worried that the flower might be poisonous or that the baby might choke. He did not relax until the remains of the flower had been fished out – it was only with difficulty that he was restrained from doing the fishing himself. After church, and the failed attempts by the press lined up outside to persuade Norma to pose giving the Prime Minister a birthday kiss, it was back to Chequers.

The Chequers staff knew that this was the last prime ministerial visit planned before the general election. They also knew where the opinion polls were pointing. Everyone was especially attentive. Alan, the chef, had made a white cake with blue candles, ostensibly to wish the Prime Minister happy birthday, but also, just in case, to say goodbye.

A bigger official party had been laid on back at Smith Square, together with the compulsory photo-call, so after lunch it was back to London. The Prime Minister, who always managed to be both an indifferent time-keeper and to fret about being late, started to fuss about how long it would take to get back. Hadn't they better be going? Norma, forgetting how long it could take to get into central London from the country on a Sunday afternoon, reassured him that they would be there in about forty minutes. In the event, it took nearly two hours.

The Prime Minister steadily became crosser and crosser. Why was nothing planned properly? There would be hundreds of people waiting for him. It was so rude. It was incompetent. It was a shambles. 'Which idiot told me it would only take forty minutes to get back to London? Do you remember, Norma?'

But, oddly, Norma didn't remember. She went strangely quiet and studied the view from her window. And the back of the detectives' heads gave nothing away.

At Central Office, a second, bigger cake, iced with the slogan 'JM4PM', was waiting. Fifteen girls each held up a letter on a big blue card which together spelled 'Happy Birthday PM' – although the girl holding the 'B' wasn't quick enough off the mark, and the photo duly appeared on the front page of *The Times* as 'HAPPY IRTHDAY'. Amongst the cards, there was one from a surprising quarter: the normally hard–bitten photographers who travelled with him on the campaign trail.[3]

The next day's press noted how resilient the Prime Minister seemed to be. They also commented on rumours of crisis meetings over the weekend, at which it had been decided to junk the existing campaign and 'chop' various key players. Jonathan and Sarah lost count of the number of times that the Prime Minister was supposed to have held a 'crunch meeting', to have 'knocked heads together', or to have taken 'personal control of the campaign'. There were stories about Chris Patten being squeezed out by John Wakeham, of Richard Ryder having been brought in to salvage the campaign, of the old guard being called back to the colours to clear up the mess made by the brat-pack. Sarah was for the chop. Chris was for the chop. Shaun Woodward was for the chop.

In fact, only one organisational change was ever considered: to take Tim Collins off the press coach and put him in charge of media relations at the centre, leaving Jonathan to take over press handling on the tour. Such a move would help strengthen press handling back at base, where there was clearly a weakness. In the event, Chris Patten agreed that how the Prime Minister did was more important than anything else. He should therefore hold on to the team he trusted.

After the Central Office birthday party, the Prime Minister went back to Downing Street. Later that evening, he gave a television interview to Bob Hawke, the ex-Prime Minister of Australia turned media personality. Jonathan was in despair – 'There are no bloody votes in Australia' – as precious briefing time was used up on a programme that wouldn't be broadcast, even in Australia, during the election period. But the Prime Minister was adamant: he had told Bob Hawke he would do it and he wasn't going to let him down.[4]

---

[3]Relations with the travelling press were generally good – although John Simpson, who had covered the Romanian revolution, did complain in the *Spectator* that dealing with Tim Collins was like dealing with Ceauşescu's *Securitate*. Tim felt extremely flattered.

[4]Even though Bob Hawke had scored more runs than the British Prime Minister at the Commonwealth Heads of Government Conference 'celebrity' cricket match in Harare the previous October.

Not all the time spent with journalists was so unproductive, but they did make huge inroads into the Prime Minister's diary. First, there were interviews with most of the national daily and weekend newspapers. Then there were appearances on all the main flagship political programmes on both television and radio. And every day out on tour, there were endless phone-ins and briefings for regional radio, television and newspapers.

There were grillings on the aeroplane, in the battlebus, in hotels, in Number 12 Downing Street, at Central Office, and up in the flat. And finally there were live interviews on all the national television news programmes at both the start and finish of the campaign. At a rough count, during the four weeks of the campaign, the Prime Minister gave at least 140 interviews, six briefings for the regional or national press, seventeen morning press conferences at Smith Square, and countless doorstep interviews for television and radio.

He made himself more available to the media than any previous party leader and was much more accessible than Neil Kinnock, who was kept well away from the press. As the *Standard* reported on 20 March:

> Nothing is being allowed to disturb the immaculately groomed image perfectly portrayed on the television screens each night. No walkabouts, no hecklers, no impromptu debates and, above all, no risk . . . clearly terrified of making that fatal gaffe, the Labour Leader has protected himself completely from exposure to the unknown.

This kind of comment reflected an odd contradiction. Journalists knew that the Neil Kinnock being presented to them was not the real thing – in other words that they themselves were being manipulated – yet they seemed to regard this as a strength. The more the Labour leader came cellophane-wrapped, the more the campaign was praised for being highly professional. By contrast, the more the Prime Minister exposed himself to the rough and tumble of politics, the more the commentators tended to criticise.

Back on the battlebus, life was almost fun. No rivalries, no back-stabbing. There were, however, moments of tension – normally when the Prime Minister discovered that he would have to wear some kind of special clothing for his next visit. He had a particular loathing of hard hats; but protective plastic spectacles, heat resistant boots, luminous jackets or white coats were all guaranteed to produce a similarly explosive reaction.[5] As successive Private Secretaries in charge of his official regional tours discovered, to arrange a visit for John Major which involved wearing an industrial hair-net was what is known in Whitehall, in best *Yes Minister* tradition, as 'very courageous'.[6]

The Prime Minister hated stunts and posed 'photo opportunities', so any photograph required very careful handling. And at the beginning of the campaign, before he had got into his stride, it was very hard work indeed. The photographers complained that they couldn't get him to do anything at all. He wouldn't pick up any machinery ('I'll break it'), pat anything ('It'll bite me'), or hold an animal or a baby ('It'll die').

But as polling day approached, so the Prime Minister relaxed. He was filmed kicking a football, using a television camera, shaking hands with a dog, sharing a joke with a shire horse. Then came the supreme test, on a visit to a hop farm in Kent – one of those farms that also have horses, and old machinery and, in this case, birds of prey. This was Shirley Stotter's great triumph. Jonathan and Sarah had both wanted to drop it. The Prime Minister was supposed to be talking about the economic recovery that day, and they couldn't work out how even Tim would be able to make the connection between barn owls and the economy. It was about time, they thought, to go somewhere a bit more hard-edged.

But Shirley had obviously reached one of those moments when people decide they have had enough. She was not going to be budged: the Prime Minister was going to visit the hop farm, come what may, and have his picture taken with a barn owl perched

---

[5]The most spectacular was when he visited an aluminium recycling plant: he had to put up with a hard hat, a donkey jacket and protective glasses.
[6]That is, completely mad.

on his arm. The more Jonathan and Sarah argued, the more she dug in. Knowing they had met their match, they backed down, predicting disaster and owl droppings. The Prime Minister agreed to the photograph. Jonathan covered his eyes and prayed. The fates smiled. To the great disappointment of the photographers, who were standing there with cameras poised, nudging each other like naughty schoolboys in church, the owl did not mess up the Prime Minister's suit and the picture got some of the best coverage of the whole campaign.

Earlier that day, the Prime Minister had made a more hard-edged visit to Medway Ports to illustrate the economic theme of the day. The first picture, of the Prime Minister standing in a sea of gleaming new tractors lined up ready for export, went well. Norman Fowler, who had arranged the visit, looked pleased – very pleased. Jonathan couldn't resist. He took Norman to one side.

'We seem to have a bit of a problem, Norman. You do realise, don't you, that those tractors you arranged are all *imports*? And I'm afraid the press are on to it. Do you want to tell the PM or shall I?'

Norman blanched – and Jonathan relented.

In the refrigerated hangar they went into next, the joke rebounded. Expecting to find crates of English produce ready for shipping abroad, to Jonathan's horror the Prime Minister stopped next to box-loads of Cape apples. Carefully positioning himself in front of the logo on the box, Jonathan looked around: there was South African produce everywhere. Even though it was refrigerated, it suddenly felt very hot.

'Let's get him out of here,' he hissed to Shirley.

The Prime Minister and the photographers were frog-marched briskly out again.

This was not, unfortunately, the only cock-up. At one of the morning press conferences to discuss defence, the phrase 'The Best Team in a Troubled World' had been chosen as the slogan. The Ministers trooped in to take their places, sitting in front of the slogan stuck up on the wall above them. No one had checked which word would be behind the Prime Minister's seat – and sure enough, in the next day's papers there appeared photographs of a pensive-looking

Prime Minister under the picture headline 'TROUBLED'. An easy enough mistake to make – but in an election campaign, attention to detail is vital. There was worse to come. A few days later, at an afternoon press conference on schools, the slogan on the stage-set spelled out in very clear terms the Conservative commitment to 'EDUCTION'.

One of the biggest potential disasters had occurred right at the beginning of the campaign – averted only by quick-thinking from the Prime Minister. Before the Bolton walkabout, he had gone to Blackpool and the Fylde College of Higher Education. The visit was passing off quietly enough, when suddenly the Prime Minister was confronted by every minder's nightmare: a pretty young A-level student dressed up – or rather undressed up – as the Blackpool Tower. She was completely naked apart from some body-paint, a bow-tie and what was described rather primly by *The Times* as 'yellow bikini briefs', and by the *Daily Telegraph* more lip-smackingly as 'knickers'.

'Was it wobbly Thursday?' one of the press wanted to know. The Prime Minister, who had spotted what was coming moments before the rest of his team, came to a halt, discreetly out of camera shot. His politician's skills had not deserted him – and nor had his manners – as he engaged her in polite conversation from a full fifteen feet away.

As the Prime Minister travelled around the country, clocking up many thousands of miles, a pattern began to develop: wherever the battlebus went, the Socialist Workers' Party always got there first, in good time to shout and scream at the Prime Minister when he arrived. Given the security surrounding the Prime Minister's programme – no advance notice of a visit was ever given – it is a reflection of the SWP's organisational skills that they always managed to have someone there to give the Prime Minister a warm welcome. But he was always pleased to see them: they were the best possible advertisement for the Conservative cause.

The SWP aside, what was striking at the time was how friendly the response on the streets seemed to be. There were moments, as at Bolton, when the Prime Minister did come across some hostility, but it was usually where it had been whipped up by local Labour or Liberal Democrat activists. For the most part, people seemed pleased to see the Prime Minister and Norma in their town, and as the coach trundled into market squares it was waves and smiles, rather than V-signs, that greeted him.

Not all his arrivals were so smooth, however. One morning, just as the aeroplane carrying the Prime Minister, Norma, the campaign team and the travelling press was touching down, one of the journalists, Patrick Wintour, was grumbling to Tim:

'It hasn't been a very exciting campaign so far, has it?'

With that, the plane crunched on to the runway, bounced up, came slamming down again and with a screeching of tyres, slewed to a stop. It was all over very quickly, but the pictures on the evening news revealed how close they had come to disaster. The pilot had misjudged the length of the runway and the plane had tilted badly on landing, with the port wing only inches from the ground before it righted itself. As the narrowness of their escape sunk in, Tim turned to Patrick Wintour:

'Was that exciting enough for you?'

Then there was a burst of ironic – and relieved – applause and laughter as the usual announcement came over the intercom: 'For your safety and comfort, please keep your seat belts on until the plane has come to a stop.'

In the closing stages of the campaign, the old debate about advertising was re-opened. Saatchi's were keen to step up the spend and have a final burst to put across positive images of the Prime Minister. For the first time ever, Labour had been spending more than the Conservatives on advertising. To tie in with a new poster that was due to appear on the hoardings over the final weekend, Saatchi's wanted the Prime Minister to set out his personal credo in a full-page advert. Their copywriter had a valiant first stab. Sarah and Jonathan took the Saatchi draft and, drawing on many of the themes and much of the language used in the 1991 party conference speech, produced a version for the Prime Minister to work on. The end result is still the best summary yet produced of what John Major stands for and believes in.[7]

[7]See illustration on page 14 of the picture section.

After the relentless diet of bombshells and boxing gloves, the new poster marked a deliberate shift of gear to something softer and more reassuring: a picture of a smiling John Major with three happy schoolchildren above the caption 'The Best Future for Britain'. What no one realised was the trouble it had taken to get that particular picture.

A couple of weeks earlier, Saatchi's had shown Jonathan and Sarah a proof of the photograph. They liked what they saw. But there was something about it which made them hesitate. It didn't look quite natural, and the more they looked at it, the more their suspicion grew: it looked as though Saatchi's had stuck together two different pictures. A quick phone call dragged out the reluctant truth. It was a fake.

Jonathan and Sarah were clear. Either the picture would have to be re-shot so that it was authentic, or the poster would have to be scrapped. Saatchi's did not at first see what the fuss was about. The picture was 'symbolic'. It was 'suggestive' of the truth. It was faithful to reality, if not literally accurate. And anyway, no one would ever find out.

But Jonathan stuck to his guns, doggedly explaining that you couldn't 'position' John Major as being honest and straightforward on the basis of a bogus picture. How could one claim that the Prime Minister did indeed offer 'The Best Future for Britain' when the image chosen to illustrate that message was itself a lie? Eventually, Maurice Saatchi was ground down. The picture would be re-shot.

The happy task of breaking this news to the Prime Minister, and of making the arrangements for the filming to be done again, fell to Jonathan. First, the same three children had to be tracked down and their agreement to be photographed secured. Then the shoot had to be organised for a day when the weather would be fine. Not surprisingly, this proved more difficult. For a while, Saatchi's explored the possibility of filming indoors, but using a backdrop to suggest that the picture had been taken outside. Finally, after huge logistical difficulties and just before the deadline for printing expired, the Prime Minister, children, photographer and sunshine were united in the garden. The picture was taken, the poster appeared. And when Jonathan drove past it on the hoardings, he had the satisfaction of knowing that it was authentic.

Three years later, Jonathan and Sarah were chuckling over the story with Maurice Saatchi, reminding him in a slightly self-satisfied way of how they had made him go to the trouble of re-shooting the picture. Maurice took a reflective sip of his coffee.

'Well, I suppose I can tell you now.' he said, 'We didn't use any of that second batch of photos taken in Downing Street. None of them were any good.'

It was his turn to look pleased with himself.

'The picture we used for the poster was a scissors and paste job after all – and you never knew.'

Jonathan's laugh could best be described as hollow.

14

Too Close To Call

We are not interested in the possibilities of defeat, they do not exist.

Queen Victoria to Arthur Balfour, December 1899

The following extract appears in the transcript of the remarks made by the Prime Minister in Downing Street on the morning of Friday 10 April 1992:

> Question: Prime Minister, you refused to comment on opinion polls throughout the campaign. Would you care to comment on them now? (*Laughter*)
> Prime Minister: They were wrong. The Conservative Party was right.

With that the Prime Minister dismissed the subject that had come to dominate the campaign – and indeed had shaped the whole way it had been reported.

There were two very good reasons why he had refused to be drawn on the opinion polls during the campaign. First, because for most of the campaign they had shown that Labour were in the lead – and that was something he could not concede. Secondly, because his political nose told him they were wrong. This did not, however, stop him poring over them, like any Roman Consul poking around the insides of a chicken.

That he should have been worried about the polls was hardly

surprising: media judgements about the campaign were shaped almost entirely by what they were showing. Thus, if Labour were ahead in the polls, this meant the Tory campaign was a shambles. If the Tories were ahead, the PM was leading a fightback. And because the nature of the reporting had an impact on the morale of party workers, particularly in Central Office which was itself feeding back its mood to the commentators, the poll ratings did matter.

The Prime Minister's public line never cracked. He would win – and that was that. The commentators could not make up their minds whether he was whistling to keep his spirits up – or whether he genuinely knew something they didn't.

He, of course, had one huge advantage over them during those four and a half weeks: he visited more parts of the country, met more people, and spoke to more constituency agents and candidates than anyone else in Britain. Those conversations, and his politician's feel, told him that things were – from the beginning – much better than the polls were saying. The kind of response he was getting on the doorstep simply did not square with being 5, 6 or 7 percentage points behind in the polls.

It was, however, extremely difficult to reconcile the political mood the Prime Minister seemed to be picking up during the day with what he saw in the early editions of the next day's newspapers when he got back to Number 10 at night. He would arrive back buoyed up after a good day on the campaign trail or a successful rally, only to read that nationally, things seemed to be swinging away from the Conservatives.

Which, the Prime Minister would ask again and again, was right? His instinct – or the polls? People seemed friendly enough – but perhaps that was just traditional British politeness. Candidates seemed fairly confident – but perhaps that was just to keep his spirits up. Maybe people weren't telling him the hard truth. Perhaps they didn't want to upset him, and messages were being softened, diluted, blurred in transmission. Many of his friends were cheerful to him, gloomy to Sarah and Jonathan. The polls could be right after all.

The Prime Minister faced his most severe test on the Tuesday evening, a week before polling day. He was flying back to London after a successful day's campaigning. Jonathan had in his pocket some of the latest opinion poll results, which were due to be published in the next day's papers. He and Norman Fowler had not wanted to show them to the Prime Minister until they were homeward bound. As they got on to the plane, one of the journalists called out: 'What do you think about being seven per cent behind in the opinion polls, Prime Minister?'

The figures Jonathan had showed the Tories 'only' 4 per cent behind. He reassured the Prime Minister that they were joking, just trying to get a rise out of him. They weren't. Three polls in Wednesday's papers put Labour between 4 and 7 points ahead – enough to give them a comfortable majority.

Then on Wednesday evening the Labour Party held their monster rally in Sheffield. While the conventional wisdom has since become that Labour's Sheffield rally was a huge blunder which swung people back to the Conservatives, it did not look that way at the time. Labour had had an audience of ten thousand in precisely the same hall where the Tories had mustered only a thousand the previous week. And anyone watching the *Nine O'Clock News* that evening would have seen John Cole, the BBC's Political Editor, beside himself with excitement, hailing the rally as the most remarkable political event since Kennedy. It certainly looked as though Labour were on a roll.

By a nice quirk of history, the low point arrived at precisely the same point that the 1987 campaign had famously 'wobbled'. Would this Prime Minister wobble too? Seven points behind and with a week to go, he might have been forgiven for a loss of nerve. After all, the outbreak of panic in 1987 had happened when the Conservative lead had fallen back to 4 per cent – a bigger lead than the Tories achieved at any point during the 1992 campaign.

The mood among the Prime Minister's team was gloomy that night. They had tried everything they could think of but it didn't seem to have made any difference. For the first time, some of them contemplated the possibility of defeat. The Prime Minister, however, stayed calm. But he certainly felt the tension. That night, he and Chris Patten worked their way through a bottle of whisky when they got back to the flat at Number 10.

Why were the opinion polls so wrong in 1992? After the election, the polling organisations sought to provide an explanation. First, it was put down to a late surge in support for the Conservatives. Then, to the fact that people had 'lied' to the pollsters. There were also some big question marks over the polling or sampling techniques used, especially in marginal constituencies.

Reports that came in to Central Office from around the country supported the idea that there was a swing to the Conservatives over the final weekend. Indeed, in those last days before 9 April, the Prime Minister said repeatedly that he wished he could have another week of campaigning. (Jonathan and Sarah tried hard to look enthusiastic.) Throughout, the bedrock of support had been there. But, in the middle of a bruising recession, the electorate were going to make the Conservatives sweat for their votes.

Before the campaign started, Central Office had had indications that this was how voters were feeling. Canvass returns were showing that a large number of people who had previously voted Conservative were now putting themselves down as 'don't knows'. Canvassers were sent out to go back and probe them on how, come the crunch, they would vote. When pressed, they conceded that they would end up voting Conservative.

Nowhere had the polls been more carefully studied than in Scotland. They showed consistently that the Tories seemed to be heading for wipe-out, possibly losing all nine seats they had held when the campaign started. Gallons of ink were spilled speculating about the crisis that would follow such a defeat. Would the Tories still be able to govern? What would the constitutional position be? Could the Union possibly survive?

Given the profile of these issues, there was, therefore, more than usual interest when, during the second week of the election campaign, the Prime Minister arrived at Bute House in Edinburgh.

Bute House is the official residence of the Secretary of State for Scotland. A fine Georgian house with a splendid drawing room and precipitous spiral staircase, it has more than a faint air of a governor's residence in the colonies. It speaks of slower, more tranquil times and a political age long since vanished. It was a wonderful place for the Prime Minister to stay – but the worst place imaginable, Jonathan found, from which to have to fight a modern election campaign.

From the moment the travelling team arrived, the atmosphere was surreal. The Prime Minister was greeted by the housekeeper with a resounding kiss. An old friend? A *very* old friend? A long-lost relation? No, just enthusiasm.

As always on arrival, there was a lot to be done: a *Newsnight* interview to be filmed in a couple of hours' time; a press notice to clear for the next morning's press conference; a photo opportunity to organise; and a speech to work on for the big rally that would round the visit off the following evening.

'Where,' Jonathan politely inquired after he had in turn disentangled himself from the housekeeper's embrace, 'would I find the fax? Could you very kindly point me towards the photocopier? And the telephone?'

Sorry. No fax. No photocopier. But would he like a drink?

Back in Number 10, Switch interrupted Sarah's round of evening phone calls.

'Sarah, Jonathan's on the line. He sounds a bit funny. I don't know *where* he can be.'

He turned out to be in a service lift – which had the only easily accessible telephone. There he had to stand, one foot in the lift, one foot out to keep the door open, while he tried to find out what had been happening in London and what had been planned for the Prime Minister in Scotland for the next day.

Press notices, briefings, the draft speech from London – all had to be sent to Scottish Central Office, from where they would then set out on the twenty-minute journey to Bute House. Any changes Jonathan wanted then had to be taken back to Scottish Central Office to be typed up there – or faxed back to London for the start of the next leg of their tortuous journey. In the middle of this, Jonathan was told about the exciting and original photo opportunity that the party in Scotland had come up with, after a great deal of careful deliberation. Yes: the Prime Minister would be photographed signing a bottle of whisky.

So the nightmare unfolded with a ghastly momentum of its own. First, an ill-tempered *Newsnight* interview with Jeremy Paxman. Then, the Prime Minister was door-stepped for his reaction to Labour's 'Jennifer's Ear' party election broadcast, about which no one had thought to inform his team. Then, when they all staggered back exhausted to Bute House, the Prime Minister promptly declared that the speech he had been sent up was undeliverable: please re-write overnight.

The next morning, Jonathan went to look for the Prime Minister to brief him before the press conference. The Prime Minister, he was told, was having breakfast. Worried that he had arrived late and expecting to find the normal pre-press-conference panic going on, Jonathan went into the dining room. Silence – broken only by the rustle of newspapers and the industrious scrape of knife and fork. The Scottish Party top brass – with their wives – were at breakfast. And they clearly weren't going to interrupt their routine just for a general election. Jonathan's attempts to broach the subject of the press conference were rebuffed by a steady Protestant crunch of teeth on toast. No briefing.

Then came the photo-call with the bottle of whisky, followed by the highlight of the day – a visit to the *Dundee Courier*, from which, to their fury, all the other Scottish and national newspapers had been excluded. (When Jonathan pointed this out, somewhat tartly, he was assured that, och no, the *Dundee Courier* had been *vairy* pleased.)

At this point, Jonathan retreated in despair to Bute House to work with Norman Fowler on re-writing the speech shredded by the Prime Minister the night before. Nick and Ronnie laboured in London, producing yet another beautifully polished and dramatic speech. At Bute House they tweaked and twiddled, buffing and honing. And meanwhile, texts whirred to and from Scottish Central Office, into the car, round to Bute House, back again, and then down the fax to Downing Street – with whom Jonathan was in regular touch from his lift-shaft.

This was all the more necessary because the storm over Labour's broadcast was erupting into a case-study in campaign follies and media overkill. The 'War of Jennifer's Ear' had begun the night before with a Labour Party election broadcast featuring a little girl waiting for an ear operation because her parents couldn't afford to pay for one.

The argument being aired here – over the privileges of wealth and the fear of a two-tier health service – was hardly new. The Tories had statistical ammunition ready to demonstrate the fall in NHS waiting times. But the original issue quickly disappeared under a torrent of argument over the child herself. Beginning as a quite serious question – was it ethical to use a child in a party election broadcast? – coverage rapidly degenerated until it had become an insiders' detective story about who revealed her name to whom, when and how. The newspapers gave over page after page to the story, and the main evening news devoted as much as twenty minutes to it.

On the use of children, the Tories were not on completely secure ground, since their own defence broadcast featured a child – admittedly an actor whose real name was both irrelevant and protected – playing war games on a computer screen. But Labour were in obvious trouble, since they could hardly make an argument purporting to be based on an individual real-life case without expecting to be questioned on the details. Labour tried to fight back with accusations that the child's name had been unscrupulously 'leaked' by the Tories, but both parties soon got entangled in an impossibly confused saga of consultants, grandparents, newspapers, television journalists, Labour press officers, and the Central Office brat-pack.

In the end, this overkill probably worked to the disadvantage of the Labour Party, since the media reacted to their own excessive coverage by losing interest in health stories thereafter. Labour efforts to raise the 'salience' of the issue again flopped dismally. (This failure was made more certain by the fact that the list of supporting cases with which they sought to follow up 'Jennifer's Ear' were quickly shown to have been riddled with errors.) But in the meantime, the Tories suffered their worst press conference of the election campaign.

At 3.30 p.m. on Thursday 26 March, William Waldegrave was supposed to be heading up a cast of doctors and nurses assembled at Central Office to tell the press about the wonders of the NHS reforms. They were ignored as the journalistic pack, scenting blood, settled into sustained pursuit of the Health Secretary. Assertions about the Hippocratic Oath, Nazi propaganda, Tory moles and

Labour lies winged their way wildly round the room. It ended in shambles, leaving William Waldegrave badly bruised. The transcript, which Sarah extracted from Central Office to fax up to Scotland, did not make happy reading.

The episode showed up the disadvantage of having a Party Chairman forced by his own electoral vulnerability to disappear from Central Office to his constituency. As Chris Patten says, that particular press conference needed a heavy hitter, able to deflect fire from William Waldegrave and answer for Central Office. But the Chairman was in Bath, and there was no one in the same league to take his place.

Meanwhile, up in Scotland, the Prime Minister had arrived back late – and irritable – from his tour. He clearly needed some red meat to chew. Unfortunately, the speech was the first thing he saw. He chewed. The drafting and re-drafting began all over again. And the clock ticked on – and on, and on.

This was all part of the by now familiar ritual. The discharge of nervous tension. The emptying of the adrenalin fuel-tank, followed by its rapid replenishment as the Prime Minister began to get himself psyched up. All a vital part of the process of preparing himself for the big occasion.

Eventually, John Major was satisfied, and the rally got under way. As his speech unfolded with its ringing defence of the Union, so the tension rose. The applause grew stronger and stronger, the atmosphere becoming supercharged as the speech wound up to its peroration. Jonathan, who remembers standing there with tears streaming down his face, as were many that night, didn't know whether the mood was so emotional because the Prime Minister's appeal to old loyalties had struck a deep and resonant chord – or whether the last thousand remaining Unionists in Scotland were all there that evening, determined to go down in flames together.

Before the election, clever minds in Whitehall had spent a lot of time worrying about the Scottish question. (Indeed, Andrew Turnbull's clearest recollection of the campaign itself was his anxiety about the constitutional position in Scotland if the Conservatives won an overall majority but did not win enough Scottish seats to staff the Scottish Office.) There was agreement about the nature of the threat to Scotland's position within the Union. There was, initially at least, none about how to address it.

From the beginning, the Prime Minister's approach to Scotland was different from that of Margaret Thatcher. For her, Scotland was a land full of moaning minnies, strangely resistant to the Thatcherite revolution. They were an ungrateful lot who never even said thank you for the subsidy they received from the (English) taxpayer.

John Major understood why the Scots were proud and why they wanted to be different. He was sensitive to the emotions that led some to argue for independence and many more to think about devolution. He argued for the Union because he believed it was good for both Scotland and England. And he went to Scotland time after time to listen, learn, and put his case.

From the autumn of 1991 onwards, some in the Conservative Party – and many in the Scottish Office establishment – had been arguing that the best way to head off a possible constitutional crisis was for the Government to offer some move towards devolution. In the wake of the jitters that broke out after the Liberal Democrats' sweeping victory at the Kincardine and Deeside by-election that November, pressure started to build for a commitment in the Conservative Manifesto to look at devolution after the election. Senior Scottish Office officials, ex-Scottish Office Ministers, MPs, local councillors and party sources were busily at work, delivering off-the-record briefings to the effect that change would have to come.

Nearly all the advice that the Prime Minister and the Secretary of State for Scotland, Ian Lang, were receiving towards the end of 1991 was that some kind of devolution had become inevitable; it would therefore surely be better to make the concession now rather than be forced into it after the expected trouncing at the general election. From a narrow party political point of view, the choice was not an easy one: there was little to be gained from being fourth and last on to the devolution bandwagon; but the Conservatives would always be likely to have a majority in Westminster if Scotland – which returned so many Labour MPs – had a separate parliament. But Ian Lang, who had inherited a Scottish Conservative Party demoralised and divided after the factionalism of the 1980s, and the Prime Minister were of one mind: the Union was not up for grabs. They were opposed to anything that would weaken that historic relationship, or undermine Britain's collective voice in Europe and the world. As John Major explained in the key-note speech he made to the Scottish Candidates Conference in Glasgow on 22 February 1992:

> It is not the Conservative Party that gains — or has gained — most from the ties between Scotland and England. And yet it is our party that supports the Union. Not because it's always been good for us, but because it has always seemed *right* to us. Not always in our political interest, but always in that of our kingdom and the countries within it.

He made his defence of the Union the centre-piece of the morning press conference on the final Monday of the campaign – overruling Central Office, where it had been planned to concentrate on tax. This clearly caused some irritation in Smith Square, which someone did not hesitate to pass on to the press. The next day, Phil Stephens of the *Financial Times* wrote: 'Miffed campaign strategists at Central Office said it was not the first time that Downing Street has upset its plans.'

The Prime Minister himself regretted the timing of his press conference on the constitutional issues: rather than leaving it to the last week, he wished that he had kicked off the campaign with it. Chris Patten, who at the time thought the Prime Minister's choice was 'mildly eccentric', now agrees that it was the right thing for the Prime Minister to do. It is difficult to prove that the Prime Minister's defence of the Union swung any votes either in Scotland or in England – although there was quite a lot of anecdotal evidence that people decided in the last week of the campaign to vote Conservative because they were more 'patriotic'. But Jonathan and Sarah always believed it had two clear benefits.

First, because it was a subject about which the Prime Minister cared deeply, he spoke about it with feeling and passion, sounding more authoritative and stirring the emotions of his audience. And secondly, by lifting him above the day-to-day small change of political knockabout, it emphasised his qualities of leadership – where there was a clear advantage over Labour. The more the Prime Minister could be seen as a statesman and leader, the more Neil Kinnock would suffer by comparison.

At that final Monday press conference, the Prime Minister set out the four threats that he believed Labour and the Liberal Democrats posed to the constitution of the United Kingdom and to the Westminster Parliament:

> Firstly, the other parties would put at risk the links between Scotland and England which have held us together for nearly three hundred years . . . Secondly, they plan a new, expensive and, I believe, unwanted layer of government in England which would drain authority from Parliament. Thirdly, their enthusiasm for a federal Europe would increasingly surrender the independence of our Parliament to Brussels. Fourthly, the voting system that the Liberals want, and that the Labour Party appear to be flirting with, would change the way that the crucial decisions as to who governs Britain would be made.

These warnings, particularly about the dangers of proportional representation (PR), need to be seen in context: over the weekend, the opinion polls had been pointing towards a hung parliament. Were that to be the outcome, the Liberal Democrats would hold the balance of power. Paddy Ashdown thought (once again) his moment had come. He set out in public the price of his support: a promise to introduce proportional representation. The Prime Minister's response was immediate and unequivocal. No deals. No promises. No pacts. No PR. But the reaction from Labour was less clear-cut. Nudges and winks were exchanged. Doors were left open. Nothing was ruled in and nothing was ruled out. One of the reasons Labour got into such a mess was that on the last Friday of the campaign, they had a 'themed day' on constitutional reform. Unable, or unwilling, to be as flexible as the Tories proved in changing their press conferences, Labour – trapped in to talking about PR at precisely the moment when it became a live political issue – became the victims of their own planning.

From the Conservatives' point of view, the timing could not have been better. The sight of Neil Kinnock and Paddy Ashdown snuggling up to each other over the final crucial weekend was the best possible illustration of the old Tory message: 'Vote Liberal and you get Labour.'

All these themes came together in the final election broadcast of the campaign. The Prime Minister had decided that he would make the broadcast himself, with a straight appeal to the electorate, speaking directly to them as they sat in their living rooms in front of the television. There was to be nothing fancy, just a simple, unvarnished approach along the lines of the broadcast he had made to the nation when Desert Storm was launched.

Saatchi's had put together a sparkling montage of the Prime Minister's time at Number 10, carried along by the Lloyd Webber/Purcell theme music. This was to fade in to a prime ministerial piece to camera, which he was to record in Number 12 on the Sunday night. A tasteful shot was arranged with a window as backdrop, and a fine sunset arrived to lend a hand, casting its glow over the Prime Minister's head. There were two problems about this arty set-up: one, the Prime Minister, silhouetted by the television lights, was a sitting duck for a sniper in St James's Park; two, with sunsets, the sun sets – and it did, long before the Prime Minister had finished recording. The lights had to be rearranged several times, dragging out the whole business until night fell. Not surprisingly, the Prime Minister's performance had a distinctly weary tone.

The following morning, when the tape was reviewed at Central Office, Sarah's spirits fell. It simply wasn't good enough. After all the palaver, she did not look forward to telling the Prime Minister it would have to be filmed again.

She had a series of agonised conversations with Jonathan on the battlebus about how best to break the bad news. When the Prime Minister got back late that Monday evening, Sarah took a deep breath and told him the crew was coming around again the next day. She waited for the explosion.

'Oh good,' said the Prime Minister, 'I knew it wasn't up to scratch. When are they coming?'

More or less as the broadcast was going out on the Tuesday

evening, a small meeting was taking place up in the flat at Number 10. Present were the Prime Minister, Chris Patten, Tony Garrett from the campaign department at Central Office, Jonathan and Sarah.

The Prime Minister had just got back from the final rally at Wembley, which had been fitted in at the last moment to give the campaign an extra boost in its last stages.[1] The speech had gone well. The response had been enthusiastic. He was in good heart.

That was about to change. The meeting had been called to give the Prime Minister Central Office's best estimate of the likely election result. Tony, who among his other responsibilities had been co-ordinating the daily reports from constituencies around the country, went steadily through his figures. They were based on the feedback he had been getting from the network of agents around the country and his own excellent political 'feel'. Hedged around, as any prediction inevitably would be, his best bet boiled down to this: come Friday morning, the Conservatives would have somewhere between 316 and 339 seats: 316 would mean no overall majority, but John Major would still be Prime Minister of a minority administration; 339 would mean he would be back with a majority of 27.

Although this was better than the polls were showing, the atmosphere had become sombre – mainly because, as Tony ran through the marginals seat by seat, it became clear who some of the losers were likely to be. As the list lengthened to include names like Francis Maude and John Maples, so the mood became gloomier.

Finally, the Prime Minister asked Tony about Bath. Tony had agreed with Chris Patten beforehand that if asked, he would come straight out with the truth:

'I am afraid, Prime Minister, that we will lose Bath.'

The Prime Minister, plainly taken aback, turned to Chris.

'Chris, is that right?'

'Absolutely, Prime Minister.'

---

[1] The decision to hold an extra rally had been taken six days before on the way back to London from a rally in Shepton Mallet. The rallies cost in the region of £200,000 each.

The Prime Minister sat there in silence as the implications of this slowly sank in. It was the first time he had really had to accept that he would lose his Chairman. Chris had been contemplating the possibility of losing for the last year, but it was only at the weekend that he finally came to terms with it. For the Prime Minister it came as a cruel shock. It was a depressing way to round off the day, and just about the worst way to prepare for the final twenty-four hours of national campaigning.

There was one big hurdle left to surmount on the Wednesday morning: *Election Call,* a phone-in programme where the party leaders answer questions live on air from members of the public – or, more accurately, from party activists masquerading as members of the public, ringing up with detailed and difficult questions designed to trip the politicians up. It was on *Election Call* that Margaret Thatcher had famously come unstuck over a question about the sinking of the *General Belgrano* during the Falklands War. So the stakes are always high. The Prime Minister, relaxed and fluent by this stage of the campaign, put in one of his best performances. There were no problems either at the final press conference held later that morning in Smith Square.

It had originally been planned that the Prime Minister would spend the afternoon touring marginal seats in Essex, ending up back at Huntingdon in the evening. But he had agreed to undertake a series of interviews for BBC, ITN, Sky and Channel 4 for their evening news programmes, and information about the intended visit had leaked. After the experience in Luton, the detectives weren't in the mood for discussion: the visit was off. So a whistlestop tour of key south London marginals was arranged instead.[2]

It was then back to Central Office in the battlebus for the last time. There was an end-of-term feeling as lockers were emptied and possessions unloaded. The Prime Minister and Norma had their photographs taken with the driver and his support team, together

---

[2]One of the constituencies the Prime Minister had originally planned to visit was Basildon. He did not, unfortunately, bring luck to the constituencies he visited instead. He spoke in support of three MPs – Colin Moynihan, John Maples and Gerald Bowden. All three lost the following day.

with those who had travelled with them day in, day out over the previous four weeks.

In the late afternoon, the Prime Minister set out on the final frenzied burst of television interviews, ending up at Channel 4. He was in buoyant, cheerful mood and stayed behind for a drink afterwards. The atmosphere was friendly, but Jonathan felt that there were not many in the room who thought the Prime Minister would still be in the job in thirty-six hours' time.

The Prime Minister arrived back at Number 10 at about 8.00 p.m. Norma had been ready to go since mid-afternoon. Most of the Majors' personal things from the flat had already been taken up to Huntingdon, or were packed away in cardboard boxes, stacked up in the little hall of the flat. Norma thought it would be tempting providence not to pack, so everything had been ready weeks before. She had not needed the insensitive reminder from the then Appointments Secretary who, halfway through the campaign, had said to her:

'Now, you won't forget to order the removal van, will you?'

The car was parked by the front door, in full view of the television cameras. So there was no question of the Prime Minister and Norma being able to slip out the back way through the garden.

At about 9.30 p.m., the Majors came down from the flat. The Prime Minister, Norma, Jonathan and Sarah stood talking by the lift, just beyond the hall. Norma was by now impatient to be off, but the Prime Minister wanted to chat. Eventually, he said, 'Well, we really must be going,' for the final time, looked around him, said goodnight and with a nod to the doorman to open the door, walked out with Norma to the car and the flashlights. The door closed behind them. Outside the car doors slammed, followed by the distinctive roar of the cars pulling away.

Number 10 suddenly felt very quiet – and very empty. It was one of those moments when the building seems to have a life of its own. It was as though it were holding its breath, its old heart giving a muffled beat through the walls.

When you start thinking like that, you know it is time to go home and get some sleep.

15

Opening the Black Box

The greatest tragedy in the world, Madam, except a defeat.
                    Wellington, in reply to the remark,
                    'What a glorious thing must be a victory.'

Long after the election, Sarah asked Douglas Hurd what he remembered most about the 1992 campaign. He paused and thought. 'Very cold,' he said.

It was a long time since the politicians had fought a campaign so early in the year. But 9 April itself wasn't cold at all. It turned out to be a fine spring day. The Prime Minister would be spending it in his constituency, doing the traditional candidate's tour of the committee rooms where his party workers were busy working to get his supporters out to vote. For most of the rest of his team there was, until the evening, nothing further they could do.

Jonathan was voting in Hammersmith, where in 1987 Labour had had a majority of only 2,415. Looking for omens, he went to his polling station. Business was slack. He and his wife were the only people voting. That was two for the Conservatives, anyway. He felt more confident, and the early morning sunshine helped. As they walked out, two mini-buses packed to the gunnels pulled up – driven by Labour Party workers. That made it about forty to two. Not so confident, after all.

Tim Collins was still on duty, looking after the press pouring into the Prime Minister's constituency. He had taken the first train up to Huntingdon, and when he arrived at the Majors' house, The Finings, there was still a cold morning mist. The Prime Minister had agreed to have his photograph taken by the *Standard*, and Tim stood shivering outside with the reporter and photographer. Suddenly, about fifteen minutes before the shoot was due, the front door opened a fraction and out shot a hand – belonging to an apparently naked Prime Minister – to pick up the milk. The *Standard* photographer never knew the scoop he had missed. Fifteen minutes later the Prime Minister appeared to have his photograph taken – clothed.

He was in high good humour, having been greatly entertained by a photograph in the *Sun* of an overweight granny in a red swimming costume under the caption: 'How Page 3 Girls Would Look Under Labour'. After breakfast, he and Norma set off on a tour of the constituency, each of them taking half, working their way round in opposite directions. The Prime Minister himself voted mid-morning. As he left the polling station, he walked under a sign marked WAY OUT. There, predictably, was the photographer from the *Daily Mirror*, camera poised. Tim kicked himself, having succeeded in avoiding similar shots all through the campaign. The picture duly appeared – but oddly only in the first edition.

Tim kept ringing Smith Square to keep the Prime Minister posted as the latest intelligence came in from the constituencies. The news filtering back was encouraging. At Eastbourne – which the Conservatives had lost badly in a by-election in October 1990[1] – voting was very brisk. The Conservative vote was turning out in force.

Meanwhile, in Downing Street, the Private Office was throwing its traditional election day drinks party in the Number 10 garden. By lunchtime it was in full swing. The girls from the Political Office were watching from one of the windows in the State Rooms. Although they had been invited, they were reluctant to join in. For most civil servants, watching the election was like going to the races. They would all have jobs the next day, whatever the

[1] The loss of Eastbourne triggered a mass outbreak of panic on the Tory benches and contributed to the downfall of Margaret Thatcher.

outcome, whoever the Prime Minister. But for the exhausted girls in the Political Office, it was not so funny: a Labour victory would mean they would be out on their ears by Friday lunchtime. The same rule applied to Nick True and Sarah – and the other members of the Policy Unit who were not career civil servants.

The girls were eventually prevailed upon to go down and have a drink, but as they walked out into the garden, they were greeted with a shout: 'And for our next game, we're going to play watching the faces of the Political Office as the results come in tonight . . .'

Sarah's secretary – although a career civil servant – had an equally unpleasant polling day. She had been told that Labour would bring in outside secretaries to the Policy Unit, and as a precaution she had applied for a job as a duty clerk. An insensitive official chose polling day to tell her she had been rejected. Robin Butler came to the rescue with friendly reassurance about her prospects, but it was an extra strain she could have done without.

After lunch at The Finings, the Prime Minister continued on his tour of the constituencies. In the afternoon, he stopped for a cup of tea at a hotel. It was a typically English scene. Perfectly manicured lawns sloping down to a lake, on which ducks were swimming; the buzz of quiet chatter; the clink of cup on saucer. People there were struck by how relaxed the Prime Minister seemed, chatting away cheerfully as his fate hung in the balance.

As Jonathan and Sarah left London for the drive up to Huntingdon, where they were going to watch the election results with the Prime Minister, Tim was about to commit his only real *faux pas* of the campaign. Having seen John Major safely back to The Finings, he had gone into the outhouse where the police rest, in order to put his feet up for an hour or two without getting in the Majors' hair. It was the end of a long day after weeks of long days. He fell asleep and started to snore. But he had unfortunately chosen to fall asleep in the middle of that week's episode of *The Bill*. The police who protect the Prime Minister's house are a friendly and hospitable lot, but not during *The Bill*. A short and ruthless jab to the ribs was rapidly administered. Tim did not fall asleep again.

At Sarah's side in the car, as she and Jonathan drove out of London, was a locked black box of official papers. It was there for a grisly purpose. During the campaign, as the polls looked bleak for the Prime Minister, the official machine had been doing its constitutional duty, preparing papers on minority governments, deals, resignation. That was right and proper. But Sarah had not wanted to show them to the Prime Minister. Confident as he was, it was bound to be disheartening to learn quite how well-prepared his officials seemed to be for life under Neil Kinnock.

In the end, Sarah went to the Cabinet Secretary to see if she could do a deal. She wanted his agreement that these papers could be kept from the Prime Minister, on the strict understanding that he would see them the minute the polls closed. Jonathan and she would meanwhile work on any statements that might be needed, and show it to the officials concerned. Robin Butler had agreed. So in the box were options for every eventuality, from victory, through hung Parliament, to outright defeat.

At ten o'clock, as the polls shut, they took the Prime Minister aside and told him the story. He was greatly amused. He spent five minutes looking at the papers. Then he tossed them back into the box, and the three of them went next door, where Tim Collins was watching the election results programme.

The first constituencies to declare were quite encouraging: the swing against the Conservatives was smaller than the exit polls had predicted, and far smaller than Labour would need to win an overall majority. Then the cameras cut to Basildon, a key marginal in the south-east, which Labour would have to win if they were going to form a Government.

The candidates were lined up on the platform waiting for the result to be declared. All eyes were on their faces, looking for clues. The Conservative candidate, David Amess, looked gloomy, his wife shattered.

'Look at her face', Sarah said. 'He's lost.'

'Look at *his* face,' the Prime Minister said. 'He's won.'

The Prime Minister had recognised the signs of a successful candidate struggling to keep his face set and expression grave.

Then the result. The Prime Minister leapt to his feet.

'That's it. We've done it. We've won the election.'

He went through to the other room where the rest of the family and Edward Llewellyn and Shirley Stotter were sitting. He punched his fist triumphantly into the palm of his hand.

'We've won. We've beaten the bastards.'[2]

The papers that Jonathan and Sarah had prepared stayed in the box. No one needed to look at them again.

But the euphoria did not last. In the kaleidoscope of results now whirling in came the news the Prime Minister least wanted: confirmation of Chris Patten's defeat at Bath. The result would have been hard enough to bear in any circumstances. It was made far worse by the behaviour of the Liberal Democrat supporters. As Chris tried to congratulate the victor and thank the people of Bath for their support over the years, he was drowned out by a barrage of jeering and barracking. Just as the Prime Minister had shared in David Amess's delight and relished his huge grin, now he had to endure watching the set of Chris's face — and that of his wife, Lavender, as she stood by his side.

A deep gloom settled on the sofa, which the steady flow of good news did little to dispel. At the time, the Prime Minister did not think beyond the fact that a close personal friend had lost his seat. It was only gradually that the full extent of the blow became apparent. Chris Patten's defeat punched a huge hole at the heart of the Government: the Prime Minister was deprived of his closest and most heavyweight political ally. Arguably, the course of the next three years would have been very different if Chris Patten had still been at the Prime Minister's side, holding one of the great offices of state.

Only one set of people behaved worse than the Bath Liberal Democrats that night — the group of Thatcherites who gathered at a house in Great College Street to watch the results coming in. When the news of Chris's defeat was announced, a cheer went up — an ugly foretaste of the factionalism with which the party was to become all too familiar over the next three years. Margaret Thatcher, who was always far bigger than her supporters, told them to behave themselves.

[2]At this stage, the word 'bastards' was still used exclusively to describe the official Opposition . . .

Round about half-past one, the Prime Minister and Norma went upstairs to change. As the Prime Minister shaved in the bathroom, Edward Llewellyn, perched on the bed next door, shouted the results through the door, as the figures inched up towards the majority.

By the time the Prime Minister and Norma arrived at the Huntingdon count,[3] the Conservatives were within sight of an overall majority. In a break with tradition, only the candidates – and not their supporters – were allowed on to the floor of the large, soulless sports hall where the count was taking place. The atmosphere was as flat as a pancake. Even the presence of Lord Buckethead and Screaming Lord Sutch as candidates could do little to liven things up.

Eventually, at about quarter-past three, the result was announced. John Major had been returned as the Member of Parliament for Huntingdon with a majority of 36,000 – the biggest anywhere in the United Kingdom.

After the acceptance speech, it was out into the throng of journalists who were besieging the hall. A battery of television cameras lay beyond the door. Jonathan was waiting to take the Prime Minister to one side and run through what he might say to the cameras. He had expected to find him buoyed up by the scale of his own victory in Huntingdon, and was ready with his congratulations. Instead, all the colour had drained from the Prime Minister's face. He looked hollow and drawn, as though he had just suffered a crushing personal defeat. The adrenalin which had powered him through the last frantic weeks had ceased to flow. He was dog-tired, and for the first time throughout the whole campaign, he had just had enough.

Jonathan knew he had to get him back to the car and on his way to London. To do that, he had to get him past the television cameras, preferably without looking like death not very warmed up. 'Come on, Prime Minister. Smile, for God's sake. You've just won. Come on. Smile.'

---

[3] Traditionally, Huntingdon had not declared until the Friday morning. This time, for obvious reasons, it had been decided to announce the result that night.

And making a final effort, the Prime Minister went out smiling into the wall of blinding white lights.

The convoy sped through the night back to London. There was no other traffic on the road. The Prime Minister travelled with Norma in the first car, his children James and Elizabeth in the second, Jonathan, Tim Collins, Shirley Stotter and Edward Llewellyn bringing up the rear. In Jonathan's car, exhaustion set in and conversation fizzled out. Just the mesmerising sound of the wheels running over the tarmac, the drone of the radio, the blurred red of the tail-lights in front. Then, the four o'clock headlines: 'The Conservatives have won the 1992 general election.' A ragged cheer went up from the back seat.

In planning for election night, one of the biggest worries had been that the Prime Minister might get back to London before his Chairman. If John Major won, he would want his Chairman to share in the glory. If he lost, he would need Chris Patten's advice more than anybody's. But there might be delays – perhaps recounts – in Bath. So they had arranged that Sarah would leave for London before the rest of the team, keep in touch, and make sure that Chris was at Central Office before the Prime Minister arrived.

Sarah had arrived back in London in the small hours. First, she went to Number 10 and checked for news there. Then she went out to Central Office, still clutching her highly sensitive black box of official papers. Smith Square had gone wild – from her driver's point of view, rather too wild. As her car turned into the square, a gang of rioters attacked it, bashing the wing and kicking the door.

She got through the crowd of Conservative supporters outside number 32 and up to the Chairman's office. It was already beginning to fill up with some familiar friendly faces, together with others last seen or heard attacking Chris Patten, the Prime Minister, or anyone else in sight. She was also given the first taste of the press's belief that they had won the election single-handedly for the Conservatives. Many who had written the Prime Minister off and derided his campaign were now turning up to lard him with praise.

Chris Patten had arrived back at Smith Square at about 3.30 a.m. He had driven back from Bath in silence, lost in his own thoughts, not really taking in the results as they continued to pour in. As his car pulled up, there was applause and cheering – but to those who had worked most closely with him, it struck an odd note. It did not feel like victory. John Gardiner, who had helped run Chris's Private Office and spent the campaign helicoptering with him to and from Bath, remembers his response to an excited member of the brat-pack who had clapped him on the back, exclaiming: 'We've won. We've won.'

'Oh really?' said John, 'Have we?'

At half-past four, Sarah spoke to Jonathan on the car-phone, and then to the Prime Minister, to reassure them that the Chairman was back. Jonathan rang her a few minutes before they arrived, so she could warn Chris to be on standby. It was just after five o'clock when the Prime Minister turned into Smith Square, but the television lights made it as bright as day. A roar went up from the crowd outside the Central Office building, well-oiled after hours of celebrating: members of the public drawn to Smith Square after their election-night parties had flagged, and party workers still dazed by the result.

The Prime Minister and Norma squeezed their way in to the building and up the stairs for the traditional pictures and speech of thanks from the Prime Minister. Now came Tim Collins's sweetest moment.

The party political broadcast made about the Prime Minister's life by John Schlesinger had shown the Prime Minister driving down Coldharbour Lane, back to the house where he had grown up. It was the first time he had been there for over thirty years. As the car drove along the road, the Prime Minister, craning his neck to look up at the flat where he had lived – and which had such mixed memories for him – had said, totally unconsciously, 'Is it still there? It is. It is.' The press, who saw this as a classic piece of prime ministerial Pooterism, used to taunt Tim with it every day. As their coach turned into Smith Square every evening and Central Office came into view, a shout would go up: 'Is it still there? It is. It is.' Each time they clambered back on to their coach after visiting a school or a hospital on the Prime Minister's tour, up would go the cry: 'Is it still there? It is. It is.' After four weeks, the joke was starting to wear a little thin.

But for Tim, there was life in it yet. As the Prime Minister walked up the stairs, with the press milling around below him, Tim shouted out loud and clear:

'Is he still there? He is. He is.'

The Prime Minister did not stay long at Central Office. A first celebratory glass of champagne in the little cubby hole next to the Chairman's office – the only quiet corner that could be found – and then back to Number 10.

Dawn was breaking as the Prime Minister's Daimler swung back into Downing Street, the television lights still burning brightly in the cold, grey light. Graham Bright, the Prime Minister's PPS, who had just held on to the highly marginal seat of Luton South – one of the results that gave the Majors the greatest pleasure – was waiting by the front door. Graham, who is not a small man, gave Norma a huge bear-hug. She survived.

It was only when Sarah and Jonathan walked back through the familiar black door that the realisation of what the Prime Minister had done really sank in. One or two of the custody guards who were nearing retirement had risked wearing 'JM4PM' badges on the backs of their lapels, which they would reveal when their managers weren't looking. Now their smiling faces brought it home. The Prime Minister was back.

Jonathan and Sarah went up to the flat for a drink with the Prime Minister and Norma. It was curiously peaceful – the briefest of lulls before events swept them all forward again. The Prime Minister switched on Ceefax, turning to Huntingdon, where his own massive majority stared him in the face. In all the glory of national success, it was this local endorsement which gave him the greatest pleasure. Ceefax stayed firmly on that page.

There was a sub-text, too. On the Monday, Peter Brown, the Prime Minister's Constituency Agent, had begun to worry. The Prime Minister had said at the start of the campaign that he expected to have a majority of 30,000 – bigger than the 27,000 he had won in 1987. The polls seemed to place this out of reach. 'I daren't tell him it may only be twenty thousand,' Peter said, 'but somebody must. We've got to depress his expectations.'

Jonathan and Sarah conferred. They knew how much Huntingdon

meant to him. They were fearful that, even if things went well nationally, he might be distracted by a disappointing Huntingdon result. So Sarah warned him that Huntingdon might be 'a bit down'. On Friday, as the screen displayed his 36,000 majority, he pointed and grinned at her.

Chris Patten had come over, and the Prime Minister was determined to take him out to share the final glory. Equally typically, Chris was extremely reluctant. He felt it was the Prime Minister's moment, to savour on his own. But the Prime Minister insisted. He knew how much he owed Chris. He knew the part his Chairman had played in making victory possible; and that in doing so, he had probably sacrificed his own political career.

Before going out, there was one final ritual to be played out – the custom by which the winning Prime Minister is applauded out into the street by the Number 10 staff. They lined up on both sides of the hall, forming a funnel through which the Prime Minister and Chris Patten had to pass. The applause was long and warm – none warmer than from those who twenty-four hours earlier had looked forward to the Prime Minister's defeat with the greatest equanimity. It made Sarah remember the story William Waldegrave had told her of how he had crept away from the Number 10 Political Office in February 1974, watching the people with whom he had worked so closely now warmly applauding the arrival of Harold Wilson.

But every triumph has such bittersweet ironies. Nothing could destroy the fact that, against the odds, the Prime Minister had pulled it off. He had done what he had longed to do since November 1990 – win his own mandate. For the first time, he was his own man. He had rid himself of his inheritance and emerged from the long shadows cast by Margaret Thatcher. The Conservative Party, which could not have won without him, lay at his feet. The tensions and strains of the last seventeen months were behind him. From now on, he could set his own course through calm waters.

Or so we thought.

AFTERWORD

———

'Put Up or Shut Up'

He will be able to put aside one issue that has preoccupied him since he took over from Margaret Thatcher; the Tories' divisions over the European Community will now not count. For the first time since Britain joined the EC in 1973, its role in Europe can be framed without regard to the minutiae of domestic politics.

The Economist, 11 April 1992

It did not seem quite like that on a cloudy July day in 1995. As the quarter-finalists slammed it out at Wimbledon, John Major was fighting for the leadership of the Conservative Party for the second time. But this contest he had called himself, to bring the trouble brewing on his backbenches to a head. The cause – or at least the focus – of that trouble was: Europe.

The Prime Minister had had only the briefest of honeymoons after his victory in April 1992. From the time of the Danish referendum in June onwards, things had not gone his way. Black Wednesday, uproar over pit closures, two tax-raising Budgets and a seemingly-endless series of ministerial resignations landed hammer-blow after hammer-blow on the Government's standing. Its opinion poll ratings had fallen to record lows, and defeat had followed defeat in local and European elections. After the rout of May 1995, Tory councillors had become an endangered species.

Fearful of following them into oblivion, the Tory parliamentary party had become hard to handle, drawn into a vicious spiral of disunity and unpopularity, each reinforcing the other. The Government's small parliamentary majority gave a rump of unrepresentative backbenchers a disproportionate influence. Fed by relentless media coverage, the habits of faction and rebellion – first learnt with the Maastricht Bill – put down their poisonous roots. Twice, the Prime Minister had to make his European policy an issue of confidence – so that Conservative rebels risked precipitating a general election if they helped Labour defeat the Government's business.

Even after the Maastricht Bill was passed, the European argument raged on. First, the Prime Minister had trouble with the left wing of his party, who jibbed at his scepticism about a single currency and robust defence of the nation state in an article for *The Economist* in 1993. Then he had problems with the right, who wanted him to commit himself to a referendum on Europe.

This pattern repeated itself with a hideous predictability. In 1994, there was a struggle with the Euro-enthusiasts, particularly among the MEPs, to bring them in line for the all-out attack on federalism on which the Prime Minister wished to base his campaign for the elections to the European Parliament. Then, more trouble with the Euro-sceptics, when he had had to compromise over the new voting system for the enlarged European Union. In the summer, however, he proved that the British veto still had power, when at the Corfu Council he wielded it against the appointment of Jean-Luc Dehaene,[1] the tubby Belgian federalist originally chosen by European central casting to succeed Jacques Delors as President of the European Commission.

Back in Britain, however, the Prime Minister's Euro-troubles rumbled on: even Rory the lion cub at London Zoo, the symbol of Britain's six-month presidency of the European Community in 1992, had sickened and died. Europe, Europe, Europe had preoccupied the Prime Minister, obsessed a part of his parliamentary party and provided a field day for the press – while no doubt

---

[1]Jean-Luc Dehaene was not without a sense of humour. After winning his own domestic election in 1995, he thanked John Major: British opposition had been just the popular platform a Belgian politician needed.

continuing to interest the rest of the country quite as little as it had in the 1992 election campaign.

Nineteen ninety-five began with a small group of Euro-rebels in exile from the Conservative parliamentary party. The Whip had been withdrawn from eight when they refused to support the Government on a vote of confidence over the European budget. A ninth backbencher – Sir Richard Body – had taken himself into voluntary exile. But with its majority over Labour in the Commons down to twelve,[2] the Government was all too obviously in need of the 'whipless wonders' back in the fold, or at least in the parliamentary lobbies. When they were accepted back, still truculent, the loyalists seethed. Mutterings and rumours about a challenge to the Prime Minister began to circulate in all parts of the party. The brew was given a further stir when the Prime Minister indicated that he was sympathetic to the recommendations of the Nolan Committee proposing restrictions on how MPs could make money, and on the jobs Ministers could take up when they left government.

In the Sunday papers on 11 June, Margaret Thatcher added another untimely mite, when her new book was promoted with well-publicised swipes at John Major. Two days later, he was speaking to the Euro-sceptic 'Fresh Start' group of Conservative MPs. Towards the end of the meeting, the Prime Minister was openly attacked by a handful of backbenchers.

The Chief Whip was known to be retiring after five hard years in the job; there was disarray in the Whips' Office; discipline in the parliamentary party seemed to have collapsed. The question on everybody's lips was: when would the Prime Minister be challenged for the leadership, and by whom? Could he limp through to November, when a formal challenge could be mounted? Or would the mythical 'men in grey suits' present him with a revolver and a tumbler of whisky before then?

On Saturday 17 June, the Prime Minister was on his way back

[2]With the death of Geoffrey Dickens, MP for Littleborough and Saddleworth, the Government's majority had fallen to ten by the time of the leadership election in June/July 1995.

from the Halifax Economic Summit. For the first time he floated
with his advisers an idea he had been turning over in his mind for
some time: instead of suffering death by a thousand cuts between
then and November, wouldn't it be better to precipitate a challenge
now? He might lose, but he would at least have his stab-wounds in
the front.

The next day he was at home in Huntingdon, talking on the
phone to one or two of his closest political allies, trying his idea
out for size. Norma, with whom he talked it over at length, was
enthusiastic. The sniping had gone on for long enough. Now was
the time to hit back. It was high-risk, high-wire stuff. But anything
– even defeat – would be better than the current back-biting. Late
on Monday evening, the Prime Minister discussed the options with
his present and past PPSs: John Ward and Graham Bright. By the
end of that meeting, Graham – who was one of those to whom
John Major had spoken on Sunday – was absolutely certain that the
Prime Minister had made up his mind to gamble all. One particular
rumour was swirling round with ever-increasing intensity: Norman
Lamont was going to challenge in November, but would declare his
candidature well before then in order to cause maximum mayhem
at the October party conference. John Ward and Graham Bright
ran through all the possible problems of precipitating a challenge
early, but the more they argued, the more the Prime Minister came
back to a simple point: he was not prepared to stand there and watch
the Conservative Party he had joined at sixteen tear itself apart at
the party conference.

The next morning, Sarah – who had left Number 10 in February
– had a summons from the Private Office: could she pop in to see
the Prime Minister, please? She found him in the garden. He quickly
came to the point. He did not intend to sit around until the autumn,
while his authority was undermined by incessant speculation. It was
time for the parliamentary party to decide whether they wanted him
to continue as leader. He was going to resign, to bring the challenge
forward. He had been working on two draft statements, one for the
executive of the 1922 Committee, the other for the press, which he
wanted Sarah to look at. What did she think?

Sarah knew why she was there. They had had this conversation before, while she had still been at Number 10. What the Prime Minister was now contemplating was a course of action she had argued against in past years. He clearly wanted to hear the counsel of caution one more time.

Having been out of Number 10 for four months, Sarah was wary about advising from a distance. Still, the Prime Minister had asked. So she ran through the arguments against. The party was always more turbulent in the summer than the autumn. Things might calm down again. He had always, in the past, gained authority in the autumn, with a good party conference. By then he would have a new Chief Whip, fresh to the task of holding the parliamentary party together.

The prospect of a challenge might simply fade away, as it had in 1994, and 1993, and 1992. But if he provoked a leadership election, although he would take the party by surprise, he must increase the risk that someone would feel obliged to stand. He – or she – would have the excuse that the Prime Minister had invited a challenge, and might secure more votes as a consequence. Backbenchers might feel that they had been bounced by the Prime Minister. What's more, once it was clear this was the only opportunity for a leadership election before the next general election, wobblers would feel more inclined to vote for change. In short, this was a tactic likely to maximise the vote against the Prime Minister.

This last point, however, she could see attracted rather than discouraged him. He actively wanted a challenge. Sarah looked again at his drafts, and urged him to make it clearer that, having resigned, he would himself be standing for re-election – and fighting all out to win. She then went through the obvious points. Who would his campaign team be? Would the rules governing the election be clear? Was it certain that there could be no further challenge in November? When she left, she did not know which way the Prime Minister would go.

Throughout Tuesday, the Prime Minister continued taking soundings from a handful of close colleagues, testing his own calculations and instincts against theirs. But it was not until Wednesday that he finally decided to go for broke. By the evening, the small Downing Street political team were at action stations. But his campaign team was not put in place until Thursday.

The Prime Minister did not talk about his plans to Robert Cranborne – the Lord Privy Seal, who was to run his campaign – until Wednesday evening. Then he asked Robert to go to tell Tony Newton, the Leader of the House of Commons, that he was going to go ahead. Very early on Thursday morning, Robert – not normally a dawn riser – went to see the Prime Minister again. If he was to run the campaign he needed a number of decisions to be taken: fast. First, could he have the Prime Minister's permission to miss Cabinet, so that he could see Sir Marcus Fox, the Chairman of the Tory backbench 1922 Committee, which was responsible for the election rules? Second, who did the Prime Minister want in his team?

The next key appointment was Ian Lang, who was to be in charge of media handling. Tony Newton and Brian Mawhinney, the Transport Secretary, were also at the first strategy meeting held in Number 12 on Thursday morning, together with the Prime Minister's Political Secretary, Howell James, and his two PPSs, John Ward and Lord McColl. The Party Chairman and the Chief Whip also sat in on that first meeting, but it was decided that neither the Whips' office nor the party machine could play an active part, as they had to remain neutral. After Cabinet, the Prime Minister asked the Home Secretary, Michael Howard, to join the core team. Alastair Goodlad, a Foreign Office Minister and former Deputy Chief Whip, Archie Hamilton, a former PPS to Margaret Thatcher, and Graham Bright were to be responsible for the most important element of all: the operation in the House of Commons.

Meanwhile, two other pieces in the planning jigsaw were snapped rapidly into place: members of the Cabinet were told of the Prime Minister's decision, and a campaign HQ was identified. The Prime Minister did not have time to tell all of his Cabinet colleagues himself. John Redwood was not singled out for special attention – or rather, inattention. He, like a number of other Cabinet Ministers, was told by one of John Major's team.

Graham Bright had been put in charge of finding a headquarters.

He had finally settled on 13 Cowley Street, which belonged to former MP Sir Neil Thorne (and a small white dog which barked excitedly at moments of tension). Graham immediately set about getting extra phone lines installed – the first of many bits of new business put BT's way by the leadership election. At the very moment the Prime Minister was announcing in Downing Street that he was standing down as leader of the Conservative Party, Cowley Street was being dug up by BT engineers.

The afternoon had to be carefully choreographed. After Prime Minister's Questions, John Major had to see the executive of the 1922 Committee to tell them of his resignation as party leader. That meeting was set for 4.15 p.m. The press were called in to Number 10 for 4.30 p.m. – even though the Prime Minister would not be ready until 5.00 p.m. at the earliest. He wanted surprise. He did not want the announcement to dribble out. It was better to keep lobby correspondents waiting in the sunshine than risk them bumping into a member of the 1922 executive in the corridors of the House of Commons.

Standing in the garden of Number 10 – only the second time he had followed this White House practice – the Prime Minister read out his statement. He was resigning – words which winged their way around the world in minutes. But he was going to fight – news which took just a little longer to percolate. He ended robustly, with words on which he had clearly been brooding: it was, he said, time for his critics to 'put up or shut up'. Those with longer memories winced at this echo of Bernard Ingham's lobby briefing in 1990, which brought Michael Heseltine out of the shadows to challenge Margaret Thatcher.

But the Prime Minister did not care: and the parallel seemed to pass the press by. Taken completely by surprise by the Prime Minister's bombshell, and always stimulated by a story, reporters and commentators on the whole reacted positively.[3] That first evening,

---

[3]There was an intriguing contrast between two commentators, Simon Jenkins and Norman Tebbit. Simon Jenkins was one of the few to criticise the gamble, while concluding that he hoped the Prime Minister would win – a position he stuck to. Norman Tebbit initially applauded the decision – but later attacked it, and gave it as one of the reasons that he was supporting John Redwood.

John Major was on a roll, with commentators noting that same sense of liberation and energy that they had witnessed during the 1992 election campaign.

But this campaign would be much shorter. Sir Marcus Fox made it known, after the press conference, that nominations would close in a week's time, on 29 June. The ballot for the first round would take place on Tuesday 4 July. To win, the Prime Minister would need to get a majority in the parliamentary party – 165 votes – and to be 15 per cent ahead of any rival: a margin of fifty votes. It was a tough combination.[4] When Margaret Thatcher was challenged in 1990, it was this second condition she failed to meet. Michael Heseltine ran her just that little bit too close.

The speed with which the Prime Minister moved certainly caught his critics by surprise. But it also caused problems for his own team. His announcement unleashed a torrent of press inquiries, which – since they concerned the leadership rather than government or straightforward party business – neither the Number 10 nor the Smith Square Press Office were permitted to handle. With no media machine at all to rely on, it was Ian Lang and Howell James who had to pick up the pieces in Cowley Street. The ground-floor front room became an information exchange for MPs, the small room at the back was given over to press handling; in the basement, Debbie de Satgé, with help from a couple of House of Commons secretaries, speedily created an engine room at the back of the kitchen. Media monitoring took place out in a little courtyard at the back of the house, while sensitive meetings were held out by the dustbins.

Friday (the 23rd) was a crazy day, as Howell James attempted to knock the Cowley Street media operation into shape. The phones were ringing non-stop, so much so that they had to be taken off the hook for an hour while the small team handling the press decided who was going to do what. Order was imposed on media handling when a roster of volunteer press officers was set up

[4]Matthew Parris, the columnist and former Tory MP, pungently described the difficulty any leader experienced in getting the overwhelming support of a bunch of parliamentarians: 'Three quarters of them are bored, half of them are stupid, a third of them are rats, a third of them are bitter and a tenth of them are mad.'

under the direction of Damian Green, while Tim Collins looked after the lobby correspondents in his spare time.[5] Tory MPs bounced in and out of the house in Cowley Street, offering to help and demanding to 'see the numbers'. In that small, panelled house, the temperature steadily rose. There was no shortage of volunteers – but there was, to start with, a lack of organisation.

There was a ripple of unease in the City when the Foreign Secretary announced he was resigning – was everyone jumping overboard? But the announcement was smoothed over – even turned to the Prime Minister's advantage. The election, it was now clear, would be followed by a big reshuffle. Hopes rose in backbench breasts.

By Saturday, the high command had settled into their roles. Robert Cranborne was Commander-in-Chief; Ian Lang, commander in the field (that is, on the airwaves); Alastair Goodlad was the campaign's head of MI5 and supplier of a 'safe house' for the high command in his Westminster home. Middle-ranking Ministers, most notably David Davis and David Maclean, rolled up their sleeves and manned the phones in Cowley Street. The strategy team met mornings and evenings, either in Alastair Goodlad's house or in the Home Secretary's room in the Commons.

The media, meanwhile, were desperately hunting for a challenger.

It was assumed, not least by the Prime Minister, that no one from the Cabinet would challenge. So Norman Lamont seemed the most likely candidate. That Friday morning, he had written an article in *The Times* criticising the Prime Minister's European policy and laying sole claim to the achievement of Britain's opt-out from monetary union – which came as something of a surprise to everyone else who had been at Maastricht. Various ripostes were prepared. But as the deadline for the Sunday papers – the natural launch-pad – passed without a Lamont challenge, they were put away again.

---

[5]Damian Green, a former member of the Number 10 Policy Unit, became Tory candidate for Ashford in 1994. Tim Collins, who also joined the Unit, became the Tory candidate for Westmorland and Lonsdale in July 1995, shortly after the end of the leadership campaign.

John Major had enjoyed warm support from a meeting of Conservative constituency chairmen at Central Office on Saturday – a fact which helped steady MPs. He spent Sunday lunching with friends in Kent. When Sarah and Jonathan went to spend Sunday evening with him and Norma, they found him relaxed and confident. He was more concerned with the next day's European summit than a challenge to his leadership – even though he knew by then that it was going to come from within the Cabinet.

Since Friday, speculation had grown that John Redwood might throw his hat into the ring. His initial statement of support for the Prime Minister had been half-hearted and ambivalent. Throughout the weekend, he had refused to comment one way or the other on the leadership election. A number of Ministers had tried to ring him to ask him about his intentions, but he had avoided ringing back. Instead, he told the press that he would make his position clear on Monday morning. That could only mean that he would stand against the Prime Minister.

John Redwood had, ironically, been the beneficiary of the downfall of his main supporter, Norman Lamont, in 1993: he was given the bottom rung of the Cabinet ladder when Norman Lamont was knocked off the top. A challenge from the Welsh Secretary was more uncomfortable than a challenge from the former Chancellor, since the Prime Minister had said – on air – that he had the support of his whole Cabinet. John Redwood was also less damaged by history than Norman Lamont; bouncing past the television cameras in his cricketing whites that Sunday evening, he offered them the attraction of novelty. But a challenge from within the Cabinet had one great advantage: the more serious the candidate, the more definitive the victory.

Shortly after 9.00 a.m. on the Monday morning, Switch rang the flat: John Redwood had called in on a mobile phone asking to speak to the Prime Minister. It would be better to speak on a fixed line, but the Prime Minister was short of time: he had to leave at 9.40 a.m. for a ceremony marking the fiftieth anniversary of the United Nations.

The Prime Minister was connected at half-past nine. The conversation was short and to the point. John Redwood said that he had been shocked by the Prime Minister's decision to stand down as party leader. He was sorry that the Prime Minister had not taken the advice on policy that he (Redwood) had offered on the previous Wednesday. He, therefore, was going to resign from the Cabinet and challenge for the leadership. The Prime Minister thanked him for the call, disagreed politely with his analysis – and accepted his resignation.

Not long after, John Major had to set off for the European Council meeting at Cannes. There were uncomfortable echoes in this trip of Margaret Thatcher's absence in Paris on the night of the first ballot in November 1990. Sarah had asked the Prime Minister if the Foreign Secretary could not do the summit job for him, as a swan-song. The Prime Minister had brushed these worries aside. It was his job to go to Cannes, and that was that. Again, the risk paid off. He had, as the *Daily Telegraph* acknowledged with surprising warmth, a successful summit.

But the timing was not good. John Redwood's declaration on the Monday morning electrified the political atmosphere. Much of the press, scenting a second round and hoping for as much blood on the carpet as possible, started to swing away from the Prime Minister. His 'bold and courageous move' of the previous week suddenly became 'a reckless gamble that had backfired'.[6]

John Redwood himself was judged to have done well, sounding more positive, more human than his robotic image had led people to expect. A fever of speculation swept the Conservative benches in the Commons. Support for John Major seemed to be melting away. Morale in the Major camp started to slip. Political correspondents were reporting back to their editors that the Prime Minister was 'finished'. In some editorial chambers, the mood was never to swing back. Relayed back to their proprietors, these early, gloomy views took root. The Major team came to learn that some of these proprietors kept in touch with each other throughout, each

[6]Tabloid interest in the contest was only muted by the coincidence of the kind of story they really enjoyed: the actor Hugh Grant's encounter with a Hollywood prostitute. 'The Week', a new weekly media summary, calculated that they devoted 86 pages to John Major between 29 June and 4 July – 99 to Hugh Grant.

reinforcing the others' perceptions in a circular process which may have led them to underestimate the swing back to the Prime Minister in the fast-changing atmosphere of Westminster.

But from the outset John Redwood's platform team had raised eyebrows in the Commons and the press lobby. Standing behind him were Teresa Gorman and Tony Marlow – who formed a vivid 'doughnut' in acid green and striped blazers respectively. John Redwood's advisers had edged these two out of shot by the second press conference, at which he launched his agenda, on the Tuesday morning. This one was, however, less of a success, and John Redwood began to get into trouble with his pledges to cut 'waste' in public spending without being able to say where. From Cannes, an unusually spruce-looking Ken Clarke gave a television interview pointing out that existing spending plans already required sharp reductions in departmental running costs.[7]

With Howell James in Cannes with the Prime Minister, Jonathan had put on harness again, to help run the Cowley Street operation and to liaise with the team in France. The first task, he realised, was to stop John Redwood commanding the field for two days. Jonathan was determined that the Prime Minister should get his own Manifesto out – and preferably ahead of John Redwood's. With Nick True's help, he put together a draft for the Prime Minister, and faxed it out to Norman Blackwell, the head of the Policy Unit, in Cannes. Jonathan wanted to get it into Tuesday's *Evening Standard*; but the Prime Minister was not able to consider it until Tuesday morning. The *Standard*'s first deadline was missed, but the article led all the other editions for the rest of the day, and ran strongly through all coverage of the election that day.

When the Prime Minister got back from Cannes late on Tuesday evening, Robert Cranborne and Jonathan were waiting at Number 10. They were able to give the Prime Minister a slightly more cheerful report. After the flurry of activity on Monday, things had been steadying down. As Ian Lang had argued, there was a lot to

[7]The Chancellor had, indeed, already begun his next battle for cost-cutting by departments – including John Redwood's – on which the chances of cutting taxes before the next election would depend.

be said for allowing the fever to rage. The hotter it burned, the quicker it would burn itself out – and the earlier in the campaign that MPs raced through the options in a frenzy, the more likely it was that they would turn back to the Prime Minister as being the only candidate who could unite the party.

Robert Cranborne delivered a stark message: from now on, it was campaigning all the way. John Major could not afford to repeat the error made by Margaret Thatcher in 1990, when she seemed to stay above the fray and take votes for granted. The Prime Minister agreed to do whatever his campaign manager thought necessary, including meeting both the Euro-enthusiast Positive Europe Group, and the Euro-sceptic '92 Group.

The next morning, the Wednesday, the Prime Minister was on the airwaves, announcing the arrangements for VJ-Day, then in the Commons to make a statement on the Cannes summit. The House was thin, and the Conservative benches subdued. The Prime Minister spent the evening in the Commons, talking to MPs and canvassing support. Thursday, he knew, would be a crucial day. Not only was it the close of nominations – the last chance for another candidate to break ranks for the first ballot – it was also Prime Minister's Questions.

If he was wounded by Tony Blair in that high-profile gladiatorial contest, John Major would go into the weekend on a low. The Sunday papers, everyone knew, would be hostile. The Redwood team had been promising 'big name' support, widely believed to be Kenneth Baker, who however kept his counsel throughout. To have any impact, that support would have to be revealed by the weekend. Meanwhile, Thursday's papers were awash with stories of preparations for a second round, including rumours that telephone lines had been installed in a Portillo base camp. To steady the ship, the Prime Minister had to win PMQs, preferably by a knockout.

As it turned out, the stories about telephone lines being installed all over Westminster gave the Prime Minister his best Questions crack. When Jonathan went into Number 10 to help out with the morning briefing, he found the Prime Minister in carnival mood. He didn't intend to waste too much time on the usual briefing; but he was in the market for good jokes, please.

The consensus was that Tony Blair would steer clear of the leadership contest. He had given a series of rather uncomfortable-looking interviews on it, evidently uneasy about being off the airwaves for too long as the Tory leadership contest dominated the news. Questions, surely, would be the opportunity for him to treat the election with lofty disdain, firing a broad attack on all Tories and their works instead.

Not so. To the delight of the Major team in the officials' box beside the Speaker's chair, Tony Blair got entangled in the contest. Why had John Redwood stood? The Prime Minister replied that he gathered John Redwood had been 'devastated because I resigned'. Score one: the Tory benches – packed this time – chortled happily. Then Tony Blair tripped up on the Portillo telephone lines. The swift installation of phone lines, said the Prime Minister, was a tribute to privatisation. Score two: the Tory benches roared with pleasure. Punch followed punch, with Tony Blair cast as Judy. Robin Oakley of the BBC and Michael Brunson of ITV both reported that it was the best performance that John Major had ever given at Prime Minister's Questions.

Thursday was again spent 'working the tea-rooms', cashing in on the success of PMQs. The next morning, the Prime Minister was in Kent on a walkabout, creating images reminiscent of his campaigning success in 1992. He went home to Huntingdon that night, but was back in London by Saturday evening, for an occasion organised by the MP Sir Fergus Montgomery – whose association dinner he had addressed on his first full day as Prime Minister, back in November 1990. Then it was back to – of all things – the Number 10 office party.

This was an event which had been proposed, on and off, ever since 1990: a dance for all members of staff. On Sunday morning, even the tireless Switch sounded a little worn. The Prime Minister's incurable interest in people had clearly not been damped down by his own situation. When Jonathan and Sarah arrived on Sunday morning, they expected to find him somewhat fed up about this ill-timed extra demand on his energies. On the contrary: he had clearly much enjoyed meeting the boy and girlfriends of his junior staff, and was full of tales of unlikely partnerships.

He had also given a strong performance on the *Frost Programme* that morning. The newspapers had been mixed, with some hostile leaders balanced by encouraging polls. In the *Sunday Times*, an NOP poll of Conservative voters showed 48 per cent in favour of John Major, with only 20 per cent for Michael Heseltine and 15 per cent for Michael Portillo, the challengers expected to emerge in any second ballot.

A *Sunday Express* survey of 160 constituency chairmen found that 96 per cent advised their MP to support John Major; Central Office's official canvass of constituencies showed the same overwhelming support, echoed by Tory Members of the European Parliament and Tory peers. A MORI poll of voters showed a leap in support for John Major: his satisfaction rating had gone up to 31 per cent, 11 percentage points higher than the previous month.

Alastair Goodlad came in to report. Norma invited Sarah, Jonathan and Howell James up to the flat for lunch. The Prime Minister was relaxed and cheerful, making teasing remarks about the reshuffle in a way which made Jonathan certain that – as in 1990 – the numbers John Major had been given made him sure he had won. The Prime Minister re-drafted an article for the *Daily Telegraph*, then started on official papers for the week ahead.

But Monday started bleakly. The *Daily Telegraph*, traditionally conservative with a small 'c' as well as a large, inclined to support the status quo, had decided to slap a leader alongside the Prime Minister's piece urging Conservative MPs in the clearest possible terms to vote him out of office. The *Sun* had torn into him, too. That evening, both John Major and John Redwood were due to speak to the '92 Group. This is a centre-right grouping which contained friends as well as enemies; but the Major team feared that the Redwood camp would have arranged for some hidden supporters to emerge claiming that they had now 'changed their minds' and would vote for John Redwood. It was their last chance to get their bandwagon rolling. But yet again, they proved short of big names.

On Tuesday morning, the newspapers were even worse. 'Time to Ditch the Captain', advised the *Daily Mail*, in vast headline type on its front page. The *Daily Telegraph*'s front-page story was headed

'Double Blow to Major as MPs back Redwood' – a somewhat over-hyped account of the support Sir George Gardiner and John Townend were giving John Redwood. 'Grim Tories Fear Verdict on Leadership' was the headline in *The Times*. The *Daily Express* and the *Evening Standard* stayed loyal to John Major. But a strong phalanx of the Tory press had declared against him.

There was much discussion in the newspapers as to what would constitute a 'win'. The rules themselves did not produce a hard and fast number, because of the requirement to beat opponents by a 15 per cent margin: the minimum number of votes necessary could be only 165 if the rest included 50 abstentions; or it could be as many as 190 if there were no abstentions. The Major campaign team had been making it crystal clear that a win by the rules was a win; a point that John Redwood had conceded the previous week. But the newspapers, with every interest in raising the hurdle, had been talking as if 200 was the real threshold. The Prime Minister had promised Robert Cranborne he would discuss numbers with no one but his high command. But it was very clear to everybody that he was not going to be satisfied with 165.

When Jonathan went into Number 10 on the Tuesday morning, to help with the briefing for Prime Minister's Questions again, he was given the campaign team's range of expectations: a vote for the Prime Minister of 205-215. But the Prime Minister was edgy. Jonathan and Howell discussed what he might say on the doorstep after the vote: it would be crazy to present an appearance of prevarication when all that was happening was a bit of backroom scribbling. Jonathan wanted him to echo the words he had used after his victory in the 1990 leadership contest, and say he was going to get on with the 'work in hand' – in this case, the reshuffle. That would move the media focus on. But in the meantime, 'work in hand' was already taking place.

That morning, the Prime Minister had a meeting with Michael Heseltine to discuss his new role. There has, inevitably, been much speculation about this meeting. Why was Michael Heseltine there for two hours? Was a dramatic deal being thrashed out, in which Michael Heseltine delivered his supporters in exchange for a fancy appointment, some gold braid, and a big office?

The answer, quite simply, is no. First of all, the Prime Minister and Michael Heseltine had been talking about the latter's new role for several weeks. Secondly, their meeting did not take as long as the door-watchers supposed. Michael Heseltine spent a good deal of the time, not with the Prime Minister, but viewing his new terrain in the Cabinet Office with the Cabinet Secretary. Having talked through the Deputy Prime Minister's role, they both came back to report to the Prime Minister.

Thirdly, Michael Heseltine had made it clear from the first that he wanted the Prime Minister to win in the first round; and that, so far as he was concerned, was that. Inevitably, down in the undergrowth, there had been some freelance activity amongst those who had long ago hitched their colours to the Heseltine mast. At the beginning of the campaign, they had been busy gauging the strength of support for a possible Heseltine challenge in round two, and – according to reports making their way back to the Major camp – trying to persuade as many as possible on the left of the party to abstain. But their soundings struck no echo, and by the Thursday of the first full week of campaigning, Major campaigners concluded that those trying to get a Heseltine bandwagon going had called it a day.

In any case, no such group is a disciplined army which switches its votes at a word from the commanding officer. Indeed, the final piece of evidence against the idea of a last-minute deal in which Heseltine supporters swung behind the Prime Minister comes from the fact that two prominent ones didn't. A Major supporter just happened to notice that, late on Tuesday afternoon, they voted – for John Redwood.

John Major, meanwhile, had to focus on Prime Minister's Questions. There was a bad omen on the way to the Commons – the Prime Minister's convoy got stuck behind a builder's van, which took over two minutes to extricate itself from a narrow turning. Tension rose. When the Prime Minister reached his room, there was barely time before Questions to take a message from Tom King, who had heard that the Labour benches would be waving John Redwood leaflets to try to put the Prime Minister off his stride.

Having learnt his lesson from the previous Thursday, Tony Blair had gone back to his own ground, and attacked on executive pay. The Prime Minister gave a somewhat distracted answer, but defended more strongly on Northern Ireland (with awkward timing, the release of Private Clegg, the British soldier jailed for the killing of a Belfast joyrider, had been announced the previous day). He came back to his room knowing that he had not ended on a high. But he did not waste time on a post-mortem.

Rumours were streaking around the Commons to the effect that the Prime Minister was planning to resign if he did not win by a clear margin – a rumour that the Major team, in order to maximise the Major vote, did nothing to damp down. Letters flooded in from MPs, urging the Prime Minister to stay. Robert Cranborne and Alastair Goodlad trooped in to see him; then Patrick Mayhew and Malcolm Rifkind. All came out looking grim.

Jonathan was struck by the stark contrast with 1990. Then, Minister after Minister had gone in to tell Margaret Thatcher that, having failed to win by the rules in the first ballot, she would have to resign, for her own sake. Today, Minister after Minister was tramping in to insist to the Prime Minister that, having won by the rules, he must stay – for all their sakes.

There was much discussion afterwards among the Prime Minister's close advisers about how serious he was in his determination to stand down unless he won by what he considered to be a decisive margin. There is no doubt that he had to win well, and that he was not prepared to cling on just for the sake of the job. He had a life outside politics, and – if the result was not clear-cut – he was not the sort of person to hang on merely for the sake of the official Daimler and the flat over the shop.

At the same time, by making his colleagues sweat, the Prime Minister was also testing the water. By worrying colleagues that he might stand down, he could gauge how anxious they were for him to stay on, and probe for some kind of consensus on what really constituted a secure 'safety margin'.

Finally, at about 4.20 p.m., John Major decided it was time to vote himself. Jonathan tried to break the tension: 'Have you made up your mind who to vote for yet?' he asked. The Prime Minister's normal sense of humour seemed momentarily to have deserted him.

Jonathan then went back to Number 10 to see Norma, tracking her down in her secretary's office. He asked her to urge the Prime Minister to stay. She said she had done all she could, but she would have one further go. With the Prime Minister and John Ward, she went to watch the results in the flat. Robert Cranborne had called in the Cabinet heavies – Douglas Hurd, Patrick Mayhew, Ian Lang, Brian Mawhinney – and the Prime Minister asked them and the rest of the campaign team up to the flat.

Like the rest of the country, they turned on the television to see a kind of carnival on College Green, the patch of grass opposite the House of Commons where the media were conducting interviews. The sun was breaking through the clouds. Crowds had built up. Behind Lord Archer, saying his final piece, a cheerful football supporter peeled off his new red Liverpool strip and waved it across the shot, convulsing his neighbours with laughter.

Up in the flat, Patrick Mayhew was operating like a kind of one-man football crowd, cheering at every positive comment, growling at every negative. The Prime Minister was worrying about his guests, offering chairs and fussing about drinks. Finally, at about ten past five, he was persuaded to look at a form of words for what he might say in Downing Street afterwards. He skimmed them quickly, without much interest.

John Ward was waiting in Norma's study for the phone call from Sir Marcus Fox. He brought the results in, showed them to the Prime Minister, and read them out – just moments before they came on television: 218 for the Prime Minister, 89 for John Redwood, 20 abstentions or spoiled ballots – later raised to 22, on the grounds that the two who had not turned up should be formally counted as having abstained.

It was far more than he needed to win by the rules;[8] it was more votes than Margaret Thatcher had secured in 1975, when she won control of the party from Edward Heath. It was more than she had got in 1990, out of a much bigger parliamentary party. It was more votes than John Major himself had got, out

[8]Against that number of votes for John Redwood, the Prime Minister could have afforded another 53 abstentions – and still have satisfied the rules.

of that same large electorate, when he was chosen as leader after her.

But Jonathan was taken back to election night in 1992. There was the same look on the victorious Prime Minister's face: stunned, tired and drawn. He didn't smile. He could hardly speak, hugging Norma while the BBC commentary went on about his 'convincing' win. Finally, he thanked everybody briefly, saying his vote was bigger than 'the figure he had had in his mind' – the threshold he had set himself for carrying on. He would say more, later.

John Major did his stuff on the doorstep of Number 10, surrounded not only by his parliamentary colleagues but – at his insistence – by the young men and women who had slaved day and night in the bowels of Number 10. He then went to the Cabinet Room to find the real evidence of his reclaimed prime ministerial status: the presence of Sir Robin Butler. He went on to Cowley Street, to thank his team, and then back to a party at Number 10. The celebration was like the political equivalent of the miracle of the loaves and fishes: there seemed to be rather more MPs than the 218 registered as having voted for him.

He reshuffled his Cabinet and went with them, two days later, to another coronation: a strange, rather anti-climactic assembly of emotionally exhausted MPs, peers and voluntary party members in the Queen Elizabeth II centre. Sarah heard the echoes of April 1992 again. The relief was palpable. Danger was past. A great political drama was over. All anyone wanted to do was to be allowed to leave the theatre and go home to sleep – and dream of summer beaches.

For a week, the leadership of Britain had been in question, put there – of his own choice – by the Prime Minister himself. As in 1990, as in 1992, John Major felt the warmth of the pleasure of friends, and heard the sharp sound of political applause. He had won a great gamble, confounded expectations, cleared the air. He had won with the good wishes of the constituency parties, and against the express wishes of the grandees of the Tory press.

He had won – for the third time – power. But only his parliamentary party could say if it would also be peace.

APPENDIX I

——— • ———

The 1992 General Election Result

Commentators and pollsters were equally confounded by the results of the 1992 election. Through the campaign, the conventional wisdom was that Paddy Ashdown was doing splendidly, Neil Kinnock pretty well and John Major's campaign was a disaster: the best the Tories could hope for was a neck-and-neck result. In fact, the Liberal Democrat vote fell by 4.8 percentage points, and the Tories ended 7.6 percentage points ahead of Labour. More people – some 14,092,891 of them in all – voted Conservative then ever before. The Tory share of an increased turnout fell only 0.4 per cent from the spectacular boom-time victory of 1987.

As David Butler and Dennis Kavanagh conclude in a psephological study of the election,[1] this result was 'totally unexpected'. And as John Curtice and Michael Steed put it in this same work, it was 'a disaster for the Labour Party'.

Messrs Curtice and Steed point out that the pundits were saved from greater public embarrassment by the fact that this time, there was no 'winner's bonus' in terms of seats. Normally, Britain's first-past-the-post electoral system translates a lead in votes into a much bigger lead in seats: had this normal pattern prevailed in 1992, they calculate, the Conservative majority in the House of Commons would have been 71 seats. The actual result was 336 Conservatives, 271 Labour, 20 Liberal Democrats, 7 Welsh

[1] *The British General Election of 1992*, Macmillan, London.

and Scottish Nationalists, and 17 others (in Northern Ireland) – a majority of 21.

Others challenged these calculations. The Tories won some marginals unexpectedly – for example, Battersea – with a swing their way. Experienced campaigners at Central Office believe that there is a trend to much greater variation in constituency results, making calculations of uniform swing less and less useful.

The majority was cut by the fact the Tories did less well in marginals than in 'safe' seats, where they piled up 'wasted' votes. Messrs Curtice and Steed found evidence of tactical anti-Tory voting, while the Tories' confidence in their traditional campaigning prowess in marginals was badly dented. Central Office also concluded that specialised polling in those constituencies, on which a good deal of money was spent, was not particularly useful.

Messrs Curtice and Steed could not find any analytical evidence to support the idea that the tabloids 'won' the election for the Prime Minister. And Bob Worcester, of the polling organisation MORI, carried out analysis which indicates that the proportion of voters who trust their newspapers' views on politics actually fell during the 1992 election – while the proportion trusting television coverage continued to rise.

Finally, what of those groups supposedly targeted by the Tories, following the 1991 Hever meeting? For information on this, one has to rely on the imperfect source of 'exit polls' – people questioned after voting – since ballot papers bear no imprint of sex or status. These exit polls suggest that the swing to Labour (2.1 per cent overall) was pretty uniform: marginally greater amongst managerial and professional groups, lower amongst skilled workers. There was a marked difference between the sexes, with barely any swing to Labour at all amongst women, while men moved quite sharply. The swing also appeared to be greatest amongst thirty-five to fifty-four-year-olds. Is it merely coincidence that the pundits who concluded John Major was losing belonged mainly to the high-swing category of middle-class, middle-aged males?

APPENDIX II

—◆—

John Major's First Cabinet – and After

John Major's first Cabinet, November 1990 (*indicates those in positions unchanged from Margaret Thatcher's last Cabinet):

PRIME MINISTER, FIRST LORD OF THE TREASURY AND MINISTER FOR THE CIVIL SERVICE
John Major

LORD PRESIDENT OF THE COUNCIL
John MacGregor★
He became Transport Secretary in 1992, and left the Government in 1994.

LORD CHANCELLOR
Lord Mackay of Clashfern★

LORD PRIVY SEAL
Lord Waddington
He left the Government in 1992.

CHANCELLOR OF THE EXCHEQUER
Norman Lamont
He left the Government in 1993.

CHIEF SECRETARY TO THE TREASURY
David Mellor
> *He became National Heritage Secretary in 1992, and left the Government later that year.*

FOREIGN SECRETARY
Douglas Hurd★
> *He left the Government in 1995.*

HOME SECRETARY
Kenneth Baker
> *He left the Government in 1992.*

MINISTER OF AGRICULTURE, FISHERIES AND FOOD
John Gummer★
> *He became Environment Secretary in 1993.*

SECRETARY OF STATE FOR DEFENCE
Tom King★
> *He left the Government in 1992.*

SECRETARY OF STATE FOR EDUCATION AND SCIENCE
Kenneth Clarke★
> *He became Home Secretary in 1992; Chancellor of the Exchequer in 1993.*

SECRETARY OF STATE FOR EMPLOYMENT
Michael Howard★
> *He became Environment Secretary in 1992; Home Secretary in 1993.*

SECRETARY OF STATE FOR ENERGY
John Wakeham★
> *He became Lord Privy Seal in 1992, and left the Government in 1994.*

SECRETARY OF STATE FOR THE ENVIRONMENT
Michael Heseltine
He became President of the Board of Trade in 1992; Deputy Prime Minister and First Secretary of State in 1995.

SECRETARY OF STATE FOR HEALTH
William Waldegrave★
He became Chancellor of the Duchy of Lancaster in 1992; Minister of Agriculture in 1994; and Chief Secretary to the Treasury in 1995.

CHANCELLOR OF THE DUCHY OF LANCASTER AND PARTY CHAIRMAN
Chris Patten
He lost his parliamentary seat in 1992, and was appointed Governor of Hong Kong.

SECRETARY OF STATE FOR NORTHERN IRELAND
Peter Brooke★
He left the Government in 1992, returned as National Heritage Secretary later that year, and left again in 1994.

SECRETARY OF STATE FOR SCOTLAND
Ian Lang
He became President of the Board of Trade in 1995.

SECRETARY OF STATE FOR SOCIAL SECURITY
Tony Newton★
He became Lord President of the Council in 1992.

SECRETARY OF STATE FOR TRADE AND INDUSTRY
Peter Lilley★
He became Social Security Secretary in 1992.

SECRETARY OF STATE FOR TRANSPORT
Malcolm Rifkind
He became Defence Secretary in 1992; Foreign Secretary in 1995.

David Hunt★
He became Employment Secretary in 1993, Chancellor of the Duchy of Lancaster in 1994, and left the Government in 1995.

In 1992, the following joined the Cabinet:

Michael Portillo, as Chief Secretary to the Treasury.
He became Employment Secretary in 1994; Defence Secretary in 1995.
John Patten, as Education Secretary.
He left the Government in 1994.
Gillian Shephard, as Employment Secretary.
She became Minister of Agriculture in 1993; Education Secretary in 1994; and Education and Employment Secretary in 1995.
Virginia Bottomley, as Health Secretary.
She became National Heritage Secretary in 1995.

In 1993, the following joined the Cabinet:

John Redwood, as Welsh Secretary.
He left the Government in 1995, to challenge John Major for the leadership of the party.

In 1994, the following joined the Cabinet:

Stephen Dorrell, as National Heritage Secretary.
He became Health Secretary in 1995.
Jonathan Aitken, as Chief Secretary to the Treasury.
He left the Government in 1995.
Brian Mawhinney, as Transport Secretary.
He became Minister without Portfolio and Party Chairman in 1995.

Jeremy Hanley, as Minister without Portfolio and Party Chairman.
> *He left the Cabinet in 1995, and became a junior Foreign Office Minister.*

Lord Cranborne, as Lord Privy Seal.

In 1995, the following joined the Cabinet:

Sir George Young, as Transport Secretary.
Roger Freeman, as Chancellor of the Duchy of Lancaster.
Douglas Hogg, as Minister of Agriculture.
Michael Forsyth, as Scottish Secretary.
William Hague, as Welsh Secretary.

By 1995, apart from the Prime Minister, only one member of his original Cabinet — Lord Mackay — was still in the place he occupied in November 1990.

Picture Credits

1 Adam Butler/Press Association.
2 Private collection.
3 Rex Features.
4 Michael Frith for the *Financial Times*.
5 Popperfoto/Reuter.
6 Associated Press/Topham.
7 Press Association/Topham (Scan Dempsey).
8 Popperfoto/Reuter.
9 Chris Harris/Times Newspapers.
10 White House photo.
11 DP Photographic.
12 Press Association/Topham (Malcolm Croft).
13 Popperfoto.
14 Press Association/Topham (John Giles).
15 Associated Press/Topham.
16 Courtesy of the *Lincolnshire Echo*.
17 Deborah de Satgé.
18 Private collection.
19 Stephen Lock/*Daily Telegraph*.
20 Shirley Stotter.
21 Adam Butler/Press Association.
22 Tim Bishop/Times Newspapers.
23 Graham Turner/*Guardian*.
24 Courtesy of Conservative Central Office.
25 Deborah de Satgé.
26 Private collection.
27 Deborah de Satgé.
28 Tony Harris/Press Association.

Index

Adam Smith Institute, 103
Allan, Alex, 22n
Alternatives to Domestic Rates (Green
    Paper), 57
Amess, David, 257
Andreotti, Giulio, 146 and n, 156
Archer, Lord (Jeffrey), 132, 173,
    209, 282
Ashdown, Paddy, 42, 249

Baker, Kenneth, 11, 45, 100, 159,
    194, 276
Baldwin, Stanley, 86
Balfour, Arthur, 29
Banham, John, 151, 154
BBC, 40n, 43, 243
Beatrix, Queen, 148
Bevins, Tony, 199–200
Billière, Sir Peter de la, 41
Black, Conrad, 74–5
Black Wednesday, 14, 47, 127
Blackwell, Norman, 275
Blair, Tony, 276, 277, 280
'Blue Chips', 4–5
Blyth, Sir James (Lord Blyth of
    Rowington), 104
Body, Sir Richard, 266
Boleat, Mark, 189
Bottomley, Virginia, 11
Bowden, Gerald, 252n
Bright, Graham, 25, 110, 225, 262,
    267, 269, 270
British Rail, 98–9, 100, 102, 181

Broek, Hans Van den, 139
Brooke, Peter, 9, 11
Brown, Peter, 262
Bruce, Brendan, 228
Brunson, Michael, 277
Budgen, Nick, 131
Budgets: (1991), 64–5, 108–9, 117;
    (1992), 120, 193–6; (1993),
    202; Labour's Shadow Budget
    (1992), 196–8, 202; traditional
    secrecy of, 193
Burns, Sir Terry, 6, 8, 64, 190n
Bush, Barbara, 51, 53
Bush, George, 8, 37–8, 49, 51–3,
    53n, 54, 164, 172
Butler, David, 284
Butler, Sir Robin, 10, 12, 25n, 95,
    98, 180, 256, 257, 283
by-elections: Kincardine and
    Deeside, 247; Monmouth, 110;
    Ribble Valley, 62–3

Cabinet committees, 60–1, 61n, 62;
    EDX (spending), 120; FLG
    (future legislation), 113–14, 115
Cabinet Office, 23n, 60
Cabinet Secretary: role of, 23,
    26
Cabinets: John Major's first, 8–15;
    layout and nature of meetings,
    12, 13; Oxford v. Cambridge
    membership analysis, 10–11,
    11n; Political, 23, 178; War,

40, 41 and n, 45; women in, 11 and n
Callaghan, James, 24, 126
Carlisle, John, 225
Cavaço Silva, Anibal, 146
CBI, *see* Confederation of British Industry
CDU, *see* Christian Democrats
Central Policy Review Staff, 23–4
Centre for Policy Studies, 103
Chalker, Lynda, 11
Channel Tunnel, 133
Chaplin, Judith, 25, 26, 28, 107, 110, 134
Chapman, William, 25n
Chequers, 87–8, 230; Prison Room, 88–9
Child Support Act, 112–13
Christian Democrats (CDU), 77–8, 78n, 147
Churchill, Sir Winston, 31; portrait of, 17 and n
Citizen's Charter, 93–105, 122, 135, 180
civil service, 203–4; *see also* staff, Prime Minister's
Clarke, Kenneth, 9, 11, 13, 27, 94, 126, 194, 228, 275 and n; career, 9n; and education reforms, 87, 89, 90, 92, 98, 100, 114, 178, 210
Cole, John, 241
Collins, Tim, 111n, 175n, 272 and n; handles media during general election campaign, 170, 175, 212, 215–16, 218, 231, 236; John Simpson's comment on, 231n; and voting day, 254–5, 256, 261–2
Commonwealth conference (1991), 137 and n
Community Charge (poll tax), 13, 14, 54, 55–7, 108–9, 117; cost of collecting, 62; relief schemes, 63, 65; search for a replacement, 57–60, 62–6; *see also* Council Tax

Confederation of British Industry (CBI), 151, 154
Congdon, Tim, 185
Conservative Central Council meeting, 66 and n
Conservative Central Office, 105, 108, 128–9, 179, 181; document on Labour's costings, 116–17; and election campaign, 107, 125, 163, 164, 165, 167–9, 204–5, 206, 207, 209, 215, 228, 248
Conservative Party Conferences, 127–9; 1991 (Blackpool), 126, 127, 128–37; 1992 (Brighton), 127 and n; ministerial disputes, 133; slogans, 128–9; use of autocue, 131–2; venues, 127–8
Conservative Research Department, 116, 129, 165, 177, 212; *Campaign Guide*, 179n, 200
Cook, Robin, 198
Cooke, Alistair, 179n
Cope, John, 110
Council of Mortgage Lenders, 189
Council Tax, 69–70, 114, 191–2; *see also* Community Charge
Cradock, Sir Percy, 27n
Craig, Sir David, 41
Cranborne, Lord (Robert), 4 and n; and leadership election, 269, 272, 275, 276, 279, 281, 282
Cresson, Edith, 147n
Criminal Justice Act, 112–13
Cunningham, Jack, 29
Currie, Edwina, 227–8, 228n
Curtice, John, 284–5

Daily Express, 103, 278, 279
Daily Mail, 79, 136, 278
Daily Mirror, 255
Daily Telegraph, 7, 26–7, 49, 65, 103, 136, 274, 278–9; on general election campaign, 217, 219, 220, 221, 224–5, 235; on Maastricht, 161; *see also Sunday Telegraph*

Dangerous Dogs Act, 113
Davis, David, 272
defence spending, 118, 119, 121
Dehaene, Jean-Luc, 265 and n
Delors, Jacques, 47, 72, 75, 143, 146, 157
Department of Education, 90–1, 99–100
Department of Employment, 90–1, 180
Department of Transport, 98, 100, 102, 104n, 181
d'Estaing, Giscard, 49
Dickens, Geoffrey, 266n
Douglas-Home, Sir Alec, 128
Downing, George, 16
Downing Street, Number 10: and election, 253, 255–6, 263; IRA attack on, 44–7; layout/decor, 16–22; staff and organisation, 22–9, 35–6
driving tests, 100–1
Dundee Courier: visit to, 244

Economist, The, 197, 264, 265
economy, 183–91, 199–202; *see also* Budgets; interest rates; public spending; taxation
education, 58–9, 86–7, 89–92, 98, 100, 101–2, 104, 114–5, 210
election, general (April 1992): deciding on timing, 106–12, 121–3, 126–7, 137, 191–2; preparing tactics, 124–6; posters, 125–6, 166, 236–8; Near Term campaign, 163–75; 'themed' visits, 169–71; Conservative Manifesto, 175–82, 194, 195; tax as an issue, 197–202; date announced, 203; final campaign team, 204–7; battlebus, 174–5, 210, 214, 215; PM's first campaign speech, 208–9; 'Meet John Major' sessions, 171–3, 209–10; education mini-Manifesto, 210; campaign routine, 210–16; Area Agents,

215n; press conferences, 211–13, 234–5, 245–6; rallies/soapbox campaigning, 216–18, 223–9, 251 and n; Manifesto launch, 218–21; *The Journey* (film of PM), 221–2; PM's broadcasts/interviews, 223, 231–2, 250–1, 252–3; rumours, 231; photo-opportunities, 233–5; opinion polls, 239–42; Scottish campaign, 242–9; proportional representation as issue, 249; voting day, 254–63; Basildon result, 257; Bath result, 251–2, 258; Huntingdon result, 259; analysis of result, 285–6
Election Call, 252
elections, general: 1983 and 1987 share of vote analysis, 107; 1987 campaign, 163–4; costs, 168n, 173n, 251n; and Ministers' adaptability, 203–4
elections, leadership: (1990), 3–8; (1995), 266–83
elections, local: (1991), 109–10; (1995), 264; *see also* by-elections
electoral register: and poll tax avoidance, 62 and n
employment, 91, 118–19, 186
Environmental Protection Agency, 115
ERM, *see* Exchange Rate Mechanism
European Community: 1990 Council meetings (Rome), 71–2; 1991 Council meetings (Luxembourg), 80–2; 1991 Edinburgh Summit, 49–50; 1995 Council meeting (Cannes), 274, 275; 'Heart of Europe' speech, 77–9; and monetary union debate, 72–6, 79–80, 149, 153, 158, 162; nature of Council meetings, 144–5, 145n; presidency, 80, 139; 'qualified majority

voting' (QMV), 143n; split
in Tory party over, 265–6;
veto by British of Dehaene's
appointment, 265; *see also*
European Parliament; Exchange
Rate Mechanism; Maastricht
negotiations
European Parliament, 141, 142,
150, 158
European People's Party, 138
Evans, David, 225
Evening Standard, 134, 220, 232, 255,
275, 279
Exchange Rate Mechanism (ERM),
72, 73, 140, 185, 187–8

Financial Times, 248
Finlay, Robina, 111n
Foreign Office, 35–6, 144
Fowler, Sir Norman, 9, 175 and n,
205, 211, 213, 234, 241, 244
Fox, Sir Marcus, 269, 271, 282
Fraser, Lord (Peter), 206
Frost Programme, 278

Gardiner, Sir George, 279
Gardiner, John, 261
Garel-Jones, Tristan, 4 and n, 5,
143–4, 153, 156, 159, 160
Garrett, Tony, 251
General Agreement on Tariffs and
Trade (GATT), 49, 53
Genscher, Hans-Dietrich, 140, 147
Gieve, John, 64
Gleeson, Dermot, 206–7
Goldsworthy, Diana, 95
Gonzalez, Felipe, 146
Goodlad, Alastair, 105, 110, 269,
272, 278, 281
Gorbachev, Mikhail, 50–1
Gorman, Teresa, 275
Green, Damian, 272 and n
Green Papers, 57n
Grey, Lady Mary, 88–9
Griffiths, Brian (Lord Griffiths of
Fforestfach), 176
Group of Seven summits, 49

Guardian, 218, 219–20, 224
Guigou, Elizabeth, 147
Gulf War, 12, 37–48, 54, 121, 136;
British death toll, 48n
Gummer, John, 9, 11, 115n, 116

Hamilton, Archie, 269
Harris, Robin, 182
Harris Hughes, Howell, 27, 88n
Haslam, Jonathan, 111n
Hastings, Max, 67
Haughey, Charles, 146
Havel, Václav, 51
Hawke, Bob, 231 and n
Healey, Denis, 42
Heath, Sir Edward, 80 and n, 142
Heiser, Sir Terry, 69
Heseltine, Michael, 11, 100, 129;
and 1990 leadership election, 5,
6, 7, 271; and 1995 leadership
election, 278, 279–80; chairs
new policy committee, 111n;
'City Challenge' scheme, 177;
Conference performances, 128,
131; on election campaigning,
166; enthusiasm of, 115, 178–9,
212; and IRA attack, 45, 46; and
John Major's first Cabinet, 8–9,
12, 13; and local government
structure, 59; on Opposition's
tax policies, 199; and poll tax
replacement, 55, 57, 65–6,
68, 69, 70; preference for
hot lunches, 178; on Shadow
Budget, 197
Hill, Alex, 133–4, 229
Hill, Jonathan, 32, 110, 126, 167;
appointed Political Secretary,
204; awaits news from
Maastricht, 144, 159; career,
27–8, 176; and Citizen's
Charter, 93, 94, 96, 100–1;
and Council Tax launch, 69;
Downing Street office, 18;
and general election campaign,
173, 174, 175, 176, 204, 205,
210–11, 213, 215, 216, 218,

224, 225, 226, 227, 229, 231,
234, 237, 238, 240–1, 243, 244;
and general election day, 254,
257, 259, 262; helps to draft
PM's speeches, 67; and 1995
leadership election, 272–3,
275, 278, 279, 281–2; and
Manifesto preparation, 179,
181–2; meeting with Heseltine,
115; and press conference
arrangements, 90; role in Policy
Unit, 88n; streamlines European
election programme, 171n
Hillmore, Peter, 227
Hilton, Brian, 104
Hogg, Douglas, 26, 44, 137
Hogg, Sarah, 32, 107, 110, 272–3,
274, 276n; advises on general
election timing, 109, 122, 191;
advises on leadership election,
267–8; and Budget meetings,
64; and Bush/Major meeting,
52, 53; on Cabinet meetings,
14; and Citizen's Charter
93, 94, 97, 98–9; and general
election campaign, 204, 207,
211–12, 213, 215, 237, 250;
and general election day, 256–7,
260, 262; helps to draft PM's
speeches, 43, 67, 79, 131; and
IRA attack, 44, 46; as journalist,
49, 128; leaves Policy Unit,
267; at Maastricht, 144, 151,
157, 159, 160; and Manifesto
preparation, 176, 179, 181–2;
meeting with Heseltine, 115;
meets Permanent Secretaries,
85; Number 10 office and
equipment, 22; offered Policy
Unit job, 26–7; and party
conference, 132–3, 134,
137; and press conference
arrangements, 90; stays in
Chequers' Prison Room, 88–9;
visits Australia, 30
Hole, Shana, 111n, 159, 206
Holland, Sir Geoffrey, 91

housing, 100, 102, 161, 185, 189
Howard, Michael, 14, 87, 89, 90, 94,
118–19, 151, 155, 269
Howe, Sir Geoffrey, 10, 71, 185
Hudson, Hugh, 163
Hume, Cardinal G. Basil, 39
Hurd, Douglas, 5, 6, 7, 8, 11,
12, 254, 282; announces
resignation, 272; and Maastricht,
140, 142–3, 144, 151, 152, 154,
162, 178

Independent, 79, 103, 197, 224
industry, 122, 186
inflation, 118, 121, 122, 184,
188, 208–9
Institute for Economic Affairs, 103
interest rates, 73, 74, 122, 185, 187,
188, 190
IRA campaign, 44–7, 172n

James, Howell, 269, 271, 275, 279
Jarvis, Fred, 92
Jay, Michael, 144, 151, 152, 153, 156
Jenkins, Simon, 270n
Jimmy Young Show, 223
Jones, Claire, 175, 227
Jones, George, 49, 217, 224–5
Jopling, Michael, 10

Kaletsky, Anatole, 197
Kaufman, Gerald, 39, 209
Kavanagh, Dennis, 284
Keating, Paul, 30
Kerr, Sir John, 71–2, 81; and
Maastricht 143, 145, 150, 151,
152–3, 154, 155, 156, 160
King, Tom, 11, 13, 37, 42, 45, 280
Kinnock, Neil, 42, 67, 126, 219;
public image, 108, 121, 163,
209, 214, 227, 232, 249
Kohl, Helmut, 51, 75, 76–7; at
Maastricht, 141, 145, 146, 147,
150, 154, 155, 156, 157

Labour Party, 103, 143, 165, 166,

188, 218, 249–50; in 1991
local elections, 109–10; and
general election result, 284;
'Jennifer's Ear' broadcast, 243,
244–5; *Opportunity Britain*,
116–17; Shadow Budget,
196–8, 202; Sheffield rally, 241;
slick election campaigns, 163,
164, 214
Labour Party Conference (1991),
125, 126–7
Lacy, John, 111n
Laing, Eleanor, 111n
Lamont, Norman, 6, 11, 59–60, 68,
161, 166n, 178, 184, 186, 200,
202, 273; appointed Chancellor,
9; favours late election, 192;
Budget (1991), 64, 65; Budget
(1992), 120, 193–4, 195; and
Citizen's Charter, 96; economic
forecast, 183; housing market
measures, 188–9; and leadership
election rumours, 267, 272; at
Maastricht, 143, 149, 151, 153,
154; and party conferences,
127n, 133
Lamont, Rosemary, 44
Lamy, Pascal, 155
Lang, Ian, 11, 12, 247–8, 269, 271,
272, 275, 282
Langdon, Julia, 105
Lansley, Andrew, 110, 165, 177
Lawson, Nigel, 5, 56, 66, 185,
187 and n
legislative programme (1990–91),
112–15
Leigh-Pemberton, Robin, 72
Liberal Democrats, 249–50, 258, 284
Lightfoot, Warwick, 116
Lilley, Peter, 11, 14, 177
Llewellyn, Edward, 175, 216,
226, 259
Lloyd Webber, Andrew, 173–4,
213n
local government, 58–9, 59n
London Business School, 190 and n
lottery, national, 194

Lubbers, Ruud, 139, 146, 147, 150,
154–5, 156, 157

Maastricht Bill, 14, 161–2
Maastricht negotiations, 138–60;
British delegation, 144; heads of
state, 146–7; immigration, 155;
Social Chapter, 143, 150–1,
152–3, 154–6, 158; subsidiarity,
142, 157; Treaty, 162
McColl, Ian, 30, 269
MacDonald, Ramsay, 29
MacGregor, John, 110, 114, 178
McKellen, Sir Ian, 130
Maclean, David, 272
Maclean, Murdo, 111n
Macmillan, Harold, 30, 84
Major, Elizabeth, 52, 260
Major, James, 48n, 260
Major, John:
  DOMESTIC POLITICS: political
  career, 4, 5, 7; wins 1990
  leadership election, 3–8;
  chooses first Cabinet, 8–11;
  first Cabinet meeting, 11–15;
  Downing Street staff, 24–5,
  25n, 26–9; gifts to, 19, 29,
  30; media interest, 29–30;
  first PMQs, 32, 33–4; work
  pressures, 35–6, 66; IRA attack,
  44–5, 47; Northern Ireland
  visits, 47; and poll tax reform,
  54, 55, 59–60, 62, 63–4, 66,
  70; plans guide to committees,
  61n; faces 'No Confidence'
  motion, 66–7; speech to Welsh
  party conference, 79–80;
  review of policies, 83–92;
  speech to Centre for Policy
  Studies, 91–2; and Citizen's
  Charter, 93–105; alarmed by
  Lib Dems' success, 109; and
  legislative programme, 110,
  115; and compensation for
  HIV victims, 117; and public
  spending, 119–20; preliminary
  election preparations, 122–3,

125, 126, 166, 169–75, 177–8;
first party conference, 127,
130, 131, 134–7; economic
policy, 184, 187, 188,
199–200, 202 and n; sets
election date, 192 and n;
allows Lamont freedom in
Budget announcement, 194;
relieved to start election
campaign, 207–8; speech to
Central Council, 208; on
constitutional issues, 209,
248–9; 'Meet John Major'
sessions, 171–4, 209–10, 225;
mini-Manifesto on education,
210; allocated code-name,
216; election rallies, 216–18,
224–9, 235–6; sends direct
mail letter, 218n; launches
Manifesto, 219, 220–1;
election broadcasts/interviews,
221–2, 222n, 223, 231–2,
243, 250–1, 252–3, 261;
walkabouts, 224, 228; photo
opportunities, 233–5, 243–4,
promotional poster, 236–8;
and opinion polls, 239–42;
Scottish campaign, 242–9; and
proportional representation,
249; on election day, 254–5,
256, 257; and Bath result,
251–2, 258; Huntingdon
majority, 262–3; 1995
leadership election, 264–83;
and Euro sceptics, 265–6, 276;
PMQs, 276–7, 280–1
INTERNATIONAL RELATIONS:
chairs international meetings,
49–50; at European Council
meetings, 71–2, 81–2; and
European monetary policy,
72–5, 79–80, 140; handling of
Gulf War, 37–48, 54; 'Heart
of Europe speech', 71, 77–9;
international statesman, 124,
137, 146, 209; and Maastricht,
139, 142, 145–6, 147, 149–61;

policy on Kurds, 80–1; quoted
on Social Chapter, 150–1;
receives foreign visitors, 35–6;
relationship with Bush, 37–8,
49, 51–3, 53n; relationship with
Gorbachev, 50–1; relationship
with Kohl, 76–7, 147;
relationship with Mitterrand,
41–2, 42n; views on federalism,
75; visits Gulf, 48, 64
QUALITIES, 7, 77n, 86, 160; and
birthday celebrations, 229–31;
broadcasts/interviews, 42–3,
43n, 105, 160, 223, 231–2,
243, 250–1, 252–3, 278; 'caring'
image, 125; convictions, 83–4;
and cricket, 124, 137, 231n; on
danger of attack, 229; dislike
of autocue, 132; dislike of
personality politics, 86; eating
habits, 28, 82, 160, 213; fond
of children, 229–30; hatred of
posed photos, 233; *The Journey*
(film), 221–2, 261–2; love of
meeting people, 131, 224, 228;
negotiating skills, 146; personal
popularity, 39–40, 108, 121–2;
preference for open criticism,
32–3; protective of family, 222;
reaction to news of 'friendly
fire' victims, 48; re-drafts
speeches, 244, 246, requires
full briefings, 36, 90; speaking
ability, 130, 131–2; views on
election speeches, 205; working
style, 12–15, 18–20, 28, 30, 33,
34–5, 90
Major, Norma, 18, 30, 192n, 222,
229–30, 255, 259, 261, 262;
campaigns with PM, 174–5,
216, 217, 224, 236, 252–3;
Edinburgh summit hostess, 50;
friendship with Bush family,
51–2; keeps Huntingdon
as base, 28; supports calling
of leadership election, 267,
278, 282

Mandela, Nelson, 137n
Maples, John, 198, 251, 252n
Marlesford, Lord, *see* Schreiber,
    Mark
Marlow, Tony, 275
Martens, Wilfried, 146, 147
Maude, Francis, 6, 96–7, 100, 162,
    181, 198–9, 251
Mawhinney, Brian, 269, 282
Mayhew, Patrick, 281, 282
media, 111–12; and election
    campaign, 164, 167–8, 170,
    199, 206, 214–15, 217–21,
    223, 231–2, 285; and election
    speculation, 126–7; and Gulf
    War, 40 and n, 41, 42–3; and
    international summits, 49–50;
    and John Major's accession
    as leader, 29–30, 84; and
    leadership election, 274 and n;
    and spending policy, 117
Mellor, David, 11, 12, 117, 120,
    121, 193–4
Michelis, Gianni de, 140, 146n
Middleton, Sir Peter, 64
Millar, Sir Ronald, 124 and n,
    129–30, 131, 132, 134, 205,
    244; election code-name, 216
Mills, John, 27, 87, 88n
Ministry of Defence, 119
Mitsotakis, Constantine, 146
Mitterrand, François, 20–1, 51, 76;
    and John Major, 41–2, 42n, 81;
    at Maastricht, 146, 147, 148,
    154, 156, 157
Montgomery, Sir Fergus, 277
Moore, John, 119n
Morris, Dominic, 25n, 67
mortgages, 189, 190
motorways, 102
Moynihan, Colin, 252n
Mulroney, Brian, 21
Myers, Sidonie, 133

National Consumers' Council,
    103
National Health Service, 99,
    102, 104–5, 110, 121, 125,
    131, 134–5
Newsnight, 243
Newton, Tony, 11, 269
Nichol, Duncan, 99
Nolan Committee, 266
Northern Ireland, 25, 47, 281
Number 12 Committee, 110–11,
    111n, 117, 159, 178

Oakley, Robin, 39, 277
Observer, 227
O'Donnell, Gus, 11, 16, 32, 52, 69,
    97, 110–11, 137, 210; and Gulf
    War broadcast, 43; liked by
    George Bush, 53; at Maastricht,
    144, 151, 157, 160; and media
    interest in new PM, 29–30;
    popular with lobby, 26
Office of Public Service and Science
    (OPSS), 180 and n
Onslow, Cranley, 7
opinion polls, 107, 108, 121, 122,
    165, 166, 184, 191, 278; during
    general election campaign, 203,
    222, 239–42
Oppenheim-Barnes, Baroness
    (Sally), 11n
Owen, Peter, 60
Oxenbury, Shirley, 206

Parkinson, Cecil, 10
Parris, Matthew, 271n
Patten, Chris, 5, 11, 55, 59, 90,
    93, 94, 110, 115–116, 117,
    124–5, 131, 180, 214, 263;
    appointed Chairman, 9–10;
    career, 5n; chooses Saatchi &
    Saatchi, 85, 108; on Council
    Tax launch, 70; on difference
    between Major and Thatcher,
    13, 14; and Europe, 77, 78n;
    and general election campaign,
    168, 175, 176–7, 178, 184, 193,
    199, 204, 207, 211–12, 213,
    231, 241, 246, 248; and general
    election timing, 106–7, 126;

gloom over election prospects, 183; on Gus O'Donnell, 26; on John Major's popularity, 83; letter on Citizen's Charter, 105; and loss of Bath, 58n, 251–2, 258, 260–1; on Michael Heseltine, 179; persuades PM to make film, 221

Paxman, Jeremy, 243

pay awards: public sector, 118

pensioners' package, 194, 196

Phillips, Sandra, 25n

Pipe, Russ, 133

Pirie, Madsen, 103, 104

PMQs, *see* Prime Minister's Questions

police forces, 100, 102

Policy Unit, 45–6, 122; and Citizen's Charter, 93–4; fields questions on PM's views, 84–5; function and staff, 23–4, 25, 26–8, 88n, 114, 256; and Manifesto, 176–7, 179; and PM's policy review, 87; and public spending, 117–18; and replacement of poll tax, 68–9; *see also* Hill, Jonathan; Hogg, Sarah

poll tax, *see* Community Charge

Poos, Jacques, 139

Portillo, Michael, 14, 69, 120, 276, 278

postal services, 100, 177

Potter, Barry, 25n, 41, 64, 67, 90

Powell, Charles, 25, 36, 38, 42, 43–4, 45, 67, 72, 78

press, *see* media

Prime Minister's Questions (PMQs), 30–2, 33–4

privatisation, 93, 94, 101, 110, 177, 181

public spending, 117–21, 122, 189, 201

rates, 55–6; *see also* Council Tax; Uniform Business Rate

Rawnsley, Andrew, 220

Redwood, John, 14, 96; and

leadership election, 269, 273–5, 275n, 276, 277, 278, 279, 280, 282 and n

Reece, Sir Gordon, 34

Reid, Sir Bob, 96, 98–9

Renwick, Sir Robin, 52

Riddell, Peter, 220

Ridley, Nicholas, 56

Rifkind, Malcolm, 94, 133, 181, 281

Robinson, Bill, 116

Rosling, Alan, 27, 88n, 179, 180, 182

Royal College of Nursing, 99

Rouncie, Robert, 39

Russia, *see* Soviet Union

Rutnam, Philip, 97

Ryder, Richard, 11, 46, 110, 111, 178

Saatchi & Saatchi, 105, 108n, 117; and general election campaign, 108, 199, 236–8, 250; initial advice to PM, 85–6

Saatchi, Maurice, 125, 164, 165, 214, 221

Saddam Hussein, 43, 48, 81

Santer, Jacques, 80, 146

Satgé, Deborah de, 134, 175, 216, 271

Schlesinger, John, 221–2, 261

Schlüter, Poul, 146

Schreiber, Mark (Lord Marlesford), 128

Scotland: in general election campaign, 242–9; and public money, 99n

Scottish Office, 99

Scowcroft, Brent, 38, 42, 43–4, 148

Screaming Lord Sutch, 259

secretaries, *see under* staff, Prime Minister's

Shephard, Gillian, 11, 110, 221

Sherbourne, Stephen, 205–6

Silver Trust, 21 and n

Simpson, John, 231n

Sinclair, Carolyn, 27, 88n, 99, 100

Slocock, Caroline, 25n

Smith, Chris, 116
Smith, John, 188, 197
Soane, Sir John, 21
Socialist Workers' Party, 226–7, 235
Soviet Union (former), 51, 122, 148
staff, Prime Minister's:
    Appointments Secretary, 24;
    on battlebus, 175; Political
    Secretary, 23, 25, 26n, 33; Press
    Secretary, 23, 26, 34; Private
    Secretaries, 22, 23, 24–5, 25n,
    33, 95; Special Advisers, 25–6,
    26n, 205; see also Cabinet
    Secretary; Policy Unit
Steed, Michael, 284–5
Stephens, Phil, 248
Stotter, Shirley, 170, 175, 213,
    226, 233–4
Stowe, Sir Kenneth, 25n
Strang, Gavin, 6
summit meetings, economic, 49–50;
    rivalry between UK and Italy, 50n
Sun, 103, 196, 255, 278
Sunday Express, 278
Sunday Telegraph, 7, 105, 158–9
Sunday Times, 278

taxation, 195–6, 197–202; see also
    Budgets; Community Charge
Tebbit, Norman, 108n, 161,
    220, 270n
Terry, Quinlan, 20
Thatcher, Margaret, 3–4, 11, 42, 61,
    84, 108n, 112–13, 119, 228,
    252, 258; and 1990 leadership
    election, 5, 6, 7, 270, 271, 274,
    276, 281; book promotion,
    266; and Bush, 52; in Cabinet,
    12–13; at Downing Street,
    16, 18n, 20, 21 and n, 24,
    46–7; and Europe, 71, 73–4,
    78–9, 80, 141, 142, 160, 161;
    and Gorbachev, 50; and Gulf
    War, 40; and John Major's first
    Conference, 127, 130–1; leaves
    House of Commons, 80n;
    and loss of Eastbourne, 255n;

neglect of economy, 185; and
    PMQs, 6, 31–2; and poll tax,
    55, 56; and Scotland, 247
Times, The, 7, 39, 92, 158, 192, 209,
    220, 221, 230, 235, 272, 278,
    279; on 1992 Budget, 196; on
    Citizen's Charter, 103; on poll
    tax, 54; on Shadow Budget, 197
Times Educational Supplement, 92
Today, 121
Townend, John, 279
trades unions: teachers', 87, 92
Training and Enterprise Councils
    (TECs), 118–19
Transforming Britain, 129
transport, 98, 102, 133; see also
    British Rail; Department of
    Transport
Treasury: 5, 81–2, 96, 144, 181,
    183, 188, 194, 195; and local
    taxation, 56, 57, 59–60, 65;
    and public spending, 117–19,
    120, 121
True, Nick, 27, 79, 93, 107, 179,
    181, 216, 244, 256, 275; and
    Citizen's Charter, 9, 95–6, 97,
    99, 100; and PM's Conference
    speech, 129, 130, 131, 134;
    and rally speeches, 205; role in
    Policy Unit, 88n, 110
Tumim, Stephen, 96–7
Turnbull, Andrew, 24–5, 25n,
    26, 28, 30, 64–5, 94–5,
    210, 246

Uff, Jane, 88
unemployment, see employment
Uniform Business Rate, 58 and
    n, 186

Waddington, David, 10, 11, 62,
    110, 178
Wakeham, John, 10, 40–1, 110, 126,
    178, 213–14
Waldegrave, William, 11, 99 and
    n, 110, 120, 121, 131, 180n,
    263; and compensation to HIV

victims, 117; election press
conference, 245–6
Wall, Stephen, 25, 36, 47, 49, 51,
52, 53, 67, 76, 210; appointed
UKREP, 71n; at Maastricht,
138, 144, 148, 153, 154, 156,
159, 160
Walpole, Sir Robert, 16, 17, 19
Ward, John, 267, 269, 282
Whetnall, Andrew, 95, 97, 100
Whips: role of, 7n
White Papers, 57n

Whitelaw, Lord (William),
10
Whitmore, Sir Clive, 25n
Wicks, Sir Nigel, 25n, 140, 141,
144, 150, 153, 162
Willetts, David, 103
Wintour, Patrick, 236
Woodward, Shaun, 110, 134
Worcester, Bob, 285

Yeltsin, Boris, 51
Young, Hugo, 219–20, 221